"Ee-Yah"

"Ee-Yah"

The Life and Times of Hughie Jennings, Baseball Hall of Famer

JACK SMILES

McFarland & Company, Inc., Publishers
Jefferson, North Carolina, and London

Library of Congress Cataloguing-in-Publication Data

Smiles, Jack, 1947–
    "Ee-Yah" : the life and times of Hughie Jennings, Baseball Hall
of Famer / Jack Smiles.
        p.   cm.
    Includes bibliographical references and index.

    ISBN 0-7864-2202-5 (softcover : 50# alkaline paper)

    1. Jennings, Hughie, 1869–1928.   2. Baseball players—
United States—Biography.   3. Baseball managers—United
States—Biography.   4. Detroit Tigers (Baseball team)—
History—20th century.   I. Title.
GV865.J39S55   2005
796.357'092—dc22   2005009062

British Library cataloguing data are available

On the cover: Hughie Jennings, coach of the Detroit Tigers

Manufactured in the United States of America

McFarland & Company, Inc., Publishers
  Box 611, Jefferson, North Carolina 28640
  www.mcfarlandpub.com

To Diane, Sadie, and Hughie Jennings'
granddaughter, Grace Doherty

Acknowledgments

Thanks to Tom Doherty, Hughie Jennings's great-grandson, for use of the family scrapbook and photographs.

Thanks to Retrosheet and to SABR.

Thanks to John Charney, Diane Studzinski and Rose Callahan for their research help; and to Mike Cotter and Ed Ackerman, who proofread the manuscript.

Special thanks to my wife, Diane, and daughter, Sadie, for helping me make the time for this project.

Contents

Preface

"Big Daddy Is Gone"

On the morning of February 3, 1928, a funeral shut down Scranton, Pennsylvania, the 55th largest city in the United States. St. Thomas College, later to be called Scranton University, canceled classes. Technical and Central high schools dismissed for the morning. County court recessed and many businesses closed in the usually bustling city of 143,000.

Hundreds of mourners packed the sanctuary of St. Peter's Cathedral for the funeral mass. Hundreds more stood outside as the cortege, led by a state police motorcycle team, arrived from the deceased's Vine Street home. His casket was borne into the church by a procession of active and honorary pallbearers made up of the city's leading citizens, including representatives of the local chapters of the Elks, Knights of Columbus, Kiwanis, Irish-American Society, Red Cross, Chamber of Commerce, and Bar Association. The Reverend Connell McHugh of Mary on the Mount Church in Mt. Pocono, who had been at the deceased's side in his final hours, was the celebrant of the Solemn High Mass. Five priests assisted on the altar and 25 more priests knelt in the first two rows of pews. During the offertory, as a sextet sang "Ave Maria," Bucky Harris—the 31-year-old manager of the Detroit Tigers and one-time "Boy Wonder" player-manager of the Washington Senators—turned to the newspaper reporter next to him, whispered "Big Daddy is gone," and openly wept.[1]

Hugh Ambrose Jennings was the kind of colorful personality who engendered nicknames. Among baseball writers he was known as "Ee-yah" for his famous coaching box cry, "The Saint Uniform" for his staunch Catholicism and "Hustling Hughie" for his style of play. In the Pittston area where he was born and raised, and the nearby Scranton area where he had lived all of his adult life, he was known simply as "Hughie." But to

1

Harris and the almost 100 other men from the Northeast corner of Pennsylvania who reached the big leagues after 1890, he was called "Big Daddy." The name came, not from his size — he was 5'-8" and 160 pounds — but from his stature as a pioneer of sorts; Jennings' success gave hope to other athletes desperate for a way out the minefields of Northeastern Pennsylvania, an area that produced ballplayers at rate far beyond any area of similar size in the country. Incredibly, six of these men reached the Hall of Fame.[2] Bucky Harris, who would one day become one of those six Hall of Famers, was the one who was most directly influenced by Hughie. In the 1880s Hughie and Harris's father, Tom, had been batterymates on a semipro club from Pittston called Our Boys. With Hughie catching, Tom Harris once struck out 19 in a game against another semipro club, the Ewings. In 1914, Hughie, then 45 and managing the Detroit Tigers, gave Bucky, then 17, his break in professional baseball by inviting him to the Tigers' training camp in Waxahachie, Texas. So Harris had plenty of reason to grieve for his old mentor Jennings, and he had plenty of company, too.[3]

Also in the St. Peter's pews that morning was Steve O'Neil, one of five brothers who reached the major leagues from Minooka, a small Scranton border town. O'Neil, as Harris had, got his break in professional baseball from Jennings. As Harris did in 1928, O'Neil would in 1943 follow Hughie's path by becoming manager of the Detroit Tigers. Other notables who came to Scranton to pay last respects to Hughie were Boston Braves shortstop Doc Farrell; former Detroit Tiger outfielder Chick Shorten; Yankee utility infielder Mike Gazella; Tiger executive William Grogan; *Detroit News* sports editor H.G. Saslinger; former Philadelphia A's outfielder Eddie Murphy; and former Orioles second baseman Jim Mullin. There were many more lesser known baseball men in the church that day to mourn Hughie Jennings, too, such as former minor league and local league teammates and opponents from such teams as Lehighton and Minooka. A continuous stream of telegrams and floral baskets poured into the Jennings' home from baseball players such as Walter Johnson, Ty Cobb, Babe Ruth, Dan Brouthers, and Roger Bresnahan; and from executives and owners including Bill Veeck, Connie Mack, Jacob Ruppert, and Clark Griffith. Boxer Jack Dempsey sent flowers. Writer Ring Lardner sent a large basket of roses from New York.

Hughie's longtime best friend and former teammate, New York Giants manager John McGraw, was in constant touch with the Jennings family by cablegram from Havana, Cuba, where he was on a baseball trip. From 1921 to 1925, in the final years of his 38-year baseball career, Jennings was McGraw's assistant manager with the Giants. Condolences and floral tributes also came into Scranton from bat boys and concessionaires, bar asso-

Though this picture was probably taken 20 years after Hughie left the mines (c. 1911), not much had changed. It's easy to picture Hughie as one of these breaker boys working at the EWEN breaker in Pittston, his birthplace. (Photograph by L. Hine, National Archives, Washington, D.C.)

ciations and bank presidents, mayors and congressmen, college presidents and vaudeville actors, and miners and breaker boys. While Hughie's funeral mass was celebrated in Scranton, the entire community of St. Bonaventure University in Allegheny, New York—where Hughie was a coaching legend—attended a mass for him in the school's chapel.

In New York City on the evening before the funeral, Mayor James Walker spoke about Hughie at the New York Baseball Writers dinner at the Hotel Commodore saying, "The hurrahs of yesterday had so short an echo," and, "He was one of the finest sportsmen who ever played the game. A player and leader of rare courage and fine ideals." He then proposed a toast to the memory of Hughie "Ee-yah" Jennings. The toast was warmly received because newspapermen across the country revered Hughie.

In the days after his death, Hughie was eulogized in editorials in all the major baseball cities. The *Detroit News* wrote, "Jennings was a great baseball player, a graceful winner, a good loser and a shining example to the youth of our country." According to the *Detroit Free Press*, "Mr. Jen-

Hughie was 11 or 12 when he went to work as a breaker boy, as pictured in this post-card. Sitting on wooden benches, breaker boys sorted slate and other waste from coal as it roared down chutes from the top of the breaker.

nings proved that it is an asset for a ball player or manager to be a cultured gentleman and a man of exemplary habits and refinement." And the *New York Herald Tribune* informed its readers, "Baseball has produced greater players, but no finer or [more] lovable character."

In Philadelphia, Richard Beamish of the *Philadelphia Inquirer* was moved to create a poem he called "Hughey Is Home":

> Hughey is home, wherever he is,
> Those freckles of his and his grin
> Are keys to unlock every front door on his way
> Be it palace or shanty or inn
> He's poking around for the lads that he knew
> And asking each stranger to tell
> Where the ballplayers hang out and where he can find
> Christy and Willie and Del
> Willie, the wee one, whose policy was
> always to hit where they ain't
> Christy whose fade away baffled them all
> Knight of the game without taint,
> Del of the wallop that rode them a mile

Who laughed at whatever befell
Lords of the ball yards where ever they are
Christy and Willie and Del
Hughey is home and gay where he is
With his "Ee-yah" and "Atta Boy" cries
And some night I'd like to drop in for a bit
On him and the gang with their lies
And their songs and their banter in Ballplayers' house
And I'd hear all of heaven's fans tell
The new plays of their Big Four, Hughey himself
And Christy and Willie and Del
(Mathewson and Delahanty a different big four)[4]

What was it about Hughie "Ee-yah" Jennings that his death produced a spontaneous buzz of sympathy and grief and newspaper tributes in prose and poetry from around the country? Who was Hughie Ambrose Jennings? First and foremost he was the son of an immigrant coal miner from Pittston, Pennsylvania.

Readers will notice two spellings for Jennings' first name. Because "Hughie" is the more common and because that is the spelling used on his Hall of Fame plaque and in various baseball encyclopedias, it is used throughout the book. In the early part of his career, especially before 1900, sportswriters often spelled the name "Hughey." In the book, the "Hughey" spelling does show up in many of the quoted passages, strictly in accord with the original version.

1

The Mule Driver

Some 500 feet under the ground, the mine car rattled down the "buggy road," with a load of coal. Perched on the front bumper of the car the smiling, redheaded, teenaged mule driver waved his hat and yelled "wa-ha" to guide the mule around a corner. The miners could only shake their heads and laugh, more than one of them probably thinking, "There goes that happy-go-lucky Jennings kid again."

Hugh Ambrose Jennings was the ninth child of James and Nora Jennings, Irish immigrants who came to Pittston, Pennsylvania in 1851. Though his mine bosses thought Hughie was born in 1869, he was really born two years later, on April 2 in 1871, in an unpainted shanty in the Brandy Patch section of Pittston. A few years later the family moved to Stark's Patch near Moosic and then Avoca, two adjacent small towns between Scranton and Pittston. Hughie was probably 11 or 12 years old, and trying to pass for 14, when he left school and went to work as breaker boy in the Pennsylvania Coal Company mine, which was walking distance from his home. His father and brothers worked at the same mine. What else, after all, was an uneducated, freckle-faced redheaded Irish boy in Pittston going to do in the 1880s?

Pittston sat at the base of the Pocono Mountains in the northeastern part of the state known as the Wyoming Valley and at the confluence of the Lackawanna and Susquehanna rivers. It might be said that Pittston was also at the center of the engine that drove the country's economy, being that it was in the middle of a huge coalfield. But this wasn't just any coalfield of common bituminous or "soft" coal. The coalfield in Northeastern Pennsylvania contained anthracite, or "hard" coal, in such quantities that three-quarters of the known deposits in the Earth were within 480 square miles. While soft coal could be more cheaply mined — and was practically unlimited in other parts of Pennsylvania and Kentucky and West Virginia — anthracite was much more in demand.

Rated chemically for hardness and luster, anthracite is the highest grade of coal in the earth. The miners called the nuggets "Black Diamonds" and they lived up to their nickname. Anthracite coal is so hard that it can be carved or sculpted. Anthracite burns cleaner, hotter and four times longer than bituminous and is virtually smoke free, while bituminous combustion emits a sooty black smoke. It was demonstrated that anthracite could be burned as fuel at the Fell Tavern in nearby Wilkes-Barre in 1728.

In 1777, the first commercial anthracite shipment left Wilkes-Barre by barge for Carlisle, Pennsylvania, where it was used to fire a forge for the manufacture of firearms. Soon the anthracite coal mined in Northeastern Pennsylvania was fueling iron blast furnaces in New York State for the production of high grade steel, driving railroads, and heating homes.[1] The U.S. Navy especially coveted anthracite. The heat gave warships speed. The lack of smoke gave them stealth. It's not a stretch to say anthracite, and the men who mined it, helped win the Civil War.[2]

As the demand for the Black Diamonds grew, so did Pittston, which was near the center of the anthracite field. Fed by thousands of English, Welsh and Irish immigrants who came specifically to work in the mines, the area grew rapidly. By 1869, the anthracite fields around Pittston were producing 25,000,000 tons of hard coal a year, double that by 1900. During this time the population of Pittston increased from 2500 to 15,000.[3]

The mines which yielded these millions of tons of anthracite were as unique as the coal itself. These were urban mines. Because the area was settled in the early 1700s, before the quantity and value of the coal was known, by the time mining began over a century later, the mines were built in and around established towns, instead of the other way around. Since many of the anthracite mines, unlike rural bituminous mines, were right in the middle of the towns such as Pittston, many of the anthracite miners worked directly below their own homes and churches and the downtown business. By the 1890s, there were five mines operating within the city limits of Pittston and over 30 in Scranton. It was possible to walk for miles underground. The urban mines gave the towns an odd appearance. The several story-high colliery breakers rose among the steeples of the churches, and the black hills of mine waste, called culm, rose in the midst of neighborhoods. Some of these monuments to mining, breakers and culm piles, still exist in the area over 50 years after the last deep mine closed.

Greater Pittston, as the 50 square miles of 15 attached and fragmented little towns around it is called, was a boom area in the late 1800s and downtown Pittston was its hub. The two-mile long Main Street was lined with storefront businesses that either directly or indirectly owed their lives to the men who risked theirs under the ground. Scores of hatters, dress shops, tailors, pharmacies, confectioneries, bakeries, banks, tobacco shops, pool halls, dance halls, hotels and restaurants, as well as stables, powder makers, and hardware stores flourished. In Pittston alone, over 50 "Mom and Pop" taverns served beer brewed in the five local breweries. Miners lined the bars for a shot and beer to wash the dust down at the end of the day, or for a miners' breakfast, a raw egg in beer, to start the day. These neighborhood taverns, where the bar was literally in the proprietors' living room, while in decline, still operate in the area. Hughie's father was one miner who was never found at a tavern. As a boy in Quest Port, Ireland, he took a temperance pledge from Father Theobald Matthew, his family's parish priest. He wore his pledge medal every day of his life.[4]

Of course, the coal had to get from Northeastern Pennsylvania to customers all over the country, and the transportation business grew exponentially. A barge canal along the river hauled coal and other goods. Over 100 railroad lines operated in Pennsylvania at the turn of the 20th century. Sometimes 45 passenger trains a day stopped in Pittston, shuttling passengers among Pittston and Wilkes-Barre and Scranton, the county seats of Luzerne and Lackawanna counties five miles to the North and South; and to and from New York City and Philadelphia, only 100 miles to the East and South.

The mines that produced all this action were called collieries. The colliery included the coal mine and all its buildings, including the breaker, where the coal was broken and separated from waste. Men and equipment were lowered down the shafts in crude elevators. The average mine was essentially a vast hall with pillars of coal 1000 feet below the surface. The actual mining of the coal was done with pick and shovel, bar, hand and machine drills, and blasting powder. Miners loosened coal from the face by blasting and knocked it down and broke it up with picks. While the word "miner" is often used to describe all colliery employees, miner was actually a specific job and it was, outside of superintendent, the best job. A breast, as the area being mined was called, was typically worked by four men, two laborers, called "butties," and two miners. The miners were independent contractors who had to furnish their own tools and powder and pay their butties. The miners' main job was to cut the coal out of the veins. Miners had to have certificates issued by the mine examining board. To get the certificates would-be miners had to have at least two years' experience as laborers and be able to answer at least twelve questions in English. While the job of miner was dangerous because of the blasting, it came with one big perk — short work days. Miners were required to cut only enough coal to fill the cars assigned by the mine bosses. Some days this could be done in three or four hours, after which the miners were free to stop at the tavern and talk politics, go home, or take in a ball game. It was left to the butties to load the cars and clean up the breast for the next day's work. And it was left to the mule drivers to haul the coal to the shafts.[5]

Before Hughie was a mule driver, his first job was breaker boy. As the coal cars were hauled from the mine they were pulled to the top of the breaker by cables, where they were dumped into a shaking machine which crushed the coal and pushed it into the chutes, which poured it down to the breaker boys waiting below. The breaker boys worked bent over on backless wooden benches picking out slate and other waste from the coal before it was loaded for shipping. They worked amid clouds of coal dust and the high-decibel roar of the rushing coal and the breaker machinery.[6]

The Jennings family, with a father and eight sons who worked in the mines at one time or another, was a typical family in the Pittston area at the time, and a lucky one in that none of the Jennings males were killed or maimed in the mines. While the ventilation tunnels and the pillars and the giant steam-fired pumps which controlled groundwater flooding were attempts at safety, the anthracite mines where Hughie and his father and brothers worked were extremely dangerous. The earliest year with comprehensive statistics was 1900. According to a Bureau of Mines report, 363 collieries in the anthracite region employed 143,826 employees in 1900, one-fourth of them boys under 16. Accidents in anthracite mines in Northeastern Pennsylvania that year killed 411, injured 1,057 and made 230 widows and 525 orphans. It is estimated that in the first half of the 19th century miners were killed at the rate of 100 per month.

Down in the mines, gas, fire, explosions, and cave-ins killed and maimed. Up in the breakers, boys sometimes fell into the chutes where they were crushed by rollers or buried in coal in the train cars being filled below. The wives and mothers of the miners lived in dread of the sound of the mine whistle during working hours. It usually meant one of their men or boys had been killed or maimed. The dead and injured were unceremoniously hauled by wagon into the patch towns and dumped on their front porches. To understand why families would send their sons to work in these conditions, consider that many of the families, as the Jenningses had, left Ireland from 1845–51 to escape the Great Famine. To them steady work of any kind was literally lifesaving. Sons working as breaker boys, even when paid as little as 15 cents a day, helped the families stay afloat, whereas boys who stayed in school cost families money. Besides, there was nothing else do to in the anthracite area. The mines and the railroad employed 80 percent of all workers in the region.

This coal breaker in Pittston is typical of the breakers that dotted the Scranton-Pittston area in the second half of the 19th century and early part of the 20th century. Hughie worked in a breaker just like this one. (National Archives, Washington, D.C.)

Though breakers sometimes operated 10 hours a day, there was still time for recreation. In the spring and summer, as early as before the Civil War, baseball was it. English and Irish immigrants, who developed baseball, made up 90 percent of the anthracite area population in the 1850s. The immigrants who settled in Pittston came through New York City, where the popularity of the Knickerbockers version of the game was spreading rapidly, or Philadelphia, where an Olympic Town Ball Club had been organized in 1833. By the time Hughie Jennings entered the breaker in the early 1880s, the game was organized into teams and leagues sponsored by collieries and athletic clubs. Hughie was fanatical about the game, and, with every minute he could steal, he played. At first he played with the other breaker boys in pickup games during lunch break and accident or machinery breakdowns. Sometimes breaker boys purposely caused these breakdowns. The breaker boys played with bats and balls crudely fashioned by helpful adults. A blacksmith might turn a hickory branch into a bat and a mine foreman might look the other way when the boys stole rubber from a coal car bumper to use for ball cores. After a slice was cut with a jackknife, it was turned over a flame on broken umbrella rod until the rough edges were smooth and a sphere produced about an inch in diameter. Then one of their mothers would wrap the sphere with yarn and old socks. When enough was put on to make it the proper size, the ball was soaked over night in water to warp the yarn. Once it dried, a knitted cover with button hole stitch was put over the yarn.[7]

Though there were undoubtedly boys at the breaker who were bigger, stronger, faster, and more talented than Hughie, none matched his exuberance, his hustle, or his fearlessness. Hughie brought these same attributes to work and the mine bosses noticed. He was quickly promoted from breaker boy to "nipper," as the boys who opened the huge wooden gangway doors for coal cars were called. When he tackled that enthusiastically, he was promoted to mule driver. Breaker boys coveted mule-driving jobs, even though it was fraught with its own dangers. A driver might fall under the mule's hoofs or the car, or, as happened to one 16-year-old from Pittston, according to a *Scranton Times* report, get his nose kicked off.

Hughie somehow escaped calamity in the mines. Years later, while at the height of his fame as manager of the Detroit Tigers and Ty Cobb, Hughie, with characteristic wit, talked about mule driving in an interview with Bozeman Bulger, a writer for the *New York Evening World*.

> Mule driving by the light of a flickering oil lamp is a job that requires patience, forbearance, and determination. That is what impressed upon me the idea of always sticking to the job until that last man is out in the ninth inning. You never know when the mule is going to kick anymore than we do when some big ball player is liable to rear up on his hind legs and shatter a ball game with a three-base wallop.
>
> While I appreciate the scientific requirements of mule driving I cannot say it has any advantages over baseball. Mule driving is art in its highest form, but I made up my mind that it was up to me to sacrifice art, and the wage of $1.10 per day, for the sake of getting $5 for playing baseball on Saturday afternoons in Lehighton.
>
> You see my father was satisfied with my association with the mule, but he feared for my future when mixed up with a lot of ballplayers. Mules did not drink and my father had heard that ballplayers did.[8]

As he gained fame as a ballplayer, manager and coach, Hughie never forgot the men back in the Scranton area who were not so lucky and he never denigrated the work. In *Rounding Third,* the book-length series of articles he wrote which was syndicated in several newspapers in 1925 and '26, Hughie talked about mining.

Many people have asked me how anyone can stand to work in the mines, but it is not so bad as you think. It is dark there, of course, but you get used to the eternal darkness. You become accustomed to the lantern light and find your way about easily. I don't think it is any hardship for the men nor the mules that are used to haul the coal. I never saw a mule that seemed to mind it in the least.

Mining has its compensations. You never get soaked by rain; there are no biting winds in the winter time; you never encounter sudden changes in weather. The temperature is about even the year around, and it is a relief from the heat of summer and the cold of winter. You appreciate being down in the mines on blistering days of summer and on the bitter days in winter. It is always comfortable down there. The mines hold dangers, but you are in danger anywhere else.[9]

Despite Hughie's claim that mining had its "compensations" and despite his whistle-while-you-work attitude, he was determined to get out. The story of how he began his escape from the mines is the stuff of legend in the Pittston-Scranton area. As Hughie worked his way up mine job ladder, he was also starting up the baseball ladder. At 13, he was recruited by the best local team, the Moosic Pounders, to be their catcher. The Pounders' next youngest player was 17 and most of them were adults. It wasn't Hughie's talent that made the Pounders seek him out, but his fearlessness. The Pounders didn't own a catcher's mitt or mask.[10] As Hughie's baseball reputation grew, his father and his mine foreman, Robert McMillian, gave him some liberty to play. But when, at age 15, he was promoted to assistant driver boss at the No. 13 shaft of the Pennsylvania Colliery, they could no longer abide his baseball. After all, as they saw it, Hughie was on the fast track to success. To them there was no better chance of promotion anywhere than in the mining business, where an energetic boy like Hughie could go from slate picker, to mule driver, to mine boss, to mining engineer or state inspector, to superintendent of collieries.

So when Hughie asked to leave work early to play for the Pounders in a big rivalry game with a nearby town team, the Minooka Barkpeelers, his father and mine boss said no. Hughie went anyway. His father caught up with him at home just as Hughie was leaving for the game. The story goes that his father forcibly stopped him, made him put on one of his sister's dresses and said, "If you go, you go in this."[11]

It was a pivotal moment in Hughie's young life. Knowing it might jeopardize his job, he went to the game in the dress and began his climb out of the mines.

2

Escape from the Mines

With the hated Baltimore Orioles in town to play the White Sox on a glorious July Sunday in 1897, the Chicago fans overflowed the West Side Grounds infield bleachers and spilled around the field. Forming a human fence five and six rows deep, they strained over and under and between bowlers and parasols for a glimpse of the famous "Big Four" of baseball's best team — Joe Kelley, Wee Willie Keeler, John McGraw, and Hughie Jennings of the Baltimore Orioles.

The fans were about to get a close-up look. With the Sox batting in the fourth and runner Bill Everett on third base, the batter hit a high foul ball over the crowd along the left field line. As the ball fell toward the crowd, the fans looked up, arms outstretched. John McGraw, the third baseman, ran over to the front line of fans and stopped. Hughie Jennings, the shortstop, didn't. Eyes burning on the ball as it fell, Jennings reached the crowd at a full sprint. With a piercing yell he launched himself over the crowd in a flat-out dive, caught the ball and dropped onto the crowd of fans. Those that didn't scatter quickly enough were knocked over. Jennings rolled to a clearing, scrambled to his feet and threw home for a double play on Everett. The fans may have hated the Orioles, and they had reason to, but they parted to let Jennings back on the field without incident.[1] It may have been that they grudgingly respected Jennings, but it may have been that they feared him, as well, as they might a crazy man, and they had reason for that too. Jennings' passion for baseball did seem to slip into mania at times, and he looked the part. Redheaded, freckled, and wide-eyed, he went through life with an impish grin that gave him the look of a man on the edge. While in later years he did have some kind of mental breakdown and spent time in a sanitarium, Hughie's dive into the crowd that Sunday in Chicago wasn't the act of a madman. It was a play that typified a code to live by — attack every challenge head-on, fearlessly, even recklessly. It was a philosophy which fueled Hughie's rise from the coal

14

mines to shortstop and captain of baseball's first dynasty team, the 1894–97 Baltimore Orioles of the National League.

Once Hughie chose baseball over honest work that day when he went to the Moosic Pounders game in his sister's dress, he was determined to escape the mines once and for all. Through 1887 and '88 Hughie continued to catch for the Pounders, now called the Anthracites. He and pitcher Martin O'Hara, who threw a wickedly unhittable drop spitball, became the hottest battery in Luzerne and Lackawanna counties. Hughie's reputation as a recklessly fierce competitor grew, and Hughie and the Anthracites drew hundreds of fans to the roped-off fields around the twin cities of Scranton and Wilkes-Barre. Many were drawn just to see Hughie throw the ball. He threw as though it were shot from a gun, even if it was not always well aimed. After Hughie knocked out a base runner trying to steal second, fans would instinctively duck whenever Hughie uncorked a throw. The Anthracites passed the hat at games, but even given Hughie's growing popularity, collected enough only to give players 50 cents or a dollar a game.[2] Hughie made more than that driving mules in the mines below the ball fields, a fact not lost on his father.

In July of '89, just when it seemed that Hughie's dream of leaving the mine would not be fulfilled after all, a stranger who would change everything arrived at the Jennings home from Lehighton, a Pocono Mountain town 50 miles to the south of Avoca.[3]

In *Rounding Third* Hughie recalled what happened.

> On a hot July day in 1889, two teams of coal miners were playing a base ball game. It was a close game; perhaps the score was tied in the ninth. Miner Mills was at bat. Maybe there were two out and the bases loaded. At that most dramatic of all possible moments in a ball game, the Miners Mills batter hit a high foul. Squinting into the blazing sun from behind his myriad freckles, the catcher ran around the backstop. The ball, he saw, was sure to clear the fence. He vaulted the fence and caught the ball.
>
> After the game (of course, Moosic won, and there are no records to disprove the statement), a man who said he was Webb Clauss and manager of the Leighton team, offered the fence-jumping Moosicer a catching job on Saturday afternoon at $5 and expenses. The catcher was me and that catch marked a turning point in my life.

Lehighton had its beginning in 1746 when the Moravian Brethren Society founded a Christian mission they called Gnadenhutten on the Lehigh River in a small Pocono Mountain valley. The missionaries did their work so well that in 1750 the local Delaware Indian war chief, Teedyuscung, was baptized as a Christian. The good will didn't last. Peace-

ful missionaries were one thing, but as German hunters and trappers settled in the area and competed with the Indians, a clash was inevitable. In
1755 Teedyuscung joined forces with the Shawnees and Mohicans and
attacked the white settlers, including the Moravian mission house. They
killed 10 and burned down the buildings. In response the colonial government built forts in the area. One was erected by a militia from Philadelphia led by Benjamin Franklin. But it wasn't until after the Revolutionary
War that settlers drove the Indians out of the area and the fighting stopped.
In 1794, Jacob Weiss, a war veteran, and Judge William Henry laid out a
town. They called it Lehighton after the Lehigh River. It became a popular way station for people traveling west from Philadelphia and New York.
The Dutch and German immigrants who gravitated to the area opened taverns and hotels to support the travelers. In the early 1800s a tannery, a
general store, and a grist mill were built. A canal completed in 1829 linked
Lehighton with the cities of Allentown and Philadelphia. In 1866 Lehighton was organized as a borough. The legendary Lehigh Valley Railroad put
the town on the map. The Lehigh Valley became the second largest coal-
carrying company in the country, after the Philadelphia and Reading.

Though there was a rich anthracite field, called the Lehigh field, in
the Lehighton area, Lehighton didn't resemble Avoca and Pittston. The
Lehighton economy was diverse. Early businesses included the Joseph
Obert Packing Company, the Lehigh Stove and Manufacturing Company,
and the Baer Silk Mill, the Lehighton Shirt Factory, and the Carbon Iron
Works, which made iron and pipes. Most of the early settlers were from
Germany, but were mistakenly described as Dutch. Even today over half
of the residents are of German ancestry.[4]

In the 1890s, affluent folks from Philadelphia and New York, both
easily accessible by train, came to the Pocono area to hunt and fish or just
escape the city heat in the summer. Lehighton's population doubled to
3000 between 1880 to 1890. In 1890 Lehighton was also a town that took
its baseball seriously. It was proud of its new ballfield with enclosed seven-
foot board fence and 400-capacity grandstand, which was filled on game
days. To help keep up the park, the town council offered a standing $5
reward to any informant providing information on vandalism at the ballpark. Lehighton's baseball team was the talk of the Pocono region. One
hundred shares of stock were sold to support the squad. There were also
fund-raisers during the season. One drawing was held for a "Chimes of
Normandy" clock, which residents were able to preview in the show window of Kutz's Cigar Store. The Lehighton team and its fans were serious
about winning. Webster Clauss, a successful tailor who owned the team,
delighted in beating other Pocono area town teams like Jeansville, Mauch

Tunnel entrance at a mine in Wilkes-Barre, Pennsylvania. Jennings likely drove a mule and coal car just like the ones shown here.

Chunk, Lansford and Tamaqua. To keep this edge Clauss scouted other areas for ballplayers. This was how he found Hughie in the summer of 1889. Clauss had seen Hughie play only that one game at Avoca, so he knew him mostly by word of mouth. Once he got to see Hughie work out and play at Lehighton, he realized Hughie was even better than advertised. Clauss was stunned by his arm, running speed, knowledge and all-out hustle. He knew Hughie was just the player to catch his ace pitcher, George W. Reichard. But as Hughie was just a teenager and decidedly under his father's influence, Clauss took a patient approach. He offered Hughie $5 a game to catch for Leighton, but only on Saturdays. From *Rounding Third*:

> When Webb Clauss offered me $5 and expenses for a single game I gasped, for that was almost as much money as I could earn in the mine all week, and imagine all the fun I was getting out of it!
>
> My father had always been strict with us boys. We had to be in bed by 9:30 every evening. I had not told my father that I agreed to catch for Lehighton on Saturday afternoons and so as soon as I got out of the mine at noon the following Saturday, I sneaked off to Lehighton. It was an extra inning game and I missed my train so had to stay in Lehighton and go back on a later one. I did not arrive home until 10:30 that night, and it was the first time in my life that I was ever out of the house after 9 o'clock.

When I reached home my father was already asleep, but he was waiting for me when I got down to breakfast the next morning. He asked me where I was the previous afternoon and I explained that I had played ball in Lehighton.

"Well, you play no more. If you do, you needn't come back home. Stay in Lehighton," my father told me.

I said no more but the next Saturday noon I again sneaked off to Lehighton. When I arrived home my father was waiting for me. He demanded to know where I had been and I told him.

"I told you last Sunday that if you ever went to Lehighton again, you could stay there and I didn't want you in this house any more. Now pack up your things and get out," said my father. He meant it, but my brother interceded for me and began arguing on my behalf.

While my brother was making his appeal I got a bright thought. Webb Clauss had given me $5 for each game and my expenses. I had saved the $5 from the first game and I had the $5 that he handed me for the second game. I pulled out the two $5 bills and handed them to my father.

"That's what I got for playing and that's better than working all week in a mine, isn't it?" I said.

My father knew nothing about base ball, strange as it may seem. He did not know men ever got money for playing ball and the sudden information took him off his feet. That anyone should pay me or anyone else a dollar for playing ball seemed ridiculous to him, but there in his hand lay $10 and he began looking at the matter from a different angle. He withdrew his objections and even agreed to come to Lehighton and watch me play.

My father, not knowing what it was all about, sat in the grandstand and pretended an unusual interest in the proceedings. Webb Clauss, a practical joker, walked over to him about the eighth inning and said, "Mr. Jennings, I don't know what's the matter with your boy today, but he's not playing his best. I think he's laying down on me."

"I'll attend to that fellow, you leave him to me," my father told Clauss.

I heard my father's shrill whistle. Whenever he wanted us, he did not call but whistled, and there was no mistaking that particular whistle. I walked over to where he was sitting and he said: "What are you layin' down for? Why don't you play ball?"

I looked startled, for I did not know at the time what Clauss had done.

"How can I lay down," I tried to explain, "when the score is 8 to 1 in our favor with only another inning to go?"

"You're not playing your best an' the score isn't any 8 to 1" my father said. "An' you got more to play. I'm going to watch you and if you don't get in there and try, you are through playing ball and I'll see that you are."

I told Clauss about it and he said that he would fix it, so he went over and told my father I was doing much better and that I was winning the game. After it was over, he told him I had won for Lehighton.

After the game Hughie's father went to the hotel where the players changed to wait for his train. He told Hughie to ask all the players to step down to the bar and have a drink on him. Hughie, who was 18 and did not yet drink, worried about the impression his teammates would make. "I told the boys it would make me a hit with the old man and help me stick with the team if they ordered soft drinks. They laughed, but all promised they would and in due time they arrived in the barroom. My father was standing at one end of the bar. I stood beside him and all the players lined up. The bartender went down the line, asking each man what he would have to drink. The bartender's look was one of puzzled wonderment as each player ordered lemonade or pop or sarsaparilla or milk, but he never cracked a smile."

"Saints an' ages, an', what a foine lot o' young men," Hughie's father said in his Irish brogue.[5]

For the rest of the 1889 season Hughie continued working in the mines driving mules and picking up coal during the week and playing for Lehighton on Saturday afternoons. The next spring, 1890, Webb Clauss came to Avoca and told Hughie and his family he wanted Hughie to be his regular catcher and live in Lehighton. He laid a contract of the table. It was for $75 a month. Hughie's father was stunned. He finally accepted that his son was going to be a ballplayer and let him go with his blessing. Clauss made the same offer to O'Hara. Clauss couldn't pay his ball players $75 a month and make money, so he worked out an agreement with the merchants in town to pay part of his players' salaries. In exchange, the players worked when the baseball schedule allowed. When Hughie and O'Hara got settled in Lehighton, the jobs were ready for them. Hughie was a painter's helper and O'Hara, a plumber's apprentice. Hughie learned that at least two Lehighton residents, an Irish saloon keeper and his sister, were not Dutch. They befriended Hughie and he took most of his meals there. Most weeks Lehighton played two or three games a week and had practices the other days. Hughie never missed. "I worked hard to make good, because I had a goal set and wanted to realize an ambition. I didn't go out and practice because it was required of me, I worked to attain a certain end. That end was to be free of the mines once and for all."[6] Clauss was so impressed he named his young catcher team captain. Soon Hughie became a Pocono celebrity. With his down time, he learned house painting and decorating and the locals lined up to hire him. He was also quite a hit with the local ladies. A blonde once presented him with a bouquet of pansies, which he reportedly wore next to his heart.

In June Hughie took another step up the baseball ladder, albeit on a broken rung. Allentown, a city 22 miles from Lehighton with a team in the Eastern Interstate League, signed Hughie. Clauss and Lehighton let him go proudly and welcomed him back happily when the Eastern Interstate League folded after just 13 games, during which Hughie batted .320 (16–50) and scored eight runs. Hughie got back to Lehighton just in time for a July 4th doubleheader. After an Independence Day parade to the ballpark, Hughie led the local team to a morning-afternoon sweep of the Jeansville team, which kept Lehighton undefeated into a third month. Lehighton finally lost a game latter in July in 10 innings at Pottstown, but there was a silver lining. The game was covered by the *Philadelphia Times*, which made note of the visitors' hard play. Hughie's reputation was reaching larger circles.[7] In 1890, Tamaqua was Lehighton's fiercest rival. Tamaqua was the unofficial champion of Schuylkill County, while Lehighton was the best from the Lehigh Valley. Lehighton won the first time they played, but in August, Tamaqua beat Lehighton to even the season series. The *Carbon Advocate* reported that jubilant Tamaqua fans celebrated with a parade, fireworks, and a general "drunk." Fans carried banners proclaiming, "We done up the Dutch" and "Lehighton is in the soup." Fans in Mauch Chunk and Lansford, who were sick of losing to Lehighton, celebrated the news nearly as rowdily as Tamaqua did. Not that Lehighton was above rowdy baseball behavior. In a September home game against Catasauqua, one of the Lehighton players got into a fist fight with an umpire and scores of fans poured onto the field. For Hughie the near riot was a preview of what was to come for him in the years ahead.

In August Hughie was signed by Harrisburg of the Eastern League for $50 a month after their catcher, minor league veteran Jack Coons, was seriously injured. Hughie finished the season in the state capital and in 69 games hit .338 with 13 steals, but not before he made some wild throws which almost got him back on the train to Lehighton. In one of his first games with Harrisburg he nailed the batter in the back of the neck trying to throw to second. The batter was knocked out, the ball ricocheted into the stands and the runner came around to score. Another time he nearly hit his pitcher, who had to dive out of the way. The ball hit the pitching box and bounced 30 feet in the air. It took Coons, who Hughie had replaced, to convince Harrisburg management to keep Hughie.

With Harrisburg Hughie played against an all-black team for only time in his career. On Oct 1, 1890 in a game between Harrisburg and the York Colored Monarchs, Hughie caught and had a double, a strikeout and a passed ball. The Monarchs won game 14–7. The game was likely an exhibition game, because according to *Sol White's History of Colored Baseball* the Monarchs left the Eastern League on July 5, 1890, and played independent ball the remainder of the season.[8]

In typical fashion, Hughie never forgot Lehighton and his supporters there. In 1906 he chose Lehighton as the place to make the biggest announcement of his career. He was managing the minor league Baltimore Orioles of the Eastern League, and he brought them to Lehighton for an exhibition game in October, where he made it known that he had been hired to manage the Detroit Tigers. Through the years, whenever Jennings spoke around the country, he always "advertised" Lehighton, calling the town the place of his baseball "beginnings." Just two weeks before his death in 1928, Jennings visited some buddies from the old Lehighton club, including Ed Nussbaum, James Yenser and Lidy Albright. After his death the Lehighton newspaper wrote of the influence Hughie had on the youth of the town in his short time there.

"He was the patron hero for several generations of Lehighton boys," the paper said, and "frequently visited old friends and companions in this town."

Hughie didn't forget his old opponents either. In 1908, now a national figure having managed the Tigers and Ty Cobb to consecutive World series appearances, Jennings agreed to an interview with the *Tamaqua Courier* and offered a theory as to why anthracite region coal miners made good baseball players.

> The ventilation is excellent, and the work is such as to develop muscle in the body, bringing out especially those muscles needed in the game. The beacon of light from the miners' lantern hats in gloom of the mine tunnels develops the eyesight. The eyes are at work constantly, but there is no strain. The men are in constant training, but never overworked. The darkness keeps them rested. A good eye means everything to a ballplayer, and a miner's eyes are wonderfully strong.

3

Hughie at the Falls

In the 18th century the major cities in America — Baltimore, Boston, Charleston, New York and Philadelphia — were all on the Atlantic coast. By the end of the century towns began to emerge in the interior. The major ones were Cincinnati, Lexington, Pittsburgh, St. Louis and, the "City at the Falls," Louisville. It is said Louisville owed its birth and early growth to the two 'Rs" — the river and the revolution. The 981-mile Ohio, a major thoroughfare in the American frontier, had only one navigational barrier: the Falls. At the Falls boats stopped to unload passengers and cargo for portage downstream, skimmed over the Falls, then stopped and reloaded on the other side. Inevitably a small settlement sprang up.

During the Revolutionary War the area of the Falls, then part of the colony of Virginia, became a staging area for General George Rogers Clark, the "George Washington of the West," and his troops for their campaign against British resistance in the vast area. Three forts were built to house Clark's troops and their families. With the end of the war more settlers arrived and a town took shape. In 1780 Thomas Jefferson, the Governor of Virginia, signed a charter incorporating a town at the Falls called Louisville for King Louis XVI of France, in gratitude for French aid in the Revolution. The area remained part of Virginia until 1792 when it became the state of Kentucky, the first western state.

In 1828, with a population at 10,000, Louisville was officially incorporated as a city. With the opening of the Portland Canal in 1830, and the large inflow of German and Irish immigrants in the 1840s, the city's population exploded. By 1850 Louisville, with 43,000 citizens, was the 12th largest city in the country, more populous than Washington or Chicago. The economy revolved around tobacco, hemp, livestock, distilling, commercial sales, warehousing, and river travel. In 1850 Kentucky granted a charter to build the Louisville & Nashville Railroad. By 1859 the line reached Nashville, 187 miles to the south. During the Civil War the city, with the river and the railroad, was considered strategic. "I may have God on my side," Lincoln said, "but I must have Kentucky." Louisville braced for invasion in the autumn of 1862, but the Battle of Louisville never happened. Instead Louisville became a center of troop movement, supplies, spies and intrigue. While other Southern cities were devastated, Louisville traded with both sides and prospered. The Louisville & Nashville, for example, transported troops for both sides.[1] During the War, with its large Irish population, and influx of often idle troops, Louisville became a hotbed of baseball. By 1874, with the city's population now over 100,000, the game was a citywide craze. Two semipro teams, the Eclipse and the Olympics, were fierce rivals. When they played each other they filled Eclipse Park and got national attention. Fans of the two teams got in so many brawls that bars banned baseball discussions.[2] In January of 1876, at the urging of William Hulbert, the president of a Chicago ballclub, Louisville hosted a meeting of representatives of ballclubs from Chicago, Cincinnati, St. Louis and Louisville to discuss the formation of what would become the first permanent professional baseball league. Hulbert's plan was to have the four Western Clubs join forces with teams from Philadelphia, Boston, Hartford, and Brooklyn in the east and create the National League of Professional baseball Clubs.

In February of 1876, five months before Custer's Last Stand, the teams met again in New York City and the National League was born. The Louisville club's president was W. M. Walderman. Its manager was John Chapman. In '76 Louisville, nicknamed the Grays, finished that inaugural National League campaign 30–36. In '77 four players—Jim Devlin, George Hall, William Craver and Al Nichols—were implicated in a gambling scandal and banished for life. Louisville was dropped from the league. Louisville was without a professional team from 1879 to '81, then fielded a team in the American Association from 1882 to 1891 before returning to the National League as the Colonels in 1893, with John Chapman again as manager. Luckily for Hughie Jennings, John Chapman liked to read.

Neither Allentown nor Harrisburg signed Hughie for 1891 and Hughie wound up back in Lehighton. Late in May, Lehighton had a few days off and Hughie went home. Chapman, the manager of the Louisville franchise, habitually took 10 newspapers a day. In Philadelphia with his team in May of '91, at the same time that Hughie was visiting home, Chapman took dinner in the hotel with his newspapers spread out in front of him. After he caught up on the news, he scoured box scores and came across an account of Lehighton game in a Philadelphia paper. The line score of the Lehighton catcher, one H. Jennings, caught his eye. In an August 1908 *Baseball Magazine* article, Chapman, in the oddly for-

mal writing style of the time, described how he discovered and signed
Hughie.

> I had taken my Louisville team of the American Association to
> Philadelphia when Jack Ryan of our club was hurt and had to be taken
> from behind the bat. We were hard pressed for a substitute and had
> pressed into service Tommy Cahill. I was put to it for a catcher and
> began skirmishing around for a man who would fit into the place.
>   Casually reading the paper the evening of my trouble I noticed an
> account of a game between the Lehightons and some other team in
> which a young man by the name of Jennings, who caught, seemed to
> be the whole show. He had 15 put outs and four-of-five hits, a home
> run among them. I rushed to the telegraph office and sent a hurry-up
> call to his home in Moosic, a little mining town six miles from Scran-
> ton, asking if he would not join my Louisville team.
>   It did not take long for his affirmative to get back. I wired I would
> give him $175 if he proved satisfactory and directed him to answer me
> in Boston and for him to report in Louisville. When we got back to
> Louisville this young man reported to me at the Fifth Avenue hotel.
>   I will have to admit that I was disappointed in his looks, for his gen-
> eral appearance was somewhat verdant. It was with fear and trembling
> that I watched him at his first tryout, for I had begun to think I had
> invested in a salted mine. But the moment he got his glove on his
> hand he was another man. A simple mitt worked wonders with him. I
> had no chance to work him out behind the bat, through, as Ryan had
> come around all right, until first baseman Taylor was injured. Here
> was an opportunity for my new man to show what stuff he was made
> of.
>   "Mr. Chapman," he answered, "I have never played the position in
> my life and I fear I cannot fill the bill."
>   "You'll have to try your hand at it, I have no one else at all."
>   "All right, I'll do the best I can."
>   Things began to happen. He tickled the crowd by the way he pulled
> down the high-sailers, reached for wild ones and dug balls out of the
> dirt. His best was amply good. I might add that I was tickled, too.
>   Jennings had earned the right to be called "Hughey."[3]

The $175 per month Chapman offered was a staggering sum beyond
the comprehension of most of the adults in Hughie's life. It was more
than even the most experienced miner could command. Even more
important than the $175 monthly salary was the $100 advance Chapman
sent. Hughie always said he never would have made it to the big leagues
without that $100.[4] When word of the offer spread, the citizens of Avoca,
Moosic, Pittston and the surrounding towns were astounded. Hundreds
accompanied him to the train station to see him off to Louisville. As the
first fully professional baseball player any of them had ever known, he
was suddenly the biggest local celebrity in coal country.[5] Hughie bought

a ticket with the $100 advance, put the change in the pocket of his jeans and climbed aboard.

There was one regret. Hughie had to leave his old batterymate, Martin O'Hara, behind. "O'Hara never advanced but that was not his fault," Hughie said. "He hurt his arm and the injury ended his career. O'Hara might now be listed with the pitching stars of all time had he escaped injury, for he had much speed and an excellent curve ball. He was also unusually intelligent. The O'Hara case impressed me with the gamble that base ball is. A player never knows when his career will be stopped. It is a precarious business, no matter how carefully the player may look after himself."[6]

Hughie made his major league debut starting at first base for Louisville on June 1 in a 14–5 loss to Washington in Louisville. He got through the game without an error, but in another respect, it was not a dignified debut. Because there was no uniform to fit him, he had to wear a uniform several times too big. A *Sporting Life* story in March of 1916 said the uniform Hughie wore that day had belonged to "Monk" Cline, who the story described as "a huge man." That's probably wrong, as Cline is listed in *Macmillan* as 5'-4" and 150 pounds. Hughie was 5'-8" and 165. So the uniform Hughie wore was likely not Cline's. In any case the story is likely true as it is recounted in several sources. The following passage is from a story in *Sporting Life.*

> The suit fitted him like a Charley Chaplin outfit. The pants flapped down around his ankles like ancient pantalets. The shirt wrapped itself around him like a pillow case and impeded every movement. In short Jennings looked as did Icabod Crane, "like a scarecrow eloped from a cornfield." To make matters worse the boy realized he looked like a fool and that everyone in the ballpark, including his own teammates, were laughing at him. His red face grew redder until it flamed like the setting sun, but he gritted his teeth and swore to show them what was in him.[7]

Hughie played 17 games at first before Taylor recovered and reclaimed his spot. Chapman then put Hughie at third, another new position. He played third for seven games filling in for another injured player, Ollie Beard. Beard came back, but then shortstop Tommy Cahill went down. Years later Ryan, the injured catcher Hughie had been signed to replace, told *Boston Herald* writer Carl Warton how Hughie wound up at shortstop.

According to Ryan, Chapman walked through the train one night looking for Beard to tell him he was going to have to play short. Ryan believed that Chapman was going to release Jennings once the train reached

Columbus. But Beard could not be found. It turned out he had sneaked off the train in Cincinnati and jumped to a team in the outlawed Western League for more money. Out of options Chapman put Hughie at shortstop. "I don't need to say anything more" Ryan said.[8]

Hughie played in 90 of the 93 available games after he joined the team on June 7, the last 70 at shortstop. For the season Hughie batted .292, scored 53 runs and batted in 58. Offering a preview of what was to become a specialty, he got hit by nine pitched balls, second on the team to a regular player who was hit 11 times. At short Hughie made a whopping 49 errors, but averaged more total chances per game, 6.6, than any shortstop in either the American Association or the National League. His 225 assists prorated to a full 139-game season would have been the second highest in the league. It was a good showing at short for a rookie who had come up as a catcher.

Reaching the major leagues with Louisville in 1891 was bad timing for Hughie when it came to salary. Had he come up just a year earlier he might have been able to jump to the Players' League for more money, as 81 National Leaguers and 28 American Association players had, in some cases for $5,000. The Players League, formed out of Johnny Ward's Brotherhood of Professional Baseball Players, was a response to the reserve clause and the $2500 salary limit the owners adopted between the 1889 and 1890 seasons. The reserve clause bound a player to one team for his entire career, unless the team released him, traded or sold him to another team. In 1890 the Players League, National League and American Association fielded 24 major league teams. Seven cities had two teams. Philadelphia and Brooklyn had three. Supply far outweighed the demand and all the teams lost money. The Players League folded in December of 1890 after just one season, leaving just the American Association and National League as the only recognized major leagues in 1891. The AA and NL owners agreed to let the players who had jumped to the Players League return to their old teams without reprisals. But when Pittsburgh and Boston of the NL didn't honor the deal and signed players belonging to the Association's Philadelphia Athletics, the Association withdrew from the agreement with the National League it had signed in 1883. With a window for player movement thus opened, each league raided players from the other. King Kelly, one of the biggest names in the game, was one who jumped leagues in 1891, from the National to the American and then back again.[9]

The New York Giants of the National League expressed an interest in the Colonels' rookie shortstop. Hughie may have entertained the thought of jumping to New York, but once his family found out about it, the idea was quickly and quietly nixed. His father, who read about the Giant offer in a newspaper, scolded Hughie about honor and wrote to Hughie's older brother James, who had moved to Colorado to be a mine foreman. James, in turn, wrote a letter to the Louisville owner, a Dr. Stuckey, and promised to use his influence to stop Hughie from dishonoring the Jennings name by jumping leagues. Chastened, Hughie stayed in Louisville.

The Association's rebellion lasted only through the 1891 season. After the season the leagues agreed to fold the four weakest AA teams and merge the four strongest — Baltimore, Washington, Philadelphia and Louisville — into the National League to form a 12-team circuit. The players gained nothing. With only one major league they had nowhere to go and the reserve clause remained in place, as it would for the next 80 years. Even so, Hughie would eventually leave Louisville. And the chain of events which would lead him away began with the fan with the leg cast. When the Colonels played a 17-game home stand in September a man with his leg in a huge plaster cast took in the games from the owner's box. He was a patient of the owner, Dr. Stuckey, who had operated on his knee. The man, as he would say in a magazine article years later, liked what he saw. "Just as soon as Dr. Stuckey put my knee in a plaster cast he permitted me to go to the ballpark every day and see the game. It was there that I saw a little fellow so full of ginger that I admired his play. He had red hair and a smiling countenance, and later became an idol of the Baltimore fans. He was Hughey Jennings."

The man in the plaster cast was Ned Hanlon.[10]

4

Harry von der Horst Finds a Manager

In 1729 the Maryland colonial government founded a town on the Patapsco River about two-thirds of the way up Chesapeake Bay on one of the largest natural harbors in the world. Though set up as a trading center for the tobacco farmers of southern Maryland, the settlement — named Baltimore Town in honor of the Lords Baltimore, the family that founded the colony of Maryland — became pivotal in the early history of the fledgling United States of America. During the Revolutionary War Baltimore served as the national capital for two months. Baltimore grew steadily as a commercial and cultural center during the 1800s. Though only 100 and 190 miles from baseball hotbeds Philadelphia and New York City, Baltimore's baseball culture was not as advanced as in the northeastern cities in the 1850s. In 1860 the city got a look at organized baseball, the New York version, when the Brooklyn Excelsiors stopped in Maryland on what some baseball historians like to call the first "road trip."[1]

After the Civil War baseball boomed at the grass roots level in Baltimore, just as it did all over the country. Local merchants and neighborhoods formed teams and leagues. In 1871 Baltimore got its first professional team, a franchise called the Lord Baltimores in the National Association of Professional Base Ball Players, which is considered the first professional league. The National Association, a player-run league, lasted from 1871 to 1875, when it was supplanted by the National League. Baltimore was not awarded a National League franchise, but the city got back into professional baseball in 1882 in a new league, the American Association of Base Ball Clubs, a rival to the National League formed in Cincinnati in the winter of 1881. The league's hooks were Sunday baseball and beer at the ballparks, banned in the National. The Baltimore AABBC franchise produced

28

the city's first stars, pitcher Matt Kilroy, who struck out 513 batters in 1886 and won 46 games in 1887, and Tommy Tucker, a hard-hitting, hard-drinking first baseman who led in batting in 1889.[2]

The Sunday baseball idea didn't fly in Baltimore, but the beer did. The Baltimore franchise was owned by Harry von der Horst, son of J.H. von der Horst of J.H. von der Horst and Sons Brewing Co, the largest of the city's 20 breweries. The brewery was known as the Eagle Brewery for the Golden Eagle statue atop the five-story brew house. Von der Horst is German for Eagle's nest.[3]

In 1890 Baltimore was the seventh largest city in the country with a population of about a half million. Though Maryland had been founded by Catholics, Baltimore was also home to poor whites from Appalachia, blacks, Germans, Irish, Russians, Anglo-Protestants, and Jews. Most of the residents lived in single-family homes. There were no tenements, and a two-story home could be had for $15 per month. There were plenty of jobs on the docks, which shipped more goods than any port the world, and in the breweries, cigar factories, and can factories, which supplied the largest oyster-canning industry in the world.

Through 1891 Baltimoreans supported Harry von der Horst's baseball team well enough to keep it going, but barely. Harry was desperate to increase attendance. The beer garden and restaurant were a draw, but what the Orioles needed was a winning team. Harry knew this, but didn't know how to build one and proved it by putting his top beer salesman, and team traveling secretary, Jack Waltz, in charge of the team in 1892. The Orioles were 1–10 under Waltz when they limped into Pittsburgh on April 29th in '92. Waltz may have been in over his head as field manager, but as he watched the Orioles get crushed by the Pirates 12–3 and then 13–1 the next day, he came up an idea which would change the face of baseball and the life of Hughie Jennings. Waltz sent von der Horst a telegram urging him to make an offer for the Pirates' 34-year-old player/manager, Ned Hanlon.[4]

Edward "Ned" Hanlon was born the son of a Irish-American carpenter in Montville, Connecticut, on August 22, 1857. His family was aghast when he quit school as a teenager to pitch for Norwich and New London baseball teams. In 1876 when he was 18, he was signed by New Providence in the New England League. He reached the National League with Cleveland 1881 and was sold to Detroit during that season. The Wolverines, as the Detroit franchise was called, converted Hanlon to a center fielder, and he became a star. A barehanded speedster, he had a knack for judging fly balls. He astounded his teammates by taking his eyes off long hits and running to the spot where the ball came down. Thin and quiet with a handlebar mustache "Silent Ned" looked, and hit, more like a librarian than a center fielder. Even so, he managed to get on base and score. One trick was to fake being hit by a close pitch, falling and pinching himself to make a red mark. In 1881, at age 24, he was voted captain of the Wolverines. With the Wolverines in 1887, he played in an early world series, a 15-game road odyssey with the St. Louis Browns. The Wolverines won 10 of the games.[5] When the Wolverines folded after the 1888 season, Pittsburgh paid $5000 for Hanlon, a princely sum for the time. He started the 1889 season as the Pirates' center fielder and by season's end, he was their manager, as well. In the off season he made a national reputation by captaining Johnny Ward's All-Americas on a world tour.

Hanlon and Ward, a second baseman for the New York Giants and a law school graduate, were early advocates of players rights. In 1887, Hanlon joined Dan Brouthers and Ward at the National League meetings and tried to negotiate with owners to recognize Ward's union, the Players' Brotherhood; agree to a free agency plan, and scrap the salary cap. When the owners, who had set a salary cap at $2,500 a year, scoffed at the Brotherhood, the Players League was launched in 1890. Hanlon, who had made some money in real estate, became player, manager and stockholder with Pittsburgh of the Players League. When the Players League folded after just one season, the Pirates took Hanlon back and made him full-time manager in 1891. This time he lasted only 78 games before he was driven out by a player rebellion against his strict insistence that the players stay in condition and drink moderately, if at all. The Pirates put him back in center field, but that plan, too, was doomed when Hanlon tore up his knee in September. Hanlon tried out his knee in spring practice in '92, but it was clear he couldn't play anymore. So the Pirates were happy to let von der Horst and Waltz talk to him about taking over as field manager of the Orioles. The three men met in Chicago on May 5, where the Orioles were playing the Colts. Hanlon insisted on full authority to run the team, including player decisions. Harry agreed and the deal was made. After a quick trip back to Pittsburgh to settle some affairs, Hanlon met von der Horst again in Cincinnati on May 8, where Hanlon officially took over the 2–16 Orioles. The Pirates were glad to get their $5000 back and unload Hanlon's salary, also believed to be close to $5000. Little could either side have known that they were ushering in a new baseball era.

When Hanlon took over the Orioles in '92, Hughie was back in Louisville as the incumbent shortstop, having signed for the same $175 a month he had been paid in '91. The Colonels, now in the National League, went 11–3 in the first 14 games and on May 3 were in second place just one-half game behind Boston. But they lost 14 of their next 17 games. When they beat the Brooklyn Bridegrooms, as they were called that season, on June 3 to end a six-game losing streak, the Colonels had dropped to ninth place in the new 12-team league National League, 10½ games behind Boston. Through the ups and downs Hughie played just well enough to not to dissuade Chapman from keeping him at short. There was one highlight for Hughie during the early part of the season. On Thursday, May 26, in 7–0 loss in Boston, he broke up a no-hit bid by the Beaneaters' John Clarkson with a single through he infield with two outs in the ninth inning. When the Colonels limped back to Louisville on June 20 after winning six and losing 19 on a 27-day, 25-game road trip, Dr. Stuckey, the president, fired Chapman. Fred Pfeffer was the new manager. The change didn't help. The Colonels were 23–35 in 54 games under Chapman and 40–54 in 100 games under Pfeffer. They finished ninth, 40 games behind Boston.

Hughie found playing and batting in the National League a little tougher than it had been in the American Association. He played all 152 games at shortstop and while he led the Colonels in RBI with 65, scored 65 runs, stole 28 bases, he batted only .222. While that was in the bottom ten among regular players in the league, .222 wasn't as anemic as it sounds, not in a season in which the league average was just .245.

5

Foxy Ned

Within days of taking over the Orioles in May of 1892, Ned Hanlon asserted his authority by suspending the team's best pitcher, Sadie McMahon, when the hard-drinking Irishman, who once had been tried and acquitted of murder, showed up drunk and cursed his new manager out.[1] Even so, McMahon was one of only three of the 17 players from '92 that Hanlon kept for '93. Another was the hard-working innovative catcher from Massachusetts, Wilbert Robinson. Known as "Robby," he was a lovable, 215-pound lug with a permanently calm and happy demeanor. Though not much of an average hitter, Robinson had qualities Hanlon adored. He was the first to arrive on game days and last to leave. He practiced long and hard and always took the lead on team runs. Robinson was one of first catchers to signal pitchers, rather than the other way around, and to position himself close behind home in a squat so his signals could be read. He recklessly stopped pitches and guarded home with his body.[2]

The third player Hanlon kept from the '92 squad was John McGraw, a skinny 5'-7", 19-year-old infielder from New York state. On paper, keeping McGraw over several of the regular players didn't make sense. McGraw had played in 76 games at six different positions and batted only .267. Hanlon left him behind on three road trips to save money. His salary of $1200 was the lowest in the league. Toughened by a rough childhood—his mother and four siblings died of diphtheria when he was 12 and he was beaten by his father—McGraw feared no man. As a rookie he fought a veteran who had pushed him off the bench and had to be restrained when he went for a bat. He played baseball crazily. It was as though each game was a challenge to his manhood. That trumped his statistical shortcomings for Hanlon.

With McGraw in the nest, Hanlon had one part in place. He needed three more to complete what was to become the famous "Big Four" of the Baltimore Orioles, the core of the dynasty to come. Part Two was Joe Kelly.

Here Hanlon showed his genius in recognizing buried talent and gauging hidden heart. Hanlon had run out of patience with center fielder George Van Haltren. In 1891, though only 25, Van Haltren had been named interim player-manager of the Orioles in the AA for the last week of the season. In '92, with the Orioles now in the National League, von der Horst kept Van Haltren on as manager. But when the Orioles started 1-14, with one of the losses being a forfeit caused by Van Haltren's failure to inform an umpire that the Orioles had to leave early to catch a train, von der Horst replaced Van Haltren with Waltz, the beer salesman, and then with Hanlon. After the demotion, Van Haltren suddenly fell apart as a player. He ran into numerous outs on the basepaths and dropped routine fly balls. Hanlon wasn't surprised. He knew from experience that it was hard to go from manager to player. By season's end Van Haltren had 52 errors in the left field. In the waning days of the season Hanlon offered Van Haltren to the Pirates for $2000. The Pirates couldn't believe their luck. They were so happy, they didn't flinch when Hanlon asked them to throw in Joe Kelley, the very man who had replaced Hanlon in the Pirate outfield after his knee injury, to complete the deal. From the Pirates' perspective they were getting a proven hitter in his prime for an untested kid barely out of his teens. From Hanlon's perspective he was getting what he coveted — youth and speed. Besides, he was wary of Van Haltren. "It's better to have a good ballplayer than a great one who, for some reason, doesn't play as well as he should," he said.

"Kelley was regarded as a comer, but Van Haltren was looked upon as a star," Hanlon said. "Some of the Baltimore fans did not like the trade very much, but I kept quiet. Of course, everyone knows how Van Haltren went down hill and Kelley became one of the greatest outfielders in the country."[3]

Kelley, a handsome and powerfully built ladies' man, was fast on and off the field. He was an athletic and aggressive runner — when he got on base. The Pirates had given up hope that Kelley would ever develop as a batter. They were wrong. From 1894–'98, Kelley would bat .357 for the Orioles. The Baltimore sports writers added a "e" to Kelly's name and he became Kelley, which was considered a classier name, lace curtain, rather than shanty Irish. The $2000 from the Kelley deal helped the team's bottom line, but the Orioles were still hurting. Hanlon loaned von der Horst $7000 of his own money for a quarter of the team's stock and full control. He was elected president and von der Horst was elected treasurer. With all the changes going down, the Baltimore writers besieged von der Horst with questions. His answer was to point to the button on his lapel. It read — "ask Hanlon."[4]

One of the things the writers might have asked Hanlon was: When were the Orioles going to win? At his first team meeting in '92 Hanlon set what sounded like a modest goal: go .500 the rest of the way. They didn't get near it. Though they won their first four under Hanlon, they won only one-third the rest of the season and finished 1892 last in the 12-team National League with a 46-101 record, 54½ games behind the first-place Boston Beaneaters. The Orioles drew only 93,000 for 70 dates. But Hanlon was undeterred by the losing and the empty seats. He had a long-range plan to change both conditions. Acquiring Kelley in the waning days of the 1892 was part one of the plan. Next he needed a shortstop. That would have to wait until the 1893 season

On March 7 in 1893 the National League held its annual meeting at Fifth Avenue Hotel in New York City. More rule changes were on the agenda. The distance from the pitching box to home plate had been moved back from 45 feet to 50 feet in 1881. Overhand pitching had been legalized in 1884. In 1889 the three-strike rule and in 1889 the four-ball rule were made permanent. At the '93 meeting, Brooklyn owner Charley Byrne was one of the leaders of a group of owners who clamored for something to be done about the dearth of batting. Batting averages had been dropping for years, reaching a league overall low of .245 in 1892. The Byrne proposal was to move the pitching box back to the center of the infield diamond, 63'-6" from home plate. Byrne and the owners who favored the move believed increased hitting and run scoring would bring more fans to the parks. But Byrne had another reason for wanting to move the pitchers back — Amos Rusie of the rival New York Giants. Rusie, a 6'-1", 215 pound pitcher known as the "Hoosier Thunderbolt," had struck out 625 batters in '91 and '92, including hundreds of Byrne's Brooklyn Trolley Dodgers. Rusie was the fastest thrower in baseball. Hughie would learn this the hard way in 1897.

Predictably, the Giants were against moving the pitchers back. So was Frank Robison of Cleveland. He had Cy Young on his team. The owners bickered for hours and finally compromised on 60'-6" measured from the closest corner of the diamond-shaped plate. They also agreed to eliminate the 5' by 4'-6" pitcher's box and install a foot-long and four-inch wide pitcher's rubber. The pitcher would have to keep his back foot on rubber. Previously they had been allowed to take a skip step in a box. The vote was 11-1. Robison was the no vote. [5]

While some, including Henry Chadwick, baseball's pre-eminent journalist, predicted the rules wouldn't change the game much, Hanlon knew better. He figured that while a few pitchers— Rusie and Young were two— threw hard enough to adjust, most were going to have their effectiveness diminished. With more time to see the ball and swing, surely batters would hit better. It made so much sense Hanlon was stunned, and happy, that many managers didn't believe it. (Hanlon would be vindicated by the numbers. Strikeouts dropped by half in '93 and the league batting average went up 35 points to .280.) If more balls were going to be put in play, Hanlon reasoned that aggressive base runners and fast fielders were a formula for success. Players like these could be taught to hit and besides, hitting was unreliable. Speed didn't have slumps. But it would take Hanlon another season to put a team together that could maximize the 60'-6" advantage.

If the new pitching distance was supposed to be an advantage for the batters, Hughie seemed determined to prove it was not. During spring practice and in the early part of the '93 season, he tired easily and was way off his form. Within a few weeks, he was diagnosed with malaria. The Colonels were sick, too. They continued to lose and attendance was dropping. They were outdrawing only Baltimore and Washington. The National League office didn't see Louisville as a good baseball town and wanted to move the franchise to Buffalo or see it sold to a group of businessmen in Milwaukee. But the Colonels resisted and in defiance opened a new field, Parkland Field, on May 22nd. It didn't help. They lost to Cincinnati 3-1. The Colonels were 3-17, and in the throes of a seven-game losing streak, when they arrived in Baltimore for a three-game set at Union Park on June 3. Their manager was "Bald Billy" Barnie, who had managed the Orioles in '91. By then, Hughie was over the malaria, but had lost so much weight he could hardly lift a bat. He had as many errors, 16, as hits, and was hitting .136. The Colonels had one player who was considered a star and Hanlon, in his continued quest to remake the Orioles, wanted that player, Harry Taylor, the beanpole first baseman. The left-handed hitting Taylor, 6'-2" and 160, had no power but was hitting .300 and was agile around the bag. Taylor was from New York State and wanted to play in the East. Hanlon offered to buy him, but Barnie wanted a player, the Orioles shortstop Tim O'Rourke, who was hitting .363. Hanlon immediately said no, but then made a counteroffer. He'd let go of O'Rourke, if Barnie would throw in that anemic-looking young shortstop with the coal dust under his nails. What was his name? Hughie Jennings? Here Hanlon was at his best as a deal maker. He may have sold Barnie on the idea that Hughie was just a minor player in a major deal for Taylor, but it was Hughie Hanlon coveted. Hanlon hadn't forgotten the fiery redhead he had watched while recuperating from his knee injury in Louisville in September of '91. Barnie liked Hughie, but as a practical matter, how could he refuse such a deal? At 27, O'Rourke was a seasoned player who seemed to be hitting his stride as a batter. Hughie, on the other hand, was batting .136. Barnie made the deal. Part Three of the "Big Four" was in place. When Chapman, by this time out of baseball and living in New York City, read about the deal, he told a New York writer, "Louisville has made a great mistake in letting Jennings go."[6]

The day after the trade was agreed to, but before the players switched teams, Hughie made a play that vindicated Chapman's and Hanlon's confidence in him and gave the Orioles a preview of things to come. Diving for a ground ball hit up the middle by Robinson, Hughie rolled onto his back and snapped a throw to first between his legs for the out. If the fans and Oriole players were stunned by the play, Hanlon wasn't. It was just what he expected from Hughie and why he wanted him. He was building a modern baseball team, one which would combat the increased batting brought on by the new pitching rules with speed and fielding. Hanlon was earning a new nickname. Soon he would be known as "Foxy Ned."

Clearly Hanlon saw something in Hughie that others didn't. Hughie bailed out on inside pitches, but he was fearless in the field and on the basepaths, diving for balls and into bases. Though he was thought to be 24, he was in fact 22. With his skinny body, thousands of freckles and startling red hair he looked even younger. [7] He had a sunny disposition, a constant grin, and an optimistic outlook. He never looked back and didn't beat himself up over his failures. He believed tomorrow would be better. He was right.

Hanlon's long-range plan was to put Hughie at shortstop, McGraw at third and Heinie Reitz at second. But as Hughie was sick, he played in only 16 games the rest of the way after joining the Orioles in June of '93. Instead Hanlon played McGraw at short and Bill Shindle at third for the rest of the '93 season. McGraw made 68 errors in 117 games and Shindle 63 in 125 games. But the errors weren't the worst of it. Given the field conditions and rudimentary gloves, errors were common. Four regular shortstops made more errors than McGraw in '93, including Washington's Joe Sullivan, who led the league with 102. A greater problem was McGraw's limited range at short. Hanlon sensed that many balls that went through the left side of the infield in '93 could have been turned into outs with Hughie at short, and McGraw, who outhit Shindle by 80 points, at third. But Hanlon was a patient man. Teaming Reitz and Hughie in the middle of the diamond with McGraw at the hot corner would have to wait until 1894.

As '93 wound down, the Orioles were not getting to Hanlon's goal of .500 and were in eighth place. Hanlon, with little to lose, started trying the plays he was dreaming about for years, the place-hit, the hit-and-run, and the bunt for a hit. As a player for the Detroit Wolverines, Hanlon had tried bunting for hits with some success, even though the tactics were scorned by his teammates as unmanly. Hanlon did his bunting when pitchers were only 50 feet away and roamed a large box, putting them in good fielding position. But in 1893, with the pitchers five feet farther back and tethered to a small rubber, they needed greater concentration and effort to throw each pitch and were vulnerable to bunts.

The new pitching distance affected everything. Because pitches took fractionally longer to reach the plate, batters put more balls in play. Because batters put more balls in play, infielders took fewer chances leaving their positions early and base runners got better jumps. Nobody realized better than Hanlon that these were perfect ingredients for the hit-and-run play. Hanlon was also a proponent of double steals, drag bunts and infield shifts. He had the Orioles work regularly on first-to-second-back-to-first double plays and schooled the pitchers in covering first base. While these tactics would become routine in the years to come, in 1893 they were undervalued by all but Foxy Ned. While Baltimore and Hanlon often get credit for inventing modern baseball, or "scientific" baseball as the sportswriters called it, the King Kelly and Boston Beaneaters were the pioneers. They won three consecutive pennants in 1891-92-93 using similar tactics. Hanlon may not have invented "scientific baseball" but he reinvented it for the 20th century. Baltimore's Union Park, because its deep fences discouraged power hitting, was better designed for such a style of play than Boston's field was. And Baltimore was better suited than Boston to accept modernity. After all, it was Baltimore where the first telegraph message was received and the crown cork stopper was invented, making it practical to bottle beer.[8]

But Hanlon still had to finish his team, especially his outfield, where, by the end of '93, he had tried 12 different players, including Hughie for one game. In September of 1893, he found an outfielder who was a keeper in Walter Scott "Steve" Brodie, a flycatcher in Hanlon's own image. Brodie had an instinct for gauging where fly balls would come down and would often take his eye off the ball to increase his speed to the spot, just as Hanlon had done in his prime. It was a tactic few players had the courage to try. Brodie was the son of a Confederate officer from Virginia. Inexplicably, he got his nickname from a Bowery bartender who jumped off the Brooklyn Bridge and lived to tell about it. A wildly inconsistent hitter, he had an oddball reputation. He talked to himself in the field, hit himself in the head when he made a bad play and shagged practice flies behind his back. For the St. Louis Browns, his strangeness made him an easy sell. Hanlon got him cheap.

Next, Hanlon went after a first baseman. He made a pitch for Dan

Brouthers, the Brooklyn first baseman, who had been Hanlon's teammate in Detroit. Brouthers was older, 35, bigger, 6'-1" and 210, and slower than Hughie and McGraw, but he had credentials as a batter. He had hit over .300 for 13 straight seasons and had led the league in home runs twice. But Hanlon knew Brouthers was near the end and wanted him as much to produce harmony as runs. Brouthers was a family man with four kids and Hanlon saw him as a mature influence for his young team. Brouthers, big and slow, may not have been a player built for Hanlon's scientific baseball, but in the deal, Hanlon lucked out and got a throw-in who would come to define it. Hanlon offered Brooklyn his right fielder George Treadway for Brouthers. Hanlon was willing to move the dark-skinned Treadway, in part, because there were rumblings among the Baltimore fans that he was black. Brooklyn manager Charlie Byrne didn't mind losing Brouthers, but wanted a third baseman in return. Since he was planning to move McGraw to third, anyway, Hanlon didn't mind losing Shindle, but insisted on a two-for-two deal. So Brooklyn threw in the 130-pound player without a position whom they had just sent to Binghamton and were planning to release. His Christian name was William O'Kelleher, but everybody called him "Wee Willie" Keeler.

6

The Big Four

John McGraw — a sober, hardworking, devout Irish-Catholic widower in his 30s — moved from New York City to Truxton in Cortland County, New York, in 1871. He got a job with the Elmira, Cortland and Northern Railroad, starting as a track-gang laborer for $9 a week. He got remarried to a local 19-year-old girl, Ellen Comfort. A son was born on April 7, 1873, and named John Joseph for his father and grandfather back in Ireland. The Truxton young John grew up in was a town of about 500 with a bank, tavern, and one Roman Catholic church, St. Patrick's, where he served as an altar boy. He worked around town doing odd jobs for spare change. He saved $1 and sent to the new Spalding Company in Chicago for a baseball. He carried the ball with him everywhere and got up games with his schoolmates in the school yard. When they went home, he stayed until dark throwing the ball against a wall.

In the winter of 1884–85 a hard life became even harder when John's mother and four of his siblings died in a diphtheria epidemic. John and his father fought over baseball. His father didn't want him playing when he could be helping out at home or doing something to earn money. In the fall of 1885 they got in a fist fight after John broke a window with a baseball. John lost the fight and left home. He wound up at the local hotel, the Truxton House. The widowed hotelkeeper, Mary Goddard, had little trouble convincing John's father to let the boy stay with her. Living with Goddard, John did well in school, worked at the hotel, and for the railroad, selling magazines and snacks on the Cortland-Elmira run. He made enough money to buy baseballs and Spalding guides. He studied the statistics and the rules and soon knew more baseball than any adult in town. At 16, and 5'-5" and 110 pounds, he was the best pitcher and best position player on his school team and the town team, the Truxton Grays. When he was asked to pitch for the town team in Homer five miles away, he agreed under two conditions — $5 a game and transportation back and forth from Truxton. A large crowd came out to see him pitch his first game. He won and rode off in the manager's buggy with $5 and to the cheers of the crowd. This, he thought, is for me.

On April 1, 1890, McGraw signed his first professional contract for $40 a month with the Olean, New York, franchise in the New York-Penn League. Six days later, McGraw turned 17. When Olean started 0–6, McGraw was the first player released in a housecleaning. The owner, Bert Kenney, gave him $70 and wished him Godspeed. Determined not to go back to Truxton, McGraw went to Wellsville, about 30 miles away, and signed on with the team there in the Western New York League. He got in 24 games before the season ended in late September. He hit .365 in 107 at bats. He caught the attention of one Alfred W. Lawson. Lawson, though just 21, was something of a minor league baseball version of P.T. Barnum. He wanted to put together a team to barnstorm in Cuba. To that end he somehow landed in Wellsville, New York, where he took a liking to the hustling McGraw kid and asked him to join his American All-Stars in Ocala, Florida, after the New Year to prepare for a trip to Cuba. McGraw went home, worked November and December at The Truxton House to save money for train fare to Florida. He spent Christmas with his family and Goddard, then boarded a coach for the week-long ride to Florida. He had made his break from Truxton and the life of a railroader. Little could he have known that within four years he would be a major force on the greatest baseball team of its era.

The rise to such lofty heights started with "El mono amarillo" or "yellow monkey." That was what the Cuban fans called McGraw because of his size and the team's yellow uniforms. Lawson's team played a series of games in a 10,000-seat park outside Havana. The Cuban series drew only enough fans to meet expenses and get the team as far as Key West, where they played a few games to get enough money for the trip to mainland Florida. By February 1891 they were back in Gainesville. The team broke up and most of the players headed back north to a normal life. McGraw, and four other players, stayed with Lawson and signed for "board, shaving expenses and a cigar once a week."[1] McGraw didn't shave or smoke. All he wanted to do was play baseball. Lawson mixed his five holdovers with some local players. When they beat a couple of other local teams, Lawson billed the team as the Champions of Central Florida and talked the Cleveland Indians, who were training in Jacksonville, into playing a game. For McGraw, Lawson's promotional ability proved serendipitous. Lee Viau, a two-time 20-game winner for Cincinnati who would go on to win 18 for the Indians that year, pitched for Cleveland. The Indians won 9–6, but McGraw played clean at short and went 3-for-5 with three doubles, three runs scored. A report of the game made it into the Cleveland papers and got mentioned in The Sporting News.[2] Based on that single game, McGraw got offers from several professional teams. The Cedar Rapids Canaries of the Illinois-Iowa League met McGraw's demand of a $75 advance and $125 per month. He made his way to Cedar Rapids, arriving in April, 1891.

As he had against Cleveland with Lawson's team in Florida, McGraw got a chance to make an impression with real major leaguers when Cap Anson and the Chicago White Stockings stopped in Cedar Rapids to play a game on their way north. McGraw made a diving stop of a Anson liner, got a single off Bill Hutchinson and scrapped and hustled. Anson took notice and McGraw's reputation grew. That reputation reached Bill Barnie, the manager of the Baltimore club in the American Association. Barnie asked a friend in the Illinois-Iowa League, Bill Gleason, to check out McGraw. Gleason asked McGraw to assess himself. "I'm just about as good as they come," was the answer.[3]

Barnie sent a wire to Cedar Rapids. That night the Canaries' manager went to McGraw's room, woke him up and handed him the telegram. McGraw made such a commotion most of his teammates woke up. They formed a delegation to see McGraw off on the 2:30 a.m. train. Gleason said of McGraw, "He was happy as a schoolboy." Small wonder. McGraw practically was a schoolboy. He was 5'-6½" and 120 pounds, had just turned 18 that April. McGraw got to Baltimore on August 24, 1891. Barnie gave him a contract for $200 a month for what was left of the season. McGraw hit .245 in 31 games and made 18 errors in 86 chances, as Baltimore finished fourth that season in the American Association. Even so Harry von der Horst signed him to a contract for 1892 when Baltimore moved to the National League.[4]

What Hughie's hometown of Pittston was to coal and McGraw's hometown of Truxton, New York, was to the railroads, Joe Kelly's hometown of Cambridge, Massachusetts, was to the garment industry. So it was that Kelly (his name would later be changed to Kelley by Baltimore writers) got his first taste of organized baseball with a team from the Woven Hose, a sock manufacturing factory. Kelley was born December 9, 1871, into a staunch Irish Catholic family. Unlike Hughie and McGraw, Kelley finished high school at a parochial school. In the summers he learned to play baseball in the public parks with his schoolmates. Before long, he was a teenaged phenom in the local garment league as a pitcher, hitter and blazing fast runner. Before long the local professional team, Lowell, Massachusetts, in the New England League, signed the 19-year-old for the 1891 season. Kelley pitched and played outfield for Lowell and was hitting .323

with 22 stolen bases in just 61 games when his contract was purchased by the Boston Beaneaters of the National League. Kelley made his big league debut on July 27, 1891, and singled off 300-game winner and Hall of Famer Mickey Welch of the Giants. But after just 12 games, during which Kelley was 12–52 batting for a .231 average, the Beaneaters made it clear that they believed they had gone after the wrong Kelly. The right one was Mike "King" Kelly. Though the former Red Stocking star was 34 and his best seasons were behind him, the Troy, New York, native was one of the biggest names, and box office draws, in the game. To understand the difference in stature of the two Kellys, follow the money: Boston paid $10,000 for King and sold Joe to Pittsburgh for $500.

At Pittsburgh, Kelley got in only two games with the Pirates at the tail end of '91 and was shipped to Omaha. In Omaha in 1892 he was made the regular left fielder. He responded with a hot start, batting .316 in 58 games with 24 extra-base hits and 19 steals and earned a ticket back to Pittsburgh, then was traded to the Orioles in the Van Haltren deal. Kelley's physical talent was surpassed only by his physical beauty, and he knew it. He carried himself with a confident air that soon earned him the nickname "Swaggering" Joe Kelley." He made his debut as an Oriole on September 25 in 1892.[5]

William Keeler was born William O'Kelleher in Brooklyn in 1872. Two years earlier, and less than a mile away, the first professional ball club, the Cincinnati Red Stockings, lost for the first time after 84 consecutive wins, beaten by the Brooklyn Atlantics. As were Hughie, McGraw and Kelley, Keeler was the son of Irish immigrants. His father Pat was a trolley driver, and mother Mary was a housewife. Willie played "one o' cat," a rudimentary bat and ball game, in the streets as a child. Though much smaller than most of the kids, even younger ones, Willie was tough and wiry. At home he boxed and beat up his much bigger brothers. But baseball was his love and in Brooklyn love was all around. Just as Willie was coming of age in Brooklyn, so was the game of baseball. Fields were being laid out in every neighborhood and amateur teams were forming. At 14 Willie, though 5'-3" and barely 100 pounds, was asked to pitch for the Rivals, a well known amateur baseball club. He had a breakout game on a field at Green Street and Broadway when he pitched the Rivals to a 12–0 win over a local legend known as "Swifty." Years later Keeler called it his most gratifying win ever. Despite that win, Keeler wasn't really a pitcher. The Rivals put him at third base, even though he threw left-handed. In school he captained and batted leadoff for the P.S. 26 team. They beat every team in the Eastern Brooklyn District. As team captain, Willie was given a red and white belt with "Captain" stitched on it. "That belt, I never took off, night or day, in the summer," he said.[6]

At 15, he left school determined to make a life in baseball. A Brooklyn factory offered him a job and a position on the factory team. He played for the team, but never reported to work. His father got him a job in a cheese factory. He worked one week and was paid $2. That weekend he was paid $3 to play a game at Staten Island. Willie may have left school, but he could do simple math. He never worked again. At 16, he traveled by trolley and ferry to play whenever he could for the Aces, Sylvans, and Allertons in New Jersey. He found time to sell scorecards at Eastern Park in Brooklyn, where a professional team played, and where the boss changed his name to Keeler because it sounded more German.

In '91 the semiprofessional Plainfield Crescents in the Central New Jersey League offered Willie $60 a month to play full-time. Plainfield, a town of 11,000, many of them transplanted from New York City, was a short ride from New York on the Jersey Central Railroad. With Willie in the lineup, the Crescents were the biggest draw in the league. He got hit after hit and stole bases at will. One day he went 12-for-13 in a doubleheader. He batted .376 and the Crescents won the pennant. No wonder the Crescents and the league had a tantrum when Willie jumped to the Binghamton Bingos in the Eastern league for $90 a month in June of '92. Willie wrote a letter to the Plainfield manager, but it didn't help. The manager told the newspapers he would do whatever he could to ban Willie from the Central New Jersey League. When Willie got to Binghamton the Bingos were in last place, where they finished in the first half of the split-season league. But, with 153 hits and 109 runs in 93 games and a league-leading .373 average, Willie turned the team around and the Bingos won the second-half pennant. It was noted that Willie also made 48 errors. Sarcastically, he was known as the best left-handed third baseman in the league. All the others were right-handed.

In late September 1892 the Giants outbid Louisville and bought Willie for $800. They signed him for a salary of $1600 per full season. He played his first game in late September. Her started at third base and thus became the second left-handed third baseman in the National League. Hick Carpenter of Cincinnati, who was in his last season in '92, was the other. Carpenter made 625 errors in 11 seasons. Willie played the rest of '92 as if he was on a mission to surpass Carpenter, but he batted .321 in 14 games and stole five bases. He was signed for '93, when he was tried in the outfield. In a game in May, Willie misplayed a ball in the outfield and was caught stealing in the bottom of the inning. The next day the *New York Sun* wrote: "Here's Keeler's record of yesterday, no runs, no hits, no putouts, no assists."

The next day Willie hit a double, triple, and home run, but in the

10th he didn't get to a ball that cost the Giants the game. Again the papers panned him. "It was painful to watch," said one of Willie's outfield play. In July he fractured an ankle with a hard slide into second. When he came back eight weeks later, he was sold to Brooklyn for $800. This was even better than playing for the Giants. The Trolley Dodgers were his home-town team, and they played in Eastern Park, where Willie had sold score-cards three years earlier and had his name changed from O'Kelleher to Keeler. But after 20 games, even though he hit .313 and scored 14 runs with only four strikeouts, Trolley Dodger president Charley Byrne sent Willie back to Binghamton, complaining that he was too small for the big leagues. When the chance came in the off season, Byrne unloaded Willie on the Ori-oles.[7] Little could Byrne have known that he had just unloaded a player who would compile eight consecutive 200-hit seasons and, in 1897, hit safely in 44 consecutive games, a major league record that stood until Joe Dimaggio hit in 56 in 1941.

When Willie reported to the Orioles in the spring of 1894, the fourth piece was in place. By the end of the season Keeler, Kelley, McGraw and Jennings would be known around the country as "The Big Four" and the Orioles, who had failed again to reach Hanlon's .500 goal in 1893, would be known as champions.

7

The Beginning of a Dynasty

John McGraw had a breakout season with the Orioles in 1893. Playing out of position at short, he batted .321 and was fourth in the league in bases on balls with 101 and on-base percentage at .454. He also made it into the top 10 in stolen bases, 48, and runs scored, 123. Something else happened in 1893 season that would have a profound, lifelong affect on McGraw. He met a new teammate, Hugh Ambrose Jennings, a coal miner from Pennsylvania.

McGraw immediately took to Hughie. They had a lot in common. Their roots were in the Northeast. Their parents were Irish-Catholic immigrants. They each seized upon baseball as a way to escape what would have been their destinies on the rails and in the mines. And they both played baseball with a take-no-prisoners intensity. That Hanlon had traded for Hughie expressly to take McGraw's position didn't bother McGraw. If Hughie at short was best for the team, so be it. Given the season McGraw had in '93, Hanlon would have to play him somewhere in '94. Within weeks of Hughie's arrival the pair became fast friends.[1] Though Hughie and McGraw had a lot in common, they were a strange pair to develop such a deep and lasting friendship. Hughie was a happy man and McGraw was not. In photographs Hughie is invariably smiling, while McGraw is expressionless. McGraw comes across as a grumpy, bitter man, while Hughie was always upbeat. McGraw made enemies. Hughie made friends. To a degree it is likely Hughie was by nature a happy fellow, while McGraw was not, but their personality differences may have been magnified by their childhood experiences. McGraw's mother and four of his siblings died in a diphtheria epidemic when he was only nine. His father drank, beat him, isolated him and never accepted baseball. Hughie grew up in a large, sober and loving family, which escaped the tragedy of early death, which was common in those days. Though his father didn't understand baseball and discouraged Hughie from pursuing it as a career, he later acquiesced and became a fan and friend to Hughie's Oriole teammates.

As much as the men were different off the field, on the field they were alike. Both men were serious, cutthroat players, who could be sarcastic to teammates and opponents and cruel to umpires. McGraw stewed over losses, assigned blame, and carried grudges off the field. For McGraw baseball was his life. But for Hughie baseball was his livelihood, and therefore the only insulation between him and the life of a miner. That's why he played as intensely as he did. But Hughie separated baseball from the rest of life. When the game was over, it was over and he reverted to the smiling, happy redhead.

Once the '93 season ended neither Hughie nor McGraw could afford to stay in Baltimore. Hughie was resigned to spending the off-season back home in Avoca, but McGraw was loath to go back to Truxton. Remembering something that had happened back in Olean in the spring of 1890, he came up with an alternative. That spring in Olean, McGraw had made friends with the Reverend Joseph F. Dolan, a faculty member at the nearby Allegheny College, a school founded by Franciscan Monks which would later be renamed St. Bonaventure. Dolan was a baseball fan and a realist. He told McGraw that he should try to get a college education in case the baseball thing didn't work out. McGraw had designs on both. He wrote to Dolan and offered himself as coach for the school's baseball team in exchange for tuition for a few classes and room and board. Dolan convinced the school's president, Reverend Joseph Butler, to accept the deal. McGraw stayed at St. Bonaventure until mid-March when he reported to the Orioles camp in Macon, Georgia.

Though Hanlon's idea to take the team south in 1894 was not unprecedented, his intense two-a-day practice sessions, which started at 10 a.m. with bunting and hit-and-run practice, were. "Work, work, work all the time," as Hughie said when asked about Hanlon's practices.[2] They practiced fouling off pitches, cutoff plays and backing up throws. Pitchers worked on pickoff plays and covering first base. After two weeks of practice the Orioles went on a well-organized 18-game tour of the South. No other National League had a spring camp in the south that spring. In the future they all would. The team started to jell at the end of the 18-game spring schedule. Keeler batted .523 in the 18 games. In the final game in Macon they scored 14 runs, then headed north for the opener in Baltimore against the New York Giants on April 19. The Giants had finished 68–64 in 1993, fifth in the 12-team National League, and a lot of scribes expected them to improve enough to contend for the pennant. The Orioles, 60–70 and eighth place in '93, were given a shot at improving to maybe .500 and fifth place. As the baseball world was about to find out, the Orioles' spring camp was the catalyst for a far more dramatic improvement than eighth to fifth. In September of 1894, when the Washington Nationals announced they would have a spring camp in Hot Springs in 1895, the *Washington Post* said the Orioles, then in first place, had started a trend: "The remarkable record of the Baltimore team this season is attributed by baseball managers to the Southern trip of the Orioles last Spring. Remember Hanlon was the only one to take his players South for practice and had grand weather for the purpose, while other teams were getting in an occasional hour or two between cold, drizzling rain and snow storms. When the season opened the Orioles were the only team in anything like condition. It is therefore dollars to dimes to bet that twelve National League clubs will journey southward next spring."[3]

Somehow, based on what happened in Baltimore on opening day, the Baltimore fans sensed that 1894 was going to be a special season. The Orioles and the Giants were paraded from the Eutaw House — a famous hotel whose staff bragged that Charles Dickens and Henry Clay slept there — to Union Park. A band and drum corps led the parade, followed by a carriage of newspapermen, then Hanlon and Giants manager Johnny Ward in a barouche, a four-wheel fancy carriage with a fold-up hood and facing seats. Next came the catchers from each team, Wilbert Robinson of the Orioles and Duke Farrell of the Giants, leading a string of smaller two-wheeled carriages with one Giant and one Oriole in each. At the end were the requisite politicians and other VIPs. Buildings along the way were decorated with orange and black bunting. Fans crowded the sidewalks, waved from balconies, and climbed lampposts for a glimpse of the ballplayers. As the last carriage passed, hundreds of fans poured into the streets and joined the parade. Over 15,000 tickets were sold, the largest amount ever for an Oriole game. Von der Horst gave away another 1000 tickets to the mayor, governor, judges, leading businessmen and other dignitaries. The outfield was opened for standing room behind a line of policemen with hand-held ropes. Fans stood on nearby rooftops. A bell in the grandstand rang in the season. Hanlon, with the Orioles as the home team, chose to bat first. This was a common practice in the 1880s and 90s. Maybe Hanlon was in a hurry to show what he had put together. This was his opening day lineup: McGraw, 3b; Keeler, rf; Kelley, lf; Brouthers, c; Brodie, cf; Reitz, 2b; Jennings, ss; Robinson c; McMahon, p. The first seven batters in that lineup missed eight games combined in 1894. Hughie played in every one.

As John McGraw strode to the plate to face the Giants' star fastball pitcher, Amos Rusie, to start the season, no one could have guessed his at-bat was the beginning of the National League's first dynasty. The Orioles unleashed "scientific baseball" and swept the series. They pulled off 13 hit-and-run plays and made several base hits by chopping down on the ball. It was an idea, Hanlon said, that came to him in his sleep during the spring. "I often got out of bed in the night to jot down plays that might be worked out," he said. Groundskeeper Tom Murphy, as per instructions, made it work by keeping the area in front of home plate hard and dry.[4] Thus was the "Baltimore Chop" born.

Sadie McMahon beat Rusie in the first game of the Giants series 8–3, and Mullane won the second game going away, 12–6. In the third game the Orioles were losing 3–1 in the seventh inning when McGraw tied it up with a 2-run single scoring Hughie and Robby. Then Keeler and McGraw pulled of the 13th hit-and-run play of the series. McGraw took off for second, Giant second baseman Monte Ward ran over to cover, and Keeler effortlessly slapped the ball into the hole. McGraw went to third and scored the winning run on a sacrifice fly. Hanlon's theory on how the 60'-6" pitching distance would change the game was proved correct in 1894, the second season of the rule. Pitchers were slow to adjust. The league batting average — which went from .245 in '92 to .280 in the first year of the longer distance — went up to .309 in 1894. Even against Rusie, the league's fastest pitcher, it was clear that batters had the advantage. They swung and missed with much less frequency and were better able to hit the ball where they wanted it to go with consistency, a perfect combination for making the hit-and-run work.

Earlier in that first game, McGraw gave another demonstration of what the N.L. was in for in '94 and beyond. When a wild pitch thrown behind him nicked his bat, he clutched the back of his head and claimed he was hit. The umpire didn't buy it and everybody laughed, including McGraw, which was a rare sight.[5] Funny or not, the tactic became regular part of the Oriole arsenal, especially for Hughie. On close pitches the Orioles would pinch themselves to make a mark and fall to the ground, as Hanlon had done when he played. Hughie flat-out refused to get out of the way and got plunked a league-leading 27 times. Houdini-like, he learned to tighten the muscles on his torso to blunt the pain.

Johnny Ward didn't take getting swept well, especially by a team using sissy tactics, as he saw it. He chastised Hanlon for the way the Orioles played and threatened to take his complaints to the league office. Whether he did or not, nothing came of it, and the Orioles played on more even more wildly as the season wore on. The Beaneaters, defending league champs, came to Baltimore after the Giants. In the first game, Boston led 2–1 going into the ninth. The Orioles scored 14 and won 15–3 for a 4–0 start. The Orioles went on to win 34 of their first 46 games. Keeler choked halfway up the bat, and no matter where they played him, he got on base. When the infielders moved in, he dropped hits over their heads. When they moved back, he beat out infield grounders. He and McGraw worked the hit-and-run multiple times a game. Brouthers hit for power. Kelly hit and made acrobatic catches in the outfield. Hughie made startling plays at shortstop and got plunked by pitches. On May 11 in a 12–7 loss to Philadelphia, Hughie was hit three times by Wilfred "Kid" Carsey, establishing a Major League record. All the players jumped into the crowd, crashed into fences, stepped into pitches, threw their bodies in front of balls, and accepted spikings as the price of making a play. If a player failed to play hard or made a mental mistake, Hanlon didn't have to scold or punish the player, the other players, especially McGraw and Hughie, gave him a roasting.

The Orioles' hit-and-run became so popular Hanlon demonstrated it for the fans in pregame practices. He put the starting infielders on the field, but even they couldn't stop the play. But the Orioles' style of play went beyond all-out hustle and brainy tactics like the hit-and-run and Baltimore chop. The Boston baseball writer Tim Murnane described it this way after an early-season series with the Beaneaters: "The dirtiest ball ever seen. Diving into the first baseman long after the ball was caught; throwing masks in front of runners at home plate; catching them by the clothes at third base; and interfering with the catcher were only a few of the tricks."

The Orioles were guilty as charged and didn't deny it. McGraw told this story of typical Oriole shenanigans: "A runner tried to steal second base. Our first baseman tried to trip him, but missed. At second Henie Reitz blocked him off while Hughie covered the bag and took the throw. The runner evaded Reitz and jumped spikes-first at Hughie, who dodged the flying spikes and threw himself bodily at the runner, knocking him flat. In the meantime the batter hit our catcher over the hands to prevent a throw, but he got the throw off and put his mitt in the umpire's face so he couldn't see the play."

Games were worked by only one umpire and the Orioles took advantage at every opportunity. When they didn't like a call, Hughie and McGraw would surround the ump and back him across the diamond. They cut bases and impeded opposing runners. In an oft-told tale, McGraw reputedly held runners by hooking a finger in belt loops. When umpire Tim Keefe ejected Hughie from a game, McGraw jumped to his friend's defense with an insult.

"Look man, you sent out for a bottle yesterday," McGraw said. Keefe said, "I was sick."

"Drunk, you mean," snarled McGraw.[6]

Fans used mirrors to reflect sunlight into the eyes of opposing batters and fielders. When an opposing batter hit a foul ball into the crowd, the fans threw back a different, deadened ball. Even Murphy, the groundskeeper, was not above a dirty trick during a game. Hughie told this story in *Rounding Third*.

> I hit a hot grounder to the Giant short stop, who fumbled. He hurried the throw and it went wild over the first baseman's head and down the right field line to the clubhouse steps.
>
> Baltimore groundskeeper Tommy Murphy was sitting alongside the open door. The ball bounded down the steps. Tommy went in after it and closed and locked the door. Roger Connor, the first baseman, banged on the door. Murphy watched through the window until I scored then opened the door and said, "Was you trying to get in, Roger."
>
> Roger said, "You crook, what are you doing?
>
> "Playing a little inside baseball."

That summer Hughie, McGraw, Keeler, Brodie, Brouthers, and Sadie McMahon lived in the same rooming hotel, the Oxford House. Hughie and McGraw grew closer as the season went on. They went to Mass at St. Ann's. They double dated and joined the Maryland Yacht Club. But baseball was always on their minds. Evenings they sat on the Oxford House porch and dreamed up plays, then tried them out at the ballpark. They timed a dash for home when the pitcher delivered and thereby, according to McGraw, invented the suicide squeeze.[7] They had Murphy contour the foul lines so that a bunted ball would be likely to stay fair. They went to the park early in the morning before home games and raked the area around third and shortstop. While the Orioles perfected the hit-and-run at bat, in the field Hughie developed a way to thwart opponents' attempts to pull off the play. With a runner on first, Hughie never tipped when he was going to cover second. Only when the ball was batted or in the catcher's glove did he dart over to the bag. He'd catch the throw with his glove on the run, and slap the tag in one motion. No other shortstop in the league would even try the play. Years later, this innovation by Hughie was noted by another pretty fair shortstop, Honus Wagner, who named Hughie his shortstop on his all-time team. "Hughie Jennings was one of the smartest shortstops that ever lived," Wagner wrote in 1924 in a syndicated story for the *North American Newspaper Alliance*. "He was always inventing new plays and was the first shortstop to take a throw from the catcher and tag the runner while on the run. Hughie was a wonderful fielder and a great student of the game."[8]

Hughie's rise to stardom in '94 was stunning. When the season began he was largely unknown. In Baltimore fans remembered him from '93 as the sickly coal miner with the .182 average and no position, except the bench. But by midseason in 1894 Hughie was a sensation as the consensus best shortstop in the league. He was suddenly a .300 hitter, but most impressive was his shortstop play. With plays like the one described by Wagner, he revolutionized the position. He ranged into the hole and up the middle, dived for any ball anywhere nearby, held the bag against the sharpest spikes and threw as hard as any fastball pitcher. Getting to foul balls down the left field line was one of his specialties. He went after them with such ferocity everybody got out of his way. Just how far and fast Hughie's star had risen was demonstrated on July 4 when the Orioles played a doubleheader in Louisville. Between games the fans presented Hughie with a floral horseshoe, honoring one of their own who had gotten away. Back in Baltimore a cigar was named after him, "Our Hughey."

On August 10 and 11 the Orioles beat the Giants in New York, 12–9 and 20–1. Hughie had five hits in the second one. But for as hot as the Orioles had been all season, on August 24 they still trailed the Beaneaters. Despite a 62–36 record and a .632 winning percentage the Orioles were tied for second place with the Giants, three games behind Boston. There were 30 games left in the season. The Orioles would lose only three of them.

On August 24 Sadie McMahon beat the Browns in St Louis, 5–2. Back in Baltimore a little over a week later the Orioles ascended into first place to stay by beating the Cleveland Spiders, 13–2 and 16–3, for their ninth and tenth consecutive wins before more than 24,000 fans, jammed into Union Park on a new national holiday, Labor Day. Kelley was 9-for-9 with five doubles. Hughie handled 15 chances with one harmless boot. And they kept on winning. They didn't lose again until the second game of a doubleheader on September 16. They had won 18 straight. During the streak Hughie's fielding drew raves. On August 28 against Louisville he handled 10 chances without an error and pulled off an unassisted double play. Game accounts noted "Jennings' marvelous work at short stop." The next day he had two hits, stole a base, scored a run and handled eight more chances without an error in a 5–1 win. When Louisville left Baltimore after that series, they left starting pitcher George Hemming behind. Hanlon bought him for cash. Hemming, 13–19 for the Colonels, went 4–0 down the stretch for the Orioles.

On September 25 the Orioles beat Cy Young and the Spiders 14–9 in

Cleveland to clinch the pennant. Hughie had one hit, scored twice and had a busy day at short with seven putouts, an assist, and one error. Back in Baltimore the play-by-play was received by telegraph and simulated in Ford's Grand Opera House on Compton's Electric Baseball Game Impersonator, a huge field diagram with movable pieces. When it was over, Harry von der Horst ran across stage with an orange and black silk flag reading "Champions, 1894" to a standing ovation from a packed house. As the news spread the streets filled with celebrating "cranks," as baseball fans were called in those days. The partying went on all night by the light of bonfires of garbage boxes and barrels.[9] Plans began immediately for a celebration, but Baltimore would have to wait a few days to party with her heroes. The Orioles had three games left to play. They beat Cleveland again the next day, then went to Chicago, where they lost one game, then ended the season with a 20–9 win on September 30. They finished 89–39, a .695 winning percentage, and three games ahead of the Giants. They averaged nearly nine runs a game and batted .343. They made the fewest errors and allowed the second lowest number of runs.

Hughie played in all 128 games. He batted .335 with a .411 on-base percentage, and a .479 slugging average. He stole 37 bases and got hit by pitches a league-leading 27 times. He led shortstops in putouts and chances per game and was second in assists, double plays and fielding percentage.

In the five days between September 25, when the Orioles clinched the pennant, and September 30, when the season ended, the joy over the Orioles' championship radiated beyond Baltimore. As the *Baltimore Morning Herald* put it, "It was the North against the South again and every man, women and child south of the Mason Dixon Line hailed the Orioles, not as champions of Baltimore alone, but of all of Maryland, Virginia and the Deep South."[10]

The truth of that account was not apparent to the Orioles until their train from Chicago stopped in Grafton, West Virginia. It was 5 o'clock in the morning and Hughie was roused from his sleep by a commotion in the Grafton station. When he realized what he was hearing, he climbed out of his berth and ran to a window and popped his head out. Surrounding the train were scores of fans, miners and their families, chanting "Jennings, Jennings, Jennings." Only after they caught a glimpse of their hero, who waved from the window, did they let the train proceed. The scene was replayed at Piedmont and Oakland.

The train stopped for breakfast in Cumberland, Maryland. As the players stepped from the train a band played "Maryland, My Maryland." The town was decked out in orange and black. A banner at the hotel proclaimed "Cumberland Welcomes the Champions." Hanlon was pre-

The 1894 Baltimore Orioles, National League Champions — Jennings is second from right in the second row. (National Baseball Library and Archive photograph.)

sented with a glass bat filled with rye whiskey and beseeched to make a speech.

In Washington D.C., a committee of 50 more Baltimore rooters were at the Baltimore and Ohio station an hour before the train was due and whiled away the minutes shouting ditties like:

> "B, B, C, "B, B, C,
> Baltimore baseball
> cranks are we
> Rah, rah, rah
> Siss, boom, bam
> Baltimore, Baltimore
> Don't give a damn.

A Mr. H. Poske was in charge of the delegation. Every man carried orange and black ribbons, medals and badges. Some had miniature pennants inscribed with "Baltimore Baseball Club, Champions of the United States." When the train arrived in Washington at 2:20 there were 150 rooters on the platform. The players came in a special car attached to the regular train with a "Baltimore Champions" banner on it with the windows draped with red, white, and blue; and orange and black bunting. When the team got off the train the rooters rushed to shake Hanlon's hand. He was wrapped in a series of wild embraces. Everyone moved across the street to the Emrich Hotel. As Mr. Emrich was an Oriole fan, the whole hotel was rented to the occasion. The team went upstairs to get out of their sweaters and bathe. A half dozen barbers were hired out to cut players' hair. At a nearby men' s store the committee bought shirts, collars and cravats. When the players came downstairs, every one was dressed in a suit and black tie. After the reception, the players hustled back to the station for the 5:30 train to Baltimore. The Mount Pleasant Drum and Bugle Corps were hired by the committee for the Baltimore festivities and they, too, boarded the 5:30 train.[11]

When the train pulled into the Camden Station on October 2, the reception was unlike anything ever before in the history of the national game. There were 50,000 fans crammed in and around the station and the nearby streets. Fireworks exploded as the players disembarked. A fife-and-drum corps escorted the team through the station. A parade ensued to the Fifth Regiment Armory. Two hundred groups had signed to march in the few days since they clinched, some on decorated floats. Half the city, 200,000 people, lined the parade route. Mounted police had to clear a path, but couldn't prevent a tragedy. Six horses attached to a heavy bus became frightened and plunged into a crowd. Eleven were injured, mostly women and children, two, Florence Ingle, 18, and Henry Kruschlen, 15, seriously. At the armory the pennant, five feet high and 25 feet long, hung across the front of the hall reading "Champion Base Ball Club of the United States, Baltimore 1894." Over 20,000 crammed into the hall, where in his remarks mayor Ferdinand Latrobe said, "we have always had the most beautiful women and the finest oysters in the world, now we have the best baseball club."[12]

At the reception, a large loving cup was filled with champagne and passed around the players' table. Captain Robby set an example for the team by refusing champagne. There was still the Temple Cup series to be played. The next day, the Orioles were followed wherever they went. In the afternoon they went to Ford's Opera House for a matinee. Fanny Rice did a hilarious impersonation of Hanlon. Theater manager Charles Ford gave each of them a gold badge. At night the *Baltimore News* sponsored a benefit performance at Harris' Academy of Music. The ballplayers occupied the stage boxes. They were introduced and the fans in the jammed theater cheered each of the champions again and again. The show included the play "The Ensign" and the balcony scene from "Romeo and Juliet." The orchestra played the "Orioles March" and the Lafayette Glee Club sang a baseball paraphrase of the opera "Ernani." At the end the Orioles appeared on stage in their new gold and black uniforms to still another ovation.[13]

8

The Temple Cup

William C. Temple, the owner of the Pittsburgh Pirates, wasn't satisfied. His Pirates finished second in the National League in 1893, but that was that. Temple yearned for more baseball. So, he came up with the idea of a postseason series between the first and second place teams in '94. As a prize for the teams' owners he commissioned an ornate $800 silver cup, 30 inches high, set on an onyx base. Temple wanted all of the ticket receipts to go the players, after expenses, on a 65–35 split for the winning and losing teams. Planning for the series began as soon as the regular season ended. Hanlon and the second-place Giants' manager Johnny Ward met in Cincinnati, where the Giants played on the last day, but couldn't agree on Temple's plan to split players' money. Hanlon refused to give a decision until he talked to his players. He went to Chicago, and after talking to the team, sent this telegram to league President Nick Young of the National League, Temple and Ward:

> The Baltimore players up to this morning understood that 65 percent went to the champions of the National League and American Association regardless of the outcome of the Temple series. The percentage is not enough to compensate us for our six months hard work if defeated. The New Yorks have nothing to lose and all to gain. Our players refuse to play under present conditions, but will play 55 per cent to the winner, 45 per cent to the loser, or winner take all.[1]

It was a curious telegram. First of all, why were Hanlon and the Orioles confused about the ticket receipts split? Temple had made it clear from the start that he wanted the series winners to get 65 percent. And Hanlon's condition at the end of the telegram made no sense. He writes that 35 percent, if Baltimore were to lose the series, was not enough to compensate his team for winning the pennant. He then offers a winner-take-all solution, which would mean the Orioles would get nothing if they lost.

The 1894 Baltimore Orioles in dress clothes — Jennings in the middle of the top row.
(National Baseball Library and Archive photograph.)

Ward and Hanlon met again and came to an agreement on 50/50 split.
Dates were set for October 4, 5, and 11 in Baltimore and October 6, 8, and
9 in New York, with the site of the seventh game, if necessary, to be decided
by a coin toss.

But Temple was adamant about the money. He refused to go along
with 50–50 split, saying no monetary incentive to win would taint the
integrity of the series. He took his case to National League President Nick
Young, who agreed. Young insisted the teams play under the terms of the
agreement made in the spring or there would be no series, at least not a
Temple Cup series. Hanlon backed down from his 50–50 position, probably because he was afraid that without the trophy and a winners' share
at stake the players would treat the games as exhibitions and the fans would
stay away. If that was the case, he was right. While 8,000 tickets had been
sold in advance for the first game, only about 2,000 tickets were sold on
the day of the game, for a total of 10,000. The weather didn't help. It was
cold and gray. Von der Horst had been planning for 15,000 or more.[2]

Officially, the series was set to be played under Temple's plan, but
privately some of the players were threatening not to unless player-to-
player agreements for a 50–50 split were made. There is no evidence that

Hughie wanted anything other than to play ball. While McGraw had to be cajoled and assured of a 50–50 split, Hughie wanted nothing more than to get the series on. McGraw was the last holdout. It wasn't until five minutes before the game that McGraw agreed to a 50–50 split with Giants' third baseman George Davis. As the first game progressed, it was obvious something was wrong with the Orioles. Gone was the high-energy intensity that had propelled them to 27 wins in their last 30 regular season games. Despite Robinson's gesture at the armory reception two days earlier when he refused the champagne, the players didn't keep up their sobriety. Two days of invitations and temptations had worn them down. Amos Rusie and the Giants won the first game in Baltimore, 4–1. The Orioles went down quietly, except in the ninth inning when they showed some life, scoring their run on singles by McGraw, Brodie and Reitz. Hughie followed and appeared to beat out an infield hit but was called out by umpire Emslie. The Orioles argued fiercely and the Oriole fans tried to hit Emslie with anything they could get their hands on. He had to be escorted from the field by police.

Hughie had a rough time in game two. In the Giants' ninth, with the score 5–5, a ground ball hit a pebble and bounded over his head, and then he booted an easy double-play ball as the Giants scored four and won 9–6. Games three and four were in New York. Rusie duplicated his game one performance in game three as the Giants again won 4–1. Attendance was 20,000. Hughie had one meaningless single and had a collision at first with the Giants' Van Haltren. Van Haltren was cut. His wound was dressed and he continued.

The fourth game, played before barely 10,000 because of winter-like weather, was an embarrassment for the Orioles. Mercifully, with the Giants leading 16–3 in the eighth, it was too dark to continue and the Giants won the series 4–0. Hughie was 2-for-14 in the four games without a run scored, just one run batted in and one costly error. He hadn't gone four consecutive games all season without scoring, when he scored 134, batted .335 and had 109 RBI. And the series was an embarrassing showing by the Orioles, a team which had scored 1171 runs in 129 regular season games, an average of 9.07 per game, and allowed just 818 and had a .695 winning percentage. The shares came to $768 for the Giants and $360 for the Orioles. Amos Rusie kept his end of the handshake deal and gave Kelley $200, but he was the only Giant who did.[3]

Within days of the end of the Temple Cup series, McGraw headed back to St. Bonaventure, this time with Hughie in tow. While sources at St. Bonaventure indicate that Hughie was with McGraw the winter of 1893–94, and while that's the implication in Alexander's book, *McGraw,* Hughie

said it wasn't until 1894–95, after that first Temple Cup season, that Hughie
joined McGraw at St. Bonaventure as an assistant.

From *Rounding Third*:

> During the winter of 1893–94 McGraw had attended St. Bonaventure
> College at Allegheny, N. Y., and he arrived in camp in the spring of
> 1894 exceedingly enthusiastic about the institution. Throughout the
> season he kept preaching to me on the subject of the advantages of
> education and finally I decided to join him. At the close of the 1894
> major league campaign, we packed our grips and went to Allegheny, N.
> Y., where I began a college career.
>
> We applied ourselves strenuously to our studies and in February we
> began to coach the base ball team. This work continued until we had
> to leave for the spring training camp of the Baltimores.
>
> Just before our departure that spring we were given a banquet. The
> Rev. Fr. Joseph Butler, then president of St. Bonaventure, made a
> speech. "Last year we had McGraw. This year we had Jennings and
> McGraw. I hope we will have both of them for 10 years more," he said.

Hughie and McGraw didn't accept college as a sweetheart deal. They
lived up to their end of the bargain. By day they went to class, first-year
English, math, and history. By night in the basement of Alumni Hall, they
ran organized practices worked out in minute detail. With McGraw acting as head coach and Hughie following his lead, they led the college players in calisthenics and fundamental repetitions. McGraw practically
invented indoor baseball workouts that winter. He hung lanterns, erected
a batting cage of chicken wire and used lumber. He drilled the team in
scientific baseball, Ned Hanlon style. They worked on the drag bunt,
squeeze play, double steal and cutoff. The college players soaked it all up
and respected McGraw like an elder, though at 19, he was younger than
most of them. All the drills weren't for the players. Determined to correct
a major flaw in Hughie's batting technique, McGraw put Hughie in the
chicken wire batting cage. Hughie was bailing out. Of course, it wasn't that
Hughie was afraid of being hit by pitches. Pulling his left foot out towards
third base was a bad habit he picked up in amateur and semiprofessional
ball where he, as did most batters, tried to pull every pitch with power
with a long swing. McGraw put Hughie in the cage with his back to the
chicken wire. For weeks he pitched to Hughie inside. Confined to the cage,
Hughie couldn't pull away, and he learned to swing without bailing. By
necessity, he also had to swing less wildly, as there was nowhere for the
ball to go in the Alumni Hall basement. To Hughie, cutting down on his
swing was as important as keeping his foot in. "I was a bad hitter because
I took a long swing. I adopted the snap style used by McGraw and Keeler
and that was the beginning of what success I might have had."[4]

When the weather allowed, McGraw took Hughie's batting lessons outside. There Hughie added another weapon to his batting arsenal, again by necessity. Since the windows in the building in left field were 25 cents a pane, Hughie hit to right field. Somehow, Hughie found time to sing tenor in the school choir. They both found time to do their classwork well enough to be given full credit for their courses and make the honor roll, even though they had to leave in March, before the semester ended, to join the Orioles.

But they didn't join the Orioles until after a holdout by the "Big Four." That was the nickname the Baltimore writers gave to Joe Kelley, Willie Keeler, Hughie, and McGraw when they held out together after the '94 season. By February, everybody but the four had signed. Hughie and the others had been paid $1,500 in '94. The numbers made a good case that the Big Four deserved a fair raise. The Orioles had drawn almost 300,000 in '94, 90,000 above the league average. With a total payroll of $35,000, the Orioles had made about $50,000. But the players got little sympathy from the fans, especially after Hanlon reminded them that the players were already making five times as much as an average factory worker. In any case, Hughie couldn't get a raise above $2400 because that was the limit imposed by the owners under the reserve clause after the collapse of the Players League. Hanlon offered Hughie a raise from $1500 to $2000. McGraw got $100 more. Out of options, Hughie and the other three signed when Hanlon threatened to go to Macon for spring training without them. Hughie and McGraw reported to Hanlon in Macon on time, sporting gold-headed canes, gifts from the St. Bonaventure players.[5]

The Orioles started '95 with a bang at home, scoring 45 runs in taking two of three from the Phillies. Hughie had six hits, three of them doubles, scored eight runs and was involved in six double plays, one unassisted, in the opening series. But something wasn't right with the Orioles. Injury and illness were part of the problem. Reitz broke his collarbone, McMahon couldn't lift his arm to comb his hair, let alone pitch, and McGraw missed several games with a cut hand and, later in the season, a long stretch with malaria. On May 9, the Orioles won their third consecutive game and stood at 7–4. But of their next 11 games, all on the road, they won just three. On the morning of May 26 in Chicago, the champions of '94 found themselves in eighth place with a 10–11 record. They beat the Cubs that day to climb back to .500, then headed home. The Orioles won 13 of 18 on the homestand and climbed back to second place, one game behind the Beaneaters and Pirates, who were tied for first place. The Orioles were a far different ball club at Union Park than they were on the road in '95. They played .818 baseball at home where they were 54–12. On the road they were

33–31. Their inability to win consistently on the road kept the pennant race close. It was called the closest race in history. On September 16, the Orioles were in first at 77–39, Cleveland was second at 77–45 and the Phillies, 73–47, were in third. The race was a boon to September attendance. Baltimore averaged 10,000 for a series with Cleveland, while 13,000 saw Philadelphia beat Louisville. The Orioles won 21 of 26 in August and 41 of their last 51, but still didn't clinch until the next-to-last game of the season, when they beat the Giants 5–2 in New York on September 28. Hughie ended that game with a leaping catch of a line drive in the ninth inning.

In 1907, after Hughie had won the American League pennant as manager of the Detroit Tigers, McGraw was asked to describe the greatest play Hughie made in the old Oriole days in an interview with the *Washington Post*. He chose that pennant-winning catch.

> There is one play which has always stuck in my mind, because it saved the pennant for Baltimore. Jennings may have made greater plays in his career, but never one that counted so much.
>
> I forget exactly the year. It was in the 90s sometime and we had been playing neck-and-neck with the New Yorks for the championship. We had been having a hard time all along the circuit, but managed to hold our lead.
>
> We finally landed in New York just a point or so ahead so that a victory for New York would have meant the pennant. I have seen a lot of big crowds in the Polo Grounds but I don't think I even saw the equal of that crowd and they were an ugly bunch, too.
>
> We weren't angels in Baltimore, I never claimed that, but the crowd in that last game was determined to knock us out if they could do it, but we were ready for them. Things went our way despite pop bottles and everything a crowd can do to make life miserable for a visiting team.
>
> Well it came along to the last inning with the score 3–1 in our favor and Pond, I think was, pitching for us and seemed to grow a little unsteady. The first two went out but then Pond gave up a base on balls, hit a man and then a wild pitch put runners on second and third.
>
> The crowd was whopping like maniacs and I confess that I felt such a case of cold feet on third base, I don't believe I could have stopped a football if it had been rolled out to me. But as it was always in a case like that Jennings came on strong and I believe he saw how it was with me and the rest of the infield. He walked over to Pond and said "easy old boy now take your time and remember nothing they can hit is going to get past this infield."
>
> I believe that steadied Pond a little, but there was a man on third waiting for any kind of chance to make a dash for home. It seemed an age before Pond pitched the ball. I think it was George Davis at bat. Pond shot the ball across. George gave one lunge and the crack could

be heard a mile, the ball going right over Hughey's head. Hughey must have jumped at the crack of the bat, otherwise he never would have got the ball. I didn't even wait to look. Knowing that the hit was good to bring two men home and give New York the pennant. I just turned my head as I walked in and there was Hughey with the ball sticking in his mitt and the pennant was ours.

Now I don't believe there was another man who could have made a play like that just at that time. Down in Baltimore they sang a song "When Hughey Caught the Ball" for two years afterward.

That illustrates that kind of player Jennings was. He has a cool head, never gets rattled and knows how to handle men. He was wonderful fielder and the quickest thrower I ever saw.

McGraw remembered the play vividly, but, as 12 years had passed, was way off on the details. The play happened in 1895, not in the last game, but in the next to last. The Giants were the opponent, but they were not in the pennant race with the Orioles. They were 20 games behind. Pond was not the pitcher and the score was 5–2, not 3–1.

Anyway, on the 30th, the Orioles ended the season with another defeat of the Giants to finish 87–43, three games ahead of the Cleveland Spiders, who would be the O's opponents in the Temple Cup series. During September, Hughie was invited to the Baltimore home of Cardinal James Gibbons, the first American Catholic Cardinal, where he was presented with a gold medallion and a small cross blessed by Pope Leo XIII.[6]

Hughie wound up batting .386, a 49-point improvement from '94, while the league average dropped 16 points. Hughie was second on the team to Keeler, who batted .391, and sixth in the league. League-wide he was third in runs scored, 159; fourth in RBI, 124; and first in runs produced, 280. He was also first in hit-by-pitch, 32; and sacrifices, 28. His fielding was brilliant, both visually and statistically. He led all shortstops in putouts, 425; double plays, 71; total chances per game, 7.2; and fielding average, .940. According to *Total Baseball* he led in fielding runs, 30.4, and had the Top Total Player rating at 5.8.

Four other Orioles batted over .300. Leadoff batter McGraw, .369 in 96 games; outfielder and cleanup hitter Joe Kelley, .365; and Steve Brodie, .348; and second baseman Kid Gleason, .309. The Spiders had two key players. Jesse Burkett, who batted an astounding .423, and a 28-year-old pitcher, who won 35 games which included a perfect 7–0 record in seven relief appearances. His name was Cy Young, and he was the starter in game one.

To avoid the hangover of a pennant celebration as happened in 1894, after the final regular-season game in '95, Hanlon took the team directly from New York to Cleveland, where the first three games of the Temple

Cup series were scheduled for October 2, 3, and 5. The plan for 1895 was to win the cup, then celebrate. The controversy of 1894 was forgotten. It was agreed to play a best of seven and to divide receipts 60–40. The entire receipts of all games were to be the sole property of the players after all expenses were paid, including payment of all necessary employees, player hotel and traveling expenses, advertising and umpires' pay.

The weather was perfect for the first game on October 2 in Cleveland, where the Orioles had been 1–4 during the regular season, and where they were hated by the fans of manager Patsy Tebeau's equally rowdy Spiders. Many of the 7000 came armed with fruit, cabbages, rotten eggs, and bottles and cans. They rained them down on the Orioles in the early innings to a serenade of horns and cow bells. A group of fanatics brought an eight-foot horn with several tubes that allowed seven fans to blow notes simultaneously. In the midst of the sideshow of fans was a ball game the Washington Post described as "the most exciting game ever played on any grounds." Six of the nine runs were scored in the eighth and ninth innings. Hughie handled eight chances without an error, ranging into the hole and up the middle. Batting in the sixth, he advanced McGraw to third with a long fly ball to center, then McGraw scored on an infield error. In the eighth, he singled home McGraw and scored on an infield out. In the ninth Hughie showed a rare bit of power, hitting a liner to deep center that Jimmy McAleer caught on the run. The O's took a 4–3 lead into the ninth, but four straight hits by the Spiders gave Cleveland a 5–4 win. The jubilant fans poured onto the field and carried the Spiders off the field. The weather was perfect again for game two, which drew 8,000, many of them drunken rowdies who continued to throw stuff at the Orioles, while the undermanned police did nothing. The Spiders scored three in the first and never were in trouble in a 7–2 win. Hughie was 1–4 and scored one Oriole run, racing home all the way from second while Brodie was run down between first and second.

The next day was Sunday, and the day off let Cy Young come back to pitch game three on Monday. It was so easy for the Spiders, their fans laid off the Orioles. Hughie was on base three times with the only walk allowed by Young and two of the Orioles' six hits. His double knocked in the only run in the eighth, but he was the only Oriole who did anything in the 7–1 loss. It was the O's seventh consecutive Temple Cup series loss.

The series moved to Baltimore for game four. The fans didn't even wait for the Spiders to get to Union Park before they got their revenge for what the Spider fans had done to the Orioles in Cleveland. A group of Oriole fans pelted the Spiders with rotten fruit and vegetables as they left the hotel for the park. The police arrested 11 of the garbage throwers. Finally, in their eighth try, the Orioles won a Temple Cup game. Pitcher Duke Esper allowed just five singles in winning 5–0. An overflow crowd of over 10,000 spilled into the outfield. It took a police line to hold them back with a rope. Hughie was wildly cheered when he came to bat in the first and flied to center. He went 3-for-4 and hooked up with Gleason on a nifty double play. In the third, after McGraw and Keeler bunted safely, the crowd surged over the rope in joy. It took five minutes for the police to get them back and restore the rope line. Hughie knocked in McGraw and Keeler scored on a fly ball. Hughie doubled down the left-field line in the fifth. In the seventh, he singled, went to second on a passed ball, and scored on Kelley's single. Hughie ended the game when he started a double play with a backhand stop of a Tebeau ground ball in the hole.

Cold weather kept the crowd down to 5,000 for game five and Cy Young kept the Orioles down. It was scoreless until the seventh, when Cleveland scored three times and went on to win 7–1 and clinch the Cup. Hundreds of the crowd, angered by an attempt by Tebeau to spike pitcher Bill Hoffer as he covered first, waited for the Spiders after the game. A pla-

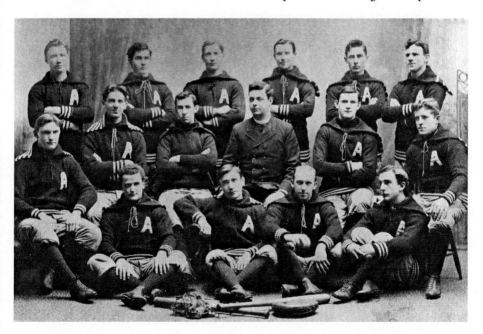

Saint Bonaventure baseball team, 1896, Hughie's second season as coach of the team with his friend John McGraw. Front row, from left, Murtaugh, Gilloegly, McClinchey, Lavin, Carroll. Second row, Tull, Curley; Father James, manager; Finn, McNamara. Third row, Hughie Jennings, Ryan, O'Malley, Conlin, Norton, John McGraw. (Courtesy Saint Bonaventure University Archives.)

toon of police formed a gauntlet to get the Spiders safely to their carriages and escorted them back to the hotel, as fans threw paper balls, peanuts, eggs and pieces of brick at their carriages.[8] Hughie was hitless in the final game, but was 7-for-19 in the series for a .368 average, second only to McGraw's 8-for-20 for .400.

The Orioles and Philadelphia had agreed to go on a Southern tour after the Temple Cup. It started in Philadelphia, then went to Baltimore, Richmond, Savannah, Augusta, Atlanta, Mobile, and New Orleans. The tour ended up in Dallas in time for the Corbett-Fitzsimmons fight.[9] The Orioles went without two of their most popular players, Hughie and McGraw. They pocketed their $385 losers' shares and headed back to St. Bonaventure. This time, McGraw lasted at school only until December 22, when he withdrew, citing nervous exhaustion, and went back to Baltimore to rest. Hughie handled the college ball club himself until March.[10]

9

The Greatest Shortstop in the Land

Hughie's signed contract for 1896 arrived at Hanlon's office on January 27. Terms were not disclosed, but it's likely Hughie signed for the same salary as he made in '95, $2000, or at best a $100 raise. In February of 1896 Hughie took a break from St. Bonaventure and went down to Baltimore to join McGraw and some of the other Orioles at the Holiday Theater for a show called "The Derby Winner." St. Louis Browns pitcher Ted Breitenstein had a small part in the show. The performance turned into a midwinter gathering of baseball fans and players. The bleachers were packed with the regular Union Park bleacher crowd. Von der Horst, Hanlon, Hughie and McGraw and the other Oriole players occupied private boxes. On one the great 1895 championship banner hung. Smaller versions of the flag adorned the other boxes.[1]

Hughie left St. Bonaventure in early March. On March 4 he stopped in Baltimore to see McGraw and Hanlon, then went on to Athens, Georgia, to coach the University of Georgia baseball team.[2] In *Rounding Third* Hughie writes about coaching at St. Bonaventure and Cornell, but makes no mention of Georgia, where he is considered the school's first baseball coach and is said to have coached beginning in 1895 through 1899. This is curious because Hughie was definitely coaching at St. Bonaventure with McGraw in the winters in '95, '96, and '97 and on his own in '98. Yet Thomas Walter Redd, the author of a university history, writes that Hughie coached at Georgia from 1895–1899. The logical explanation is that Hughie coached at both schools during those years. The Orioles' spring camp was in Macon in those years, which is 90 miles from the university at Athens. Hughie must have coached the Georgia team before and during the Orioles spring camp and on their spring tour. It is known that the Orioles

played at least one game in Athens in '95. But certainly Hughie was with
the Georgia Red and Black in 1897. From Redd's book:

> The University of Georgia in the spring of 1897 had a great baseball
> team and coach. It is doubtful whether the Red and Black ever had a
> greater team or coach. The ace pitcher was Will Stanford. Behind the
> bat was Threatt Moore, one of Georgia's all time receivers. The team
> was captained by George W. Price, who in addition to being a great
> football player was a demon at the bat and was a sure fielder. And who
> was the coach? Why none other than the famous Hughey Jennings of
> the Baltimore Orioles.

The team played 15 games and won 10. They beat both the University of Pennsylvania and the University of Virginia in what were considered major upsets. The Pennsylvania game was played in Atlanta on April
13. The Orioles' last spring game was in Norfolk on April 9. The Orioles'
regular season didn't start until April 22.

From the university history:

> Pennsylvania was top team in the North. Very few believed Georgia
> could win. Those who left to the game with long faces had not taken
> into account Hughie Jennings, Bill Sanford and the other boys. Young
> ladies were there by the hundreds gaily attired in their Easter dresses
> and swathed in red and black ribbons.
>   The PA boys were rather cocksure and never dreamed of what was
> coming to them. Sanford retired them in order in the first on ten
> pitches and hit a home run over the fence in the second inning. Geor-
> gia won 4–0. Sanford gave up one hit and faced only 29 batters.

When camp opened on March 18, Hanlon put the Orioles through 12
days of uninterrupted practice before they played any spring games. Hanlon's latest innovation was bat "blanks." These were unfinished baseball
bats, essentially elongated rectangles of ash wood with handles, which he
bought in New York State in the off-season. At camp the players selected
blanks and had them lathed into custom-finished bats.[3]

It was clear from the start of camp that Hughie, at 25, was at the peak
of his power. He had not missed a game in two seasons, during which time
he seemed to get better with each passing game. And he was in peak physical condition. Whereas many of the players had spent the off-seasons giving into the temptations of celebrity back in their hometowns, Hughie had
kept in shape working out with the St. Bonaventure team and with daily
swims in the college pool. Hughie was poised for a good year, but would
surprise even himself by turning in the greatest season ever by a major
league shortstop. By the end of the regular season, he was being dubbed

"The Greatest Shortstop in the Land" by the scribes, but he almost didn't make it out of the spring season.

On April 8 in the seventh inning of a game at Petersburg, Virginia, against the local club, several of the Orioles surrounded the umpire to protest a call. Hughie was on the fringe of the rhubarb when he was sucker-punched in the eye and knocked to the ground by a Petersburg player. The Orioles then refused to finish the game and left for their hotel. An angry mob from the game caught up with the Orioles at the hotel where a brawl broke out in the lobby, which was thoroughly trashed. In the melee, Brodie threw one of the Petersburg fans through a glass door. It took a police escort to get the Orioles out of town safely.[4]

The Orioles were at a disadvantage in the fight. They were without McGraw. He was back in Georgia in another fight—for his life. After a game in Athens in late March, McGraw's temperature soared to danger-ous levels. When the Orioles left, McGraw stayed behind at St. Joseph's infirmary at the University of Georgia, where he was diagnosed with typhoid fever. The fever almost killed McGraw twice before it finally broke in May.

The fight in Petersburg was just what the Orioles' new first baseman needed to sell himself to his new teammates. Hanlon got "Dirty" Jack Doyle in a deal with the Giants in the off-season. And while it was true that Doyle, an aggressive, speedy baserunner and a "scientific" batter, was an Oriole-type player, there was a problem. He had been one of the Giants who reneged on the 50–50 split agreement after the '94 Temple Cup, and the Baltimore fans never forgot. When the Giants played in Baltimore in '95, Doyle was ridiculed with taunts of "Jack the Welsher." But once the fans learned Doyle had been the first player to jump to Hughie's defense in the Petersburg fight, the fans forgave him. The fans forgave Doyle because Hughie was their hero. As Hughie was at the height of his physi-cal ability in 1896, he was also at the height of his popularity. His coal miner toughness and constant cheerfulness endeared him to the fans, while his unrelenting hustle, energy and willingness to sacrifice his body to get on base or make a play, earned him the respect of the players.

The season opened in Baltimore on April 16. The Orioles' lineup and batting order of Doyle, 1b; Keeler, rf; Jennings, ss; Kelley, lf; Brodie, cf; Donnelly, 3b; Reitz, 2b; Robinson, c, and pitcher Sadie McMahon lost the opener to Brooklyn. Bill Hoffer started and lost the second game. Dr. Arlie Pond salvaged the third game, then the Orioles went to Boston for the first game of a home-and-away series with the Beaneaters. They lost again and almost got lost themselves. The Orioles and Beaneaters, en route to Bal-timore on different steamboat lines, got stuck in heavy fog nine miles south of New York City. The teams were rowed ashore at 5:30 in the morning and didn't get to Baltimore until 2:30 for a 3 o'clock game. The game went off as scheduled.

The first six games drew 82,000 fans, an average of 14,000, the best ever. But with McGraw out, the Orioles got off to a slow start, losing three of four. It fell to Hughie, the team captain, to motivate the Orioles to play as a team, to keep mentally alert, to hustle on each play, as McGraw had done. It wasn't that McGraw was a natural leader of men. He could be surly and insulting. Rather, he led by being unyielding in his demands, by wearing players down. Hughie led by spreading optimism with his constant upbeat cheerfulness and by his play.[5] On April 21 in a 14–2 rout of the Beaneaters, Hughie went 3-for-4 with a double and two runs scored and, for the first of what would be a record-setting 51 times, he was hit by a pitch. On April 25 he was 2-for-2 with a triple and was plunked two more times by Washington's Jake Boyd in a 10–2 win. On May 5 in Pittsburgh he knocked in Keeler with the winning run in the 11th inning. The next day in an 8–0 win, Hughie hit a ground ball to first, then collided with Pirate pitcher "Cold Water" Jim Hughie at first base and knocked the ball loose. "Cold Water" returned the favor by plunking Hughie with a pitch in his next at bat. Hughie also made a fielding gem in the game. "Jennings robbed Donavan of a hit by a one-handed stop and remarkable throw from deep short."[6]

Hughie had his mishaps, too. On May 10 he misplayed a grounder in the 10th inning at Boston, then threw the ball away leading to the tying and winning runs in a 10–9 loss. Typically, he shrugged it off and kept playing his game. On May 4 he was hit by pitches twice, stole two bases and knocked in the winning run in the 11th in a 5–4 win over the Pirates. The next day he was 4-for-6 in a 12–2 win. On May 9 in the bottom of the 10th in Cincinnati (the Reds chose to bat first as the home team) Hughie was on third and Brodie was on first with two outs. Brodie took off for second. The Reds' pitcher turned and threw to Bid McPhee, the second baseman, who threw to third to try to get Hughie. Just as the throw was getting there, Hughie knocked down Reds third baseman Charlie Irwin with a hard slide and the ball went into the crowd. Hughie scored the winning run. The Reds appealed to umpire Bob Emslie, but he let the play stand. For giving Hughie a pass, Emslie had to be escorted out of the ballpark by Cincinnati police. Hughie's play early in '96 didn't go unnoticed by league brass. On April 27, National League president Nick Young was in Washington and watched the Nationals play the Orioles game in the press gallery. "That Jennings is a daisy, isn't he?" Young asked the writers, rhetorically. "Jennings could have been had for 50 cents when he was with Louisville, now Hanlon wouldn't let him go for $5000."[7]

Hughie led by example with his new bat, too. He started the season with a 24-game hitting streak that stretched into the middle of May. Hughie didn't go hitless until Sunday, May 17, in Chicago, before a Chicago record crowd of 19,000, in one of only four N.L. cities which allowed Sunday baseball in 1896. St Louis, Louisville and Cincinnati were the others. Hughie's lack of hitting hardly mattered. The Orioles won 13–1 to raise their record to 15–9 and put them in a four-way tie for first place with Cleveland, Boston and Cincinnati. But it did matter the next four days as Hughie had three more hitless games in the next four and the Orioles lost them all, two in Cleveland and two in Louisville. But even when he didn't hit, his fielding dazzled everyone. In one of the losses at Cleveland *Sporting Life* said, "Jennings' work at short was gilt edge." The Orioles salvaged the last game of the Louisville series and limped home with a 16–13 record, 3½ games behind the first-place Beaneaters.

Back in Baltimore Hughie heated up, and so did the team. They won 10 straight. Hughie seemed to be on base all the time. Batting third, as he would all season, he hit .525 during the winning streak and was hit by three pitches. Memorial Day was the biggest day ever in the short history of the National League as over 100,000 attended games around the league. Hughie went 5-for-9 in the two games,

This is how Hughie looked when he was captain of the Baltimore Orioles in 1896. (This studio portrait from Baltimore is courtesy of John Loftus, Jennings' descendant.)

6–5 and 9–6 wins over Cincinnati, stole a base and started a double play. The morning game drew 8,000 and the afternoon game, 11,000. On June 2 during a 10–3 thrashing of the Pirates Hughie laid a hard tag on Pirate outfielder Jake Stenzel. As Hughie went back to his position at short, Stenzel followed him screaming in his ear, itching for a fight. Hughie calmly told Stenzel that he bore a striking resemblance to Ananias. [Ananias was a wealthy Biblical figure who, as described in The Acts of Apostles (5:1–10), when asked to give all his wealth to God, lied about how much he had and then fell down and died.] But Stenzel wouldn't back off. Though the fans egged Hughie on, he refused to take the first swing and a brawl was avoided.[8]

On June 3, with the bases loaded in the bottom of the ninth and the Pirates and Orioles tied 4–4, Hughie, as the *Pittsburgh Press* described it, "stepped on home plate, allowed a pitched ball to hit him and the game was over." The 10-game winning streak had the Orioles in first place, 1½ games ahead of the Beaneaters and Reds. But a mini-slump — they lost five of the next eight — put them behind the Spiders by percentage points on June 15. Beginning the next day, the Orioles won 12 of 13. In two wins in Philadelphia Hughie went 7-for-9, scored four runs and took part in four double plays. But as hot as the Orioles were, they were matched by the Spiders. On July 4 in New York Hughie went 6-for-8 in a doubleheader, but the Orioles lost the second game and at the end of the day still trailed the Spiders by percentage points. The Spiders were 39–19. The Orioles were 40–20.

After the July 4 doubleheader in New York the Orioles went on a 21-game Western road trip to Chicago, Cleveland, Louisville, St Louis and Cincinnati. They started the streak losing two of three wild games in Chicago, 14–13 and 15–13, and winning 13–11. From Chicago they went to Cleveland, where on July 8 they were shut out by Cy Young, 7–0. After a day of rain they were shut out again by Nig Cuppy, 12–0, in the first game of a doubleheader to fall to third place, three games behind the Spiders and percentage points behind the second-place Reds. The Orioles were in trouble. If Cleveland could sweep the next two games they'd go up by five games. But the second game of the doubleheader was a turning point for the Orioles. They were losing 6–5 in the ninth, but, aided by two hits lost in the twilight by Spider outfielders, scored four times to win 9–6. Hughie was 2-for-5, scored two runs, stole a base and turned a double play. The next day the Orioles won 10–1. Hughie was 2-for-5 with two runs and two more double plays. Instead of leaving Cleveland five out, they left for Louisville down by just one game. The Orioles swept three games from the Colonels. In the second one Hughie was 3-for-3 and was hit by a pitch in a 12–5 win. He got plunked again in the third game, a 10–1 win. On their next three stops on the Western swing the Orioles took two of-three in Cincinnati, Pittsburgh and St. Louis to finish their Western swing 12–6 and $20,000 richer.

That was the Orioles' take from the trip, where they drew 120,000 for 15 dates.[9] By far they were the best road draw in the league and in no small part due to Hughie.

On June 30, the editor of the *Sporting Life* put a poetic spin on Hughie's popularity. "Hughey Jennings, brilliant Hughey — brilliant from hair to toe-plate — the white-plummed, scarlet-tipped knight of the emerald diamond. There was never his equal and fantasy can hardly paint his equal in the future. Such a cheerful, modest, painstaking, intellectual, skillful, combination was never before seem on a ballfield."

While the Orioles were winning those 12 of 16 on the road, they passed Cleveland in the standings. They now trailed the Reds by 3½. Cincinnati had won 19 of 21 on a home stand. The two losses were to the Orioles on July 19 and 21. The second of those games drew 20,000, a record crowd in Cincinnati. Baseball wasn't the only sensation in Cincinnati at the time. A celebrated murder trial of a man named Scott Jackson was also going on. Hughie, who would enter Cornell law school in a few years, and several of the other Orioles attended.

Hughie batted .425 on the Western trip, which ended in St. Louis on July 26. But the Orioles were not going home. They headed to Boston where they lost 3–2 on July 28, before launching a 10-game winning streak, all but one on the road, and six of them against Washington, who they outscored 68–27 in the six games. In the only home game in the stretch, they beat Washington 5–4 with a run in the ninth in a game which was controversial because of the umpire. Oriole pitcher "Chick" Hoffer called the game after Tim Horst took sick. Outrageous by today's standards, it was acceptable in 1896, when only one umpire worked the games. From the *Sporting Life* account of the game: "Baltimore managed to win the game by one run, but if Hoffer, who was calling the ball and strikes in the absence of Horst, had not been partial to his own club in the ninth inning, the score would have at least been tied."

In four games between August 7 and 11, one in New York and three in Washington, the Orioles scored 65 runs. Hughie was 10-for-18 in the four games with 10 runs and was hit by a pitch in three of the four games. The August 8 game, a 21–16 win over Washington, featured the season debut of John McGraw. He pinch-hit in the third to a two-minute ovation.

Hughie's season was appreciated by opposing fans. On August 12, during a 3–0 shutout loss to Brooklyn, Hughie made a play that was described this way in a game account: "O'Brien hit a fly beyond Jennings that was worth a single but for an aerial flight of Hughie's. He captured the ball in midair, a parachute specialty that was awarded with several rounds of applause."[10] He also had the only two hits allowed by the Giants Harley Payne. On August 19 the Orioles completed a four-game sweep of the Phillies in Philadelphia and then headed back to Baltimore to begin a 31-game homestand. They deserved it. Beginning on July 3 and continuing for a stretch of 41 games, the Orioles had played just six at home. So hungry were the Baltimore fans to see their Orioles again, thousands came out for the morning practices. On August 20 as the Orioles started their homestands, they were one-half game behind the Reds. The Spiders, having lost 8 of 12, were six games out. The Orioles lost the first game of the homestand to the Browns and the Reds won to go up by a 1½ games. But then the Reds collapsed. Playing in the East they lost their next 10 and the pennant race was effectively over. The batting race, however, was heating up. When Hughie had that 10-for-18 stretch the second week of August, he took over the batting lead over Cleveland's Jesse Burkett. But Hughie stayed on top for only a few days. When the homestand started on August 20, Burkett was back on top with a .403 average. Hughie was at .401. On August 22 the Spiders came to Baltimore for a three-game set. The Spiders won the first game. The next day the Spiders won the morning game of a doubleheader. In the afternoon game, 11,505 fans created a rowdy scene over the batting race between Hughie and Burkett. When Hughie hit a fly ball toward Burkett in left field in the ninth inning, the crowd broke through the outfield rope and tried to stop Burkett from catching the ball. Umpire Horst wisely called the game and it ended in a 4–4 tie.[11] Hughie did get back ahead of Burkett again in early September, and Baltimore bookies were offering 3-to-2 that Hughie would win the batting championship.

On September 4 in a doubleheader against Chicago, Hughie was hit by pitches twice in each game and some observers began to wonder about his sanity. Taking one for the team was one thing, but to his refusal to get out of the way, even after the pennant was all but won, seemed crazy. He wore crude pads under his uniform, but by August he was black and blue. From the Baltimore Bulletin section of an August *Sporting Life*: "His name and gameness were praised, but some said he was foolhardy. The later opinion was almost universal when after Baltimore clinched he continued to get hit. He seemed unable to convey the sense of danger from his brain to his limbs."

But Hughie wasn't as reckless as all that. He was hit a record 51 times in 1896, more than double the next highest total in the league, but never missed a game. The balls were not as hard then as they are now, and fewer of them were used in a game, so they softened up. Pitchers, with a few exceptions like Rusie and Young, did not throw as hard as they do today.

And as the *Sporting Life* pointed out in a subsequent article, Hughie didn't get hit with just any pitch. "There is considerable of the fox about Jennings and he knows when to get hit. It is the slow ball, one thrown at the lobster rate, that visits Jennings' form. He was never known to overlook a slow inshoot, which somehow or other — Jennings can explain it — tickles him in the ribs or on the legs."

On Labor Day, September 7, after rainouts on the 5th and 6th, the Orioles played and won a tripleheader from Louisville. The next day they won two more from the Colonels. On September 12 they beat Brooklyn 9–5 to clinch their third consecutive pennant. Hughie went 2-for-4, stole two bases and had three putouts and seven assists in the field. After the game on September 21 against Philadelphia, Hughie asked Hanlon for a leave. He was going back to Avoca to make arrangements to get married. Hanlon agreed. The next day the Orioles took the field without Hughie Jennings at shortstop for the first time since 1893. Hughie took care of business at home and then caught up with the Orioles in New York and played in the last game against the Giants. By giving up those three games, he may have also given up a chance to catch Burkett for the batting title, but, according to the writers, he didn't care.

"Hughie was right up there at the top this season and yet for all anyone could see by his actions in the games he was unconscious of a possible batting record and wholly conscious of the desirability of using the bat so that a run would result," wrote one in the *Sporting Life* late that season.

Another, in a bit of exaggeration, put it this way: "If Hughey heads the batting contingent, why, he just can't help it. He tries not to. He sacrifices and works for the man on the bases and the team and believes it is almost a disgrace to be at the top." Hughie batted .401, second to Burkett's .410. For Hughie there was no shame in finishing second to Burkett. Before he reached the major leagues Hughie, though only three years younger than "the Crab," had called Burkett his favorite player. A West Virginia native, Burkett broke in with the Giants in 1890. One of only three players to bat over .400 three times, Burkett was inducted into the Hall of Fame with Hughie in 1945.[12]

While Hughie was home for those few days, he was interviewed by the *Wilkes-Barre Record*. Typically, he tried to downplay his own contributions to the Orioles' success. "Many a time it has been my luck to make an error at a critical point, but in an instant Donnelly, Reitz, Clark or for that matter Keeler or Kelley in the outfield would sing out, 'never mind Hughey, we'll pull the game out yet.' Then I would go at it with determination, encouraged wonderfully by such an exhibition of friendly interest. This sort of encouragement was offered to every man from the pitcher on down and do you wonder at it that the Orioles occupy their present exalted position."

Hughie also lamented that it was the Spiders, and not the Reds, who finished second and would be the Orioles opponents in the Temple Cup. "We much preferred Cincinnati be the competitor, knowing the crowds would be larger out in Porkopolis and the receipts would unquestionably exceed those possible in Cleveland. Then, too, Young and Cuppy wouldn't be against us."

Hughie had reason to fear Cy Young. The Spiders had won 8 of 11 against the Orioles during the season and Young had won five of the eight without a loss. Though publicly Hanlon and the Orioles tried to play down the team's Temple Cup failures in '94 and '95, telling anyone who would listen that only the National League regular-season championship mattered, privately the Temple Cup losses rankled. Everyone from von der Horst on down wanted desperately to win. There were five days between the end of the season and the first game of the Cup series, and if the Orioles believed in omens, there were good ones. The intervening five days were so wintry and rainy in Cleveland the Spiders couldn't even get in a practice. When they left for Baltimore, where the first three games were to be played, a train wreck forced them to make a 20-hour trip in coach without a sleeper. Meanwhile, the Orioles were cozy in their homes in warm and sunny Baltimore where they practiced daily. Young started game one for the Spiders and Bill Hoffer started for the Orioles. With the first batter of the game the Orioles' good luck continued. McGraw lined one flush into Young's right wrist. Young recovered and got the out. He finished the game, but pitched like a human as the Orioles got to him for 13 hits and seven runs. After the game Young's wrist was stiff and swollen. He did not pitch again in the series. Hoffer scattered five hits and the Orioles won 7–1. In the second inning Cleveland's starting first baseman, Patsy Tebeau, who had not missed a game all season and was considered the league's best fielder at first, was lost for the series with a back injury. Hughie was 3-for-5 with two runs scored and handled nine chances in the field with one harmless error and a sharp double play.

For the second game Hanlon shocked everyone by passing on his regular starting pitchers and selecting 20-year-old Joe Corbett to start the game. Corbett, the younger brother of heavyweight boxing champion Jack Corbett, had pitched in just 11 games during the season. The Orioles staked the kid to a 6–0 lead with four in the first and two in the second. Hughie was in the middle of both rallies. He was hit by a pitch in the midst of their four-run first and singled and scored in the Orioles' two-run third.

Corbett gave up just seven hits. The final was 7–2. Hughie was 1-for-3, was plunked twice and scored two runs. In the field he had four putouts and four assists. The game was called after eight innings on account of darkness. Hanlon pitched Hoffer again in game three and Tebeau, managing from the bench wrapped in a heavy winter coat, pitched Nig Cuppy. Hughie didn't have a great game. Though he knocked in a run with a sacrifice fly, he was 0-for-4 with an error, but it didn't matter. The Orioles won 6–2 to take a 3–0 lead. After the game the teams traveled together and played exhibition games in Newark, and in Pennsylvania in Wilkes-Barre and Scranton, the later two arranged by Hughie.

In Cleveland for game four on October 8 Hanlon pitched Corbett again. Without Young, Tebeau came back with Cuppy on two days rest. Game four was the most competitive of the series and Hughie made two key plays. In the Cleveland fifth with the score 0–0, Hughie booted a sure double-play ball. The Spiders then pulled off a double steal to put runners on second and third with one out. Next, Burkett hit a hard grounder to short and Hughie fielded it cleanly and made a perfect throw to the plate to nail the runner for the second out. The Orioles got out of the inning. The Orioles broke the scoreless tie with two runs in the eighth. In the top of the ninth Hughie hit a two-run double and scored on Doyle's single, and the Orioles won the game 5–0 and the Temple Cup series in a four-game sweep. Corbett gave up just four hits and struck out eight. Hughie was 5-for-15 in the series with five runs, two doubles, three RBI, and a base on balls. He was hit by two pitches and his on-base percentage was .444.[13]

The next day the headline in the Baltimore American blared: "WHO NOW DISPUTES THE ORIOLES ARE THE GREATEST BASEBALL TEAM IN THE WORLD"

No one did. In the four-game sweep the Orioles had outhit the Spiders .298 to .195 and outscored them 25–5 to justify their regular season, when they played .697 baseball (90–39) and won the pennant by 9½ games. The Orioles were happy to win, but their joy was tempered by the poor gate. Cold and cloudy weather was blamed for the turnout of only 3,995 for game one, but the real culprit was the ticket prices. Hanlon and von der Horst raised them from the regular-season rate, a move which backfired. When attendance dropped to 3,100 for game two on a warm and sunny day, Temple and the league office considered playing the third game in either Pittsburgh or Cincinnati. Instead, von der Horst lowered admission to 25 cents for game three. It didn't help much, as only 4,240 paid to see game three. Attendance hit bottom for the fourth game in Cleveland on October 8 when only 1500 came out to see the Orioles complete the sweep. Fewer than 13,000 fans paid to see the four games, a pitiful total considering 10,000 had turned out for just one of the '95 games. Each winners' share of the gate receipts was only $198.88, over $100 less than the Orioles had made as losers in the '94 and '95 Cups. The exhibition games netted each player $48 and a benefit at Ford's Theater another $31, bringing each Orioles' total purse to $274. The Spiders got about $115. On October 13, Hughie picked up another $17.50 in postseason money. That was his prize winnings at the annual Oriole field day. Hughie won the long distance fungo batting contest with a 402'-10" blast and was second in baserunning to Keeler by one-half second. Keeler rounded the bags in 15 flat and Hughie in 15.5.[14]

By the end of 1896 Hughie was, by consensus of his peers and according to the numbers, baseball's best shortstop. He had batted .401 and in the field led all shortstops in putouts, double plays and fielding percentage. He was second, by three, in shortstop assists to Washington's Rabbit DeMontreville, who committed 29 more errors. Had there been a most valuable player award in 1896, Hughie, as shortstop and captain of baseball's best team, would have been tough to vote against. Life was good for Hughie in the fall of 1896. He was at the peak of his ability and popularity, but, oddly, there was a report that he was drinking.

"From Baltimore comes the report that Hughey Jennings has been dallying with the jollying fluid that makes a difference in the morning and is viewing the world through the bottom of a fizz glass, all of which began to happen after the Orioles clinched the pennant."[15]

Hughie wasn't a teetotaler like his father, but this was a strange report. Evidence that Hughie drank more than socially with McGraw and the boys after games would not surface again for 20 years, when Hughie was in his last season managing the Detroit Tigers.

10

Hughie the Honeymooner

Down in the hold of the steamship *Templemore*, Hughie grabbed a steer by the horns and tried to wrestle it into a stall, slipping and sliding in the beast's waste. Meanwhile, up on the deck, Wee Willie hung over the side in the throes of interminable seasickness. That's how the newspaper cartoonists characterized the two ballplayers' passage to England late in October of 1896 after the Temple Cup series, but it wasn't true.

Hughie and Keeler did sign on as cattlemen on the ship, but that was just a technicality. They were on board as honored guests of the captain, not as cowpunchers. That didn't stop the writers from taking their shots, "I was sorry to see the Orioles go to Europe in cattleships," wrote one in the *Sporting Life* on October 16. "It robs me of one of my stock-in-trade arguments. I have vigorously maintained that the men who play baseball in the National League were not an aggregation of Plebeians, accustomed to 15 cent meals and smoking cars, and only living in fancy hotels and riding in sleeping cars when someone else paid the bills. Jack Doyle told me the boys could go to Europe and return, first cabin, for $100 each. I don't get a ball player's salary or get a ball player's long vacation, but if I were going to Europe and could go in the first cabin of a liner, I wouldn't ride in a cattleship, not by a jugful."[1]

But Hughie and Keeler were treated royally. They were greeted with a gun salute when they boarded, played cards in the captain's cabin, watched whales, and thanks to beautiful weather and calm seas, didn't get sick once on the eight-day voyage. On October 26 they landed in Liverpool. Hughie registered in a Liverpool hotel "in very large letters for fear they would not know who we were and where we came from."[2] From Liverpool they went to London where they met up with McGraw, Kelley and Pond, who had traveled on the passenger liner *St. Louis*. The original plan had been to make the trip as a team and play a series of exhibition games, but when the plan fell through the Big Four and Pond went anyway on a pleasure trip. Together they went to their ancestral homeland, Ireland, and saw the international exposition in Brussels. In Paris they saw the seven-year old Eiffel Tower and toured the catacombs. In Rome Hughie fulfilled a lifelong dream by meeting Pope Leo XIII. They sailed home on the *Majestic*, arriving in New York on December 9 wearing Prince Albert coats, silk top hats and London-made boots.[3]

Hughie went home for Christmas and New Year's, but his marriage to his local sweetheart, Elizabeth Dixon, was put on hold. Instead of being a groom, Hughie was a best man. On February 3, 1897 he went back to Baltimore to stand up for McGraw at his wedding and reveled in the part. McGraw married Minnie Doyle, a Baltimore woman, in St. Vincent's Church on Front Street. For baseball fans the wedding was a rare chance to see their Oriole heroes during the winter. Fans jammed the aisles of the church and the sidewalk in front despite the cold weather. Keeler and Kelley were the groomsmen.

"Members of the championship team cut a fashionable figure in their full dress suits," wrote the *Washington Post*. "Hughey Jennings as best man looked as happy as the groom himself as he marched up the aisle with Miss Margaret Tighe on his arm and his face full of blushes as it is when the girls applaud him for a grandstand play."[4]

The 1897 season opened on April 22 at Union Park with the Orioles as favorites to win an unprecedented fourth straight National League pennant. McGraw was revved up for a full season of mayhem. Corbett was ready to go as a full-time starter. The new center fielder, Jake Stenzel, was coming off a .361 season at Pittsburgh. And, of course, Hughie, Keeler, and Kelley were runs in the bank. But the Boston Beaneaters—with future Hall of Famers in batsmen Hugh Duffy, Jimmy Collins and "Sliding" Billy Hamilton and pitcher Kid Nichols—were formidable rivals. Fittingly, they were the Orioles' opponents in the season-opening series. The Orioles passed that test with a three-game sweep, outscoring the Beaneaters 24–11 in the three games. In the second game Keeler and Hughie pulled off two perfect hit-and-run plays. Twice Keeler broke for second, and as the Beaneater second baseman covered, Hughie slapped a base hit to right field.

As 1896 had been to Hughie, when he started the season with a 24-game hitting streak, so 1897 was to Keeler, plus 20. Willie hit in a record 44 consecutive games before he was stopped by the Pirates' Frank Killen on June 19. For the first 22 games the Orioles were nearly as perfect as Willie. On May 19 the Orioles stood at 19–3. The Beaneaters were 11–10 in sixth place. But the Beaneaters went on an incredible tear, going 24–2 over 26 games. Between May 31 and June 21, a span of 17 games, all but one of them at home, the Beaneaters did not lose. When they finally did lose on June 22 at Brooklyn, they were in second place, just ½ game behind the Orioles, who were beset with injuries. McGraw missed time with a badly sprained ankle. Robinson missed nine weeks with an infected finger and came back without all of the digit. The tip had to be amputated.

On Monday, June 28, the Orioles were in New York playing the Giants. On the mound for the Giants was Amos Rusie, "the Hoosier Thunderbolt." Batting in the first inning, Hughie crowded the plate, practically daring Rusie to throw inside. Hughie had been plunked so many times to that point that the joke in the dugout was that he enjoyed it. He wouldn't enjoy this one. Rusie uncorked a fastball that rammed into Hughie's skull just above his ear with a sickening crack. The 12,000 fans at the Polo Grounds, the largest Monday crowd of the season, let out an gasp of horror in unison and then fell silent as Hughie went down and out, bleeding from the ear. He was revived with a large dose of ice water, and to the amazement of all, got up and wobbled toward first base. Somebody in the bleachers yelled, "that's putting the wood to it, Hughey ole boy."[5]

Hanlon and the team's trainer intercepted him and pleaded with him to come to the dugout, but Hughie flat-out refused to leave the game. Somehow he made it around to score a run on an infield error and a Keeler single. After the third out Hughie took his place in the field and staggered around like a drunk. Even when he was ordered to stop playing by a doctor, he refused and had to be led from the field by his teammates. Keeler took him to a downtown hotel and put him to bed. It was later determined he had a concussion. Years later, Doyle recalled the beaning in an interview. "Hughey had a way of riding the plate, standing up as close as he could get and shoving his body out over it. Rusie was determined to put a stop to this. Amos cut loose one of those terrible inshoots. The ball hit Jennings flush on the side on the nose and everybody in the stands could hear the bones snap."[6]

While some reports said Hughie hovered between life and death for five days after the beaning, the injury may not have been as serious as that. On July 6 he was back in the lineup, having missed just 7 games. If anyone thought that the beaning would cure him of crowding the plate, they were wrong. He resorted to his old trick of getting hit in the first game back, when he was plunked by Ted Breitenstein in a 10–3 loss at Cincinnati. Beginning on August 21, the Orioles won 22 of 26 on a homestand with only one loss. Three of the games were called for darkness and ended in ties. The Orioles made up seven games during the hot streak and on September 2 they were 73–33 and back in first place, but by just ½ game over the Beaneaters, who were 75–34.

Hughie got a treat during the homestand, a visit from his father, James Jennings, Sr. On Monday, August 30 the 73-year-old retired miner joked with the Orioles during pregame practice. Hanlon gave Hughie the day off and he and his dad watched the Orioles beat the Reds 7–1. Joe Quinn played short. The umpire, Jack O. "Kick" Kelly, described Hughie's father's visit in a newspaper interview.

> Hughey Jennings' father is a land leaguer. He wears a pair of fire-escape whiskers that skirt his chin a la Galway. Hughey had the elderly gentleman on the bench during Monday's game with the Reds. He's quite a comedian is the old man. Joe Quinn who was playing short as a sub for Hughey wore a red sweater in practice, and Hughey's father didn't like the look of it. "Who's that bloke in shortfield, Hughey? He looks like an Irishman but he's flashing the wrong color," he asked Hughey.
> "That's Joe Quinn," Hughey said. "He is Irish, father."
> Quinn took the sweater off and had it draped over his arm. The member of the Jennings family with the fire escape face jumped from the bench and pulled the sweater from Joe's shoulder and said in oily Galway, "Quinn, I don't know you personally, but you're flashing the wrong colors. A red sweater on a Mick makes a turncoat out of him. It's a disgrace to your country." Quinn threw the sweater on the ground and borrowed Joe Corbett's which is green.[7]

With the win the day Hughie's father visited, the Orioles went back into first place, ½ game ahead of the Beaneaters. For the next 24 days Baltimore and Boston bounced back and forth between first and second place. When the Beaneaters came to Baltimore on September 24 for a three-game series the Orioles were leading by ½ game. Though each team had another series to play before the season ended on October 2, everyone believed the Orioles-Beaneaters series would determine the National League pennant — and everyone was right. Over 13,000 fans jammed into Union Park for the first game, which fell on Friday. One hundred fifty seats behind the Boston bench were reserved for their rooters, who attracted a lot of attention at the Eutaw House, where they stayed, and with the caravan of eight horse-drawn omnibuses that brought them to the park. Blowing horns and shaking noisemakers, they tried to keep up with the Oriole rooters and gave a hearty greeting to Joe Kelley, who they saw as a native son. Kid Nichols, who had already won 29 games, pitched for Boston. Corbett, 24–8, pitched for the Orioles. Hughie staked the Orioles to a 2–0 lead in the first inning. He lined a single to center to score McGraw, stole second and scored on Kelley's double. One writer described the reception Hughie got after he scored: "Hundreds of enthusiastic young women in the grand stand arose in their seats, screamed with delight and called Hughey a darling."[8]

The lead held up until the fifth, when Boston scored two to lead 3–2. It was 6–2 when the Orioles came up for their last chance in the ninth. They loaded the bases with no outs, but Quinn, batting for Pond, who had relieved Corbett, popped out. McGraw then hit a single, scoring two runs and leaving runners at first and second. Keeler then came to bat representing the potential winning run with just one out, while Hughie, who already had two hits, waited on deck. The crowd roared as the line drive left Keeler's bat, put the roar turned to a groan as Herman Long leaped and snared the ball with a spectacular catch and doubled the runner off second to end the game. Now the Beaneaters led by ½ game. The next day the Orioles regained first place with a 6–3 win before 18,000 fans, who began lining up at 8 o'clock in the morning. Hughie knocked in two runs with a pair of doubles and handled 10 chances without an error and one double play. The Orioles' win set the stage for what would be the most anticipated baseball game in the history of the National League to that time. Never before had a game of such importance been played so late in the season. But everyone would have to wait a day. There was no Sunday baseball in Baltimore in 1897. On Monday, lines started at the ticket office before daybreak, but soon disintegrated into an unorganized free-for-all. By the time the gates opened at 2 o'clock, the 50 policemen assigned to control the crowd had given up. Before the gate could be opened it broke down from the weight of the crowd and thousands of fans rushed in without tickets. The paid attendance was said to be 25,390, the largest crowd in the history of the league. Another 4000 squeezed in without tickets and thousands more watched, as best they could, from outside the park. By game time order was restored outside and the gate was repaired. Scalpers sold reserved tickets for $5, five times their face value.

One writer described the scene this way: "In addition to the thousands of people on the stands and lined down left field five rows deep, every house top from which even a glimpse of the diamond could be caught was covered with men and women. Hundreds of pairs of opera and field glasses were leveled at the teams from elevated positions blocks away."[9]

Nichols and Corbett both were both back on the mound for the decisive game. Corbett did not last the first inning. He was hit on the thumb by a batted ball and couldn't continue. Nichols was hit hard for 10 runs on 13 hits, but it didn't matter. Boston made 23 hits against a succession of Baltimore pitchers. In the eighth they hit six doubles into the roped-off crowd and scored nine runs. They won 19–10. Hughie was 7-for-11 in the three games, but it was for naught. Two days later the Beaneaters clinched the pennant and the Orioles' three-season reign as National League champions was over. The Orioles lost a lot of star time to injuries over the course of the season, but the Beaneaters' pennant was no fluke. Boston had won by playing an amazing .821 ball at home (53–12.) They led the league in runs with 1025, fewest runs allowed, 665, and outscored their opponents by 2.73 runs per game.

A lot of players and fans around the National League were glad the Orioles lost. Henry Chadwick, a pioneer baseball journalist then in his 80s, was an Oriole basher. Though the Orioles had toned down their rowdy rule-bending style of play from what it had been in 1894, Chadwick was happy they lost and said the Orioles had long ago "forfeited the good will of every lover of manly ball playing."[10]

Chadwick's comment notwithstanding, the Orioles and their fans, with the exception of the ticket crush before game three, had been sporting during the decisive series. There was no kicking with the umpires. The Boston rooters were extended respect and hospitality. There were no spiking incidents or other examples of player animosity.

The pennant lost, Hughie did not play in the last two games in Washington. Instead he went home to prepare for his wedding. He finished with a .355 average and again led the league in being hit by pitches with 46. He stole 60 bases and scored 133 runs in just 117 games. Keeler led the league in hits with 239, a record for any league, and average at .424.

After a few days at home Hughie met up with the Orioles in Boston on October 4 for the start of the fourth Temple Cup series. Sam Augustine's brass band played "Yankee Doodle Dandy" and "Maryland My Maryland" as the fans filed into the South End Grounds in Boston for game one, but that was about excited as anybody got for the Temple Cup series. A 300-page history of the Boston baseball club on sale at the gate sold out.[11] The author, one George Touhey, and the players split the take. As things turned out, they would need it. The 9,600 who turned out for the first game would be the biggest crowd of the five-game series, which could not match the tense three-game series which had decided the pennant. There was an anticlimactic feel, a lack of urgency to win, from the beginning. Rumors that the players had agreed to a 50–50 split of receipts in defiance of Temple's dictum didn't help.

Kid Nichols started the first game of the series, opposed by the Orioles' Jerry Nops. Hughie had one of the best games of his career. In the Orioles four-run first inning, he hit a two-run double and scored from second when Keeler got into a rundown. It was the first of five hits in a 5-for-6 game with two doubles and three singles. No player would get five hits in a postseason game again until Paul Molitor did it in the 1982 World Series. Nichols left after the sixth with a sore arm and did not pitch again in the series. Boston came back to win the error-filled game 13–12, but did not win again.

Joe Corbett pitched game two for the Orioles. He walked four, hit a batter, threw two wild pitches, gave up 16 hits and 11 runs, and won. The Orioles scored 13 on 17 hits off two Boston pitchers. Hughie had one hit and scored a run. Attendance dropped to just 6,000. Hughie went hitless in game three and made an error, but Boston won easily 8–3, before just 4,000 fans at the South End Grounds on October 6. The series was set to resume on October 9 in Baltimore. The teams agreed to stop for two exhibition games on the way. At Worcester, Massachusetts Hughie received an unexpected honor when admirers from Holy Cross College presented him with a gold-headed ebony cane during the game.[12] Only 2,626 came out for game four. Despite the close score — the Orioles won 12–11— the game provided little drama. The Orioles scored 11 runs in the first two innings and went through the motions the rest of the way. If the players were indifferent, so were the fans. Fewer than 1,000 showed up to watch the Orioles clinch their second consecutive Temple Cup series with a 9–3 win on October 10. Hughie went 7-for-22 in the five games with two doubles, four runs, five RBI and four bases on balls in what would be the last Temple Cup series. The winners' shares were $310, while the losers got $207. Each made an extra $77 for the two exhibitions.

On October 14, Hughie married his hometown sweetheart, Elizabeth Dixon, at St. Mary's Catholic Church in Avoca. The ceremony was performed by Father George Dixon, the bride's brother. Hughie's brother, Dr. J.A. Jennings of Pittston, was the best man. The Baltimore Club sent the bride a silver dinner service. The players sent a mahogany cabinet.[13] What a honeymoon Hughie had in store for his young bride — a trip to San Francisco disguised as a baseball barnstorming tour. Immediately after the reception Hughie and his bride left for Columbus, Ohio, where they joined the Orioles for a series of exhibitions against the All-Americans, a team of all-stars which included Chicago shortstop Bill Dahlen, Cleveland player/manger Patsy Tebeau, and Boston third baseman Jimmy Collins. The teams played games in Columbus on October 15 and Cincinnati on the 16th, then made their way to San Francisco with stops in Indianapolis, Peoria, Topeka, and Kansas City. They played the first of a series of games in San Francisco on November 6 before 12,000 fans. Baltimore lost, and according to a newspaper report, "the only feature in the playing of Baltimore was Jennings' quick and clean fielding. He made a remarkable double play catching a straight liner by jumping high in the air and throwing the runner out at first."[14]

The teams played seven games in San Francisco and Mr. and Mrs. Jennings got back to Avoca in mid-December. After the holidays he and his bride moved to Allegheny, where Hughie resumed his studies and coaching duties at St. Bonaventure, this time without McGraw, who was back in Baltimore starting a pool hall business with Wilbert Robinson. Hughie found his contract from Hanlon for 1898 in the mail when he got home from San Francisco. This time Hughie didn't sign it.

11

The Big Four, No More

Hughie had a simple question for Hanlon in March of 1898: Why shouldn't more work come with more pay? The league had increased the schedule for 1898 from 132 to 154 games to pay for a second umpire. Even without the extra games, Hughie had a good case for a raise in 1898, even though he had reached the official salary limit of $2,400. Not only had he batted .355, he was fourth in the league in on-base percentage (just one point behind Keeler) and fifth in runs. He was the consensus peer of short-stops, having led the league in fielding percentage for the fourth consecutive season. The country was coming out of a recession which had started in '93. With a total attendance of over 2.2 million in 1897, baseball was more popular than ever. The Orioles had drawn 273,046, up from the '96 total of 249,448, and they were easily the best road draw in the league.

Hanlon wouldn't budge. Still unsigned, Hughie went to Baltimore in March and boarded the train to go south with the team. Kelley and Keeler, who were also holding out, did not. Corbett, another holdout, was still in California. But when the train got to Macon, Hughie went on to Athens to work with the University of Georgia team. Hanlon pleaded with him, but this time it was Hughie who refused to budge. After camp, the Orioles played their way north without three of the "Big Four." McGraw, who was coming off two injury-filled seasons, broke down and signed. On April 12, four days before the season opener, with Hughie still in Georgia, Hanlon met with Keeler and Kelley and agreed to pay Keeler $2,600 and Kelley, $2,700. Summoned by wire, Hughie arrived the next day and signed to play for $2,600.[1] Corbett, though, continued to hold out, and when Hanlon refused to offer a raise, he quit baseball for good and went to work for his brother, "Gentleman Jim," the famous boxer.

Though baseball had been surging in popularity through the mid-90s, in no small part thanks to the Orioles, something else occupied the minds of Americans that summer — war. Just one a week into the season, on April

25, President McKinley signed a declaration of war against Spain. The war was sparked by the sinking of the USS *Maine*, which had been sent to Havana in January 1898 to protect American interests during the long-standing revolt of the Cubans against the Spanish government. On the night of February 15, while most of the crew slept, the USS *Maine* sank when her forward gunpowder magazines exploded. Nearly three-quarters of the battleship's crew was killed. While the cause of the mysterious explosion was never pinpointed, American popular opinion blamed Spain. Hughie was stunned by the news. He had visited the battleship, and met with the crew baseball team, during the spring of '97 when the ship was anchored in the James River at Newport News, Virginia.[2]

The 1898 season opened under the "Brush Rule." The rule, which was clearly aimed at the Orioles and specifically at McGraw, was an attempt to curtail rowdy play and cursing. Named for Cincinnati president John T. Brush, the rule said that any player who talked to an umpire or another player in a "villainously filthy manner" could be banned for life if found guilty by a board of discipline. The Orioles' season opened at Union Park on April 16. Though only 6,518 fans paid to see the Orioles and Senators, Hanlon and von der Horst were confident the crowds would be back once they saw the strong club they had put together. But it never happened. The opening day draw would turn out to be the best home gate of the season. Doc McJames, acquired from Washington, started the opener and beat his old club in the opening game 8–3. (With McJames and Arlie Pond on the staff, the 1898 Orioles had the only major league pitching staff which could double as a medical staff. Both men were medical doctors. Pond left the team during the season and joined a medical unit in the Army.) The next day, the teams went to Washington. James Jay Hughes, a 24-year-old rookie from California who had been signed on Hughie's recommendation, threw a shutout in a 9–0 win.

Though he tried to hide it, something was wrong with Hughie. Some days he could barely throw across the diamond. During the past four seasons he had handled more chances and made more hard throws than any man alive. By May of '98 there was a lump as big as an egg on Hughie's arm directly opposite the elbow. The pain was so excruciating when he threw, he stopped trying. Doctors said the lump could be removed but Hughie didn't want surgery. Instead, he tried treatments which today would be considered quackery. He went to Philadelphia to be treated by a man with a reputation for helping rehabilitate ball players' arms with a "ball and chain treatment."[3] He missed nine games. When he came back, he seemed better initially, but the pain and weakness came back. On the bad days, he played second base, which he did for 27 games. In Chicago

Hughie saw Harley Parker. Parker had invented a method to treat ballplayers' arms called the "cupping system." Copper suction cups with rubber rims were worked over the body. Air was extracted and the suction was worked over the injured part to increase circulation. At least that was the theory.[4]

Despite all the injuries, the Orioles won 96 games in '98, but once again they finished behind the Beaneaters, who won 102. Though Hughie's average dropped to .328, he got on base more than he ever had. Again he led the league in getting hit by pitches, 46, and was fifth in bases on balls with 78. He was third in on-base percentage at .454 and second to McGraw in runs with 135. For the first time since 1894 there was no postseason championship series or barnstorming tour planned, and the Orioles disbanded right after the season. As the Orioles went their separate ways, there were hints that the "Big Four" era of the Baltimore Orioles was over, as was the era of Hughie Jennings as "The Greatest Shortstop in the Land." From '94 through '98 the Orioles had played .690 ball, which would translate to 110 wins per season in a 162-game schedule. But even that wasn't enough for the fans. While attendance was down all over because of the war, it took a terrible plunge in Baltimore. Toward the end of the season it got so bad that Hanlon and von der Horst stopped releasing official figures. In September, most of the home crowds were under 1000. In the end the official tally reported to the league was 123,416, less than half of the Temple Cup years. The Orioles were again the most popular team on the road, where they drew double what they had at Union Park, but even that was not enough for the Orioles to get out of the red. As much as von der Horst did not want to treat his team strictly as a business, he had to do something. The solution seemed bizarre, but really made sense. In keeping with a national trend of business mergers (von der Horst's own brewery had merged with several others) the Orioles merged with Brooklyn and the team was renamed the Superbas. The Oriole owners bought half of the Brooklyn franchise while the Brooklyn owners bought half of the Baltimore franchise. The deal became official on February 7, 1899. The idea was to move Hanlon and the best of the Baltimore players to join with the best Brooklyn players and form a team which, it was estimated, would make $100,000 in the world's largest city. After all, Brooklyn had drawn 300,000 as a 10th-place club in '98, more than the Orioles ever had. And Brooklyn alone was twice the size of Baltimore. The Orioles would then be left with the weaker players from both teams.[5] If the Baltimore fans would not even support a winner anymore, what fate awaited a team of sure losers? Predictably, the National League Orioles had only two seasons of existence left.

Under different circumstances Hughie would have railed against the breakup of the team, but he had much graver problems. Hughie and Elizabeth had set up housekeeping in Baltimore in April. In August they had a baby. They named her Grace. On November 21 his father died in Avoca. He was 75. Hughie left immediately for home, while Elizabeth, who was still feeling the effects of a difficult childbirth, stayed in Baltimore in care of a nurse. Hughie's father was buried wearing the temperance medal he had worn for 61 years. After the funeral Hughie hurried back to Baltimore to be with Elizabeth and was at her side when she died on November 26. She was 22. Grace was four months. Hughie took Elizabeth home and buried her in St. Mary's cemetery in Avoca, just as he had his father just five days earlier.[6] Hughie stayed secluded in Avoca until December, when he went back to Baltimore and said he was already resigned to a move to Brooklyn, even though it did not become official until February 7. "I think the Baltimore fans have been treated shamefully. If there is any way in which I could remain here I would do so. If I am put in Brooklyn I suppose I would be forced to go, but it would be with great regret. I had expected to make my home here permanently in this city. The time is rapidly approaching when players must break away from the National League and its arbitrary decisions."[7]

In February, Hughie left Grace in care of his wife's relatives and went back to college, this time at Cornell University in Ithaca, New York, where he had worked out a deal to coach the baseball team in exchange for tuition at the law school. With 65 men out for the team, Hughie earned his credits. He had a batting cage built in the local armory, and with intense daily workouts, weeded the team down. He stayed in Ithaca until late March, then took the Cornell team to Macon during the Easter break for a series of exhibition games. The Brooklyn Superbas were also in Georgia, headquartered at Augusta, and Hughie split time between the two teams until he went north with the big league squad. In an exhibition game on April 6 Hughie took his old place at shortstop for Hanlon's Superbas and handled 10 chances without an error, giving hope that his arm was healed. But it was a false hope and Hughie knew it. He had admitted as much to McGraw in Augusta when they went out to celebrate their birthdays, as was their tradition. Their birth dates were five days apart in early April.

Hanlon wanted to keep the "Big Four" together in Brooklyn. And the "Big Four" were willing to go, at a price. Keeler was thrilled to go. Brooklyn was his home. But he and Hughie tried to make the case they deserved more money since the new team was expected to make $100,000.

"We believe we can play as well as ever and we believe we should be entitled to some of the profits which accrue from this change. We like Baltimore, but we are dependent on the game for our livelihood and should be given a share of prosperity when it comes. We will stand together in this matter and the 'Big Four' will be a consideration again," Hughie told a Brooklyn newspaper.[8]

But, as the players had no real leverage, Hanlon waited them out. Kelley was mollified by being named captain and the $200 raise that came with it. Hughie, despite his public protest, was still reeling from the double tragedy in November and was in no mood for a fight. He signed at 1898 prices. Keeler held out longer, but just before the team went south, he, too, signed for no raise. But McGraw and Robinson refused to go. In a compromise, McGraw was named manager of the Orioles and Robinson his player/coach. Thus the "Big Four" of the Old Orioles became the big three — Keeler, Kelley and Jennings — of the renamed Brooklyn Superbas. McGraw tried to get some investors to buy the Orioles, but it was a tough sell because it was rumored the National League was going to drop four teams and go with an eight-team league in 1900. Though it took a year longer, the rumors would prove to be true.

On April 15, 1899, the revamped Baltimore and Brooklyn teams were both home on opening day, but all the fanfare was in New York, where a band playing "The Star Spangled Banner" marched players in from center field to a roar from 20,000 fans in Washington Park. Meanwhile in Baltimore there was no band, no parade, and just 4,000 fans, who cheered every move McGraw made. In Brooklyn the first ball was thrown at 3:30, beginning a new era in Hughie's career. Hanlon's lineup: Joe Kelley, lf, Willie Keeler, rf; Hughie Jennings, ss; Honest John Anderson, cf; Bill Dahlen, 3b; Dan McGann, 1b; Con Daly, 2b; Alex Smith, c; Brickyard Kennedy, p. For the first time since the middle of '93, when he was traded to the Orioles from Louisville, Hughie would be without John McGraw. In his accustomed place batting third and playing shortstop, Hughie took a pitch from Kid Nichols in the stomach in the first inning. The Beaneaters protested that he took the hit purposely, but the umpire sent him to first base. In the field, Hughie made a diving stop and strong throw to first for an out. It was a good start, but the first game of the post–McGraw era did not end well for Hughie, now 28, as this passage from a newspaper account of the Superbas' 11-inning, 1–0 loss to the Beaneaters colorfully explained:

"Ten innings of as pretty baseball as the most exacting crank could demand had been played when Hughie Jennings, he of the brick colored hair and anxious disposition, had the misfortune to juggle with an apparent easy grounder and in trying the get the ball to first in advance of the runner perpetrated a throw that brought great agony to the 20,000 and a few more of highly wrought up enthusiasts who today visited Washington Park to welcome the Bridegrooms of '99 in the opening tussle with the refined representatives of the refined city of Boston."[9]

The writer was kind to say Hughie threw the ball away in haste. In fact, Hughie's arm was seriously injured. After just three games, Hanlon took him out of the lineup. When May came and went and Hughie still did not play, Hanlon didn't say anything to the writers, but Harry von der Horst did. "I fear that Hughey is out of it and that his arm will never round into form. He is too brainy a ball player to be overlooked and he may be tried at first base in the near future."[10]

Cy Young doubted that Hughie could play first base. "The transfer to first base will not keep him in the game if his arm is played out. A crippled throwing arm is like a stiff neck. Every sudden twitch awakens pain as sharp as a cut from a knife."[11]

Hughie didn't get back in the lineup until June 26 in Chicago, when Hanlon put him at first base, batting fifth. At that point the Superbas were in first place by six games over the Beaneaters. Hughie didn't get out of the first inning in his first game. Umpire Emsile ordered him from the game for refusing to stop arguing a call. Finally, on June 28 and 29 in Pittsburgh, he started and played full games for the first time since the first week of the season, again batting fifth and playing first. He went hitless in the two games and made an error. It didn't help that the Superbas lost both games. On June 29, Hughie was on the bench again. Fearing that Hughie was finished as a productive player, Hanlon offered to trade him and $2500 to Louisville for the Colonels' 24-year-old third baseman, Honus Wagner, who was showing promise as a batter in his second full year in the majors. Hughie didn't want to go to Louisville, and took it upon himself to make sure the trade didn't go through. He sent a wire to Louisville team secretary Harry Pulliam. On July 17, Pulliam made the telegram public. It read: *Don't consent to deal. Am in no condition. Will play no more this season. Bad arm.*

Asked about the telegram by a *Brooklyn Eagle* reporter, Hughie offered no spin. "I am not opposed to figuring in a deal, but I most certainly object to going to Louisville. With the reports that are going around regarding new leagues and the reduction of the National League, a player don't know where he is at. It isn't certain that Louisville will be in the league next year and I want to stay in the big organization. I am looking out for my own interest and if Louisville were to be dropped next season, I might be frozen out."

But it's unlikely Pulliam, though a great admirer of Hughie, would have made the deal even without the telegram. Pulliam wasn't going to be conned by Hanlon a second time in a deal involving Hughie. It was Pulliam who had signed off on the trade of Hughie to Baltimore for Tim O'Rourke in '93. "I have great respect for Hanlon's ability," Pulliam said, "but I think he overplayed himself in this case. Wagner is younger and even if Jennings were in perfect trim, it is doubtful he would prove as valuable in the long run as Wagner. Hanlon talked as if it would be a special favor to me if I gave him Wagner for Jennings."[12]

However, since the Colonels didn't make a positive refusal until after the telegram, Hanlon, and the Brooklyn president, Charley Byrne, were furious. They appealed to the league office, which considered suspending Hughie for sending the telegram. Hanlon was angry enough to release Hughie, but von der Horst insisted on a trade. Meanwhile in Baltimore, McGraw missed his friend and lobbied for a trade that would reunite them. Von der Horst wired McGraw that he was bringing Hughie to Baltimore to trade him for infielder Topsy Magoon. But McGraw, without telling Hanlon or von der Horst, had already traded Magoon. Hanlon, now even madder, got revenge on McGraw by sending him Hughie and taking two players, including the Orioles' best pitcher, Jerry Nops. Now McGraw was hot. As much as he wanted Hughie back at his side, he felt ripped off. Hanlon had said he wouldn't treat the Orioles like a Superbas farm team, but now he was doing just that. After the Superbas' game in Cincinnati on August 2, Hughie took a train to Pittsburgh to join the Orioles. McGraw put him in the lineup at second base and batting third. As the headline in the *Baltimore American* read the next day: "Jennings Brought His Bat." Hughie hit two triples, twice driving home McGraw, and made three assists without a mishap in a 5–4 win. From the story: "With the smiling face of Hugh Jennings on second base the Birds of this afternoon recalled the three-time winners. The Pittsburgh people barely had time to recover from the shock occasioned by Jennings' appearance as an Oriole before he was in the game with both feet."[13]

McGraw was happy with Hughie's showing, but still resented Hanlon's taking of Nops. "Jennings will strengthen our team. He showed that today, but taking away Nops is a hard blow. When in shape he is the best left hander living."[14]

The subplot to Hughie's return to the Orioles was that he was returning to a team which was just six games behind the league-leading Superbas from which he had come. How McGraw had the Orioles winning was the talk of the league. As a manager he had a knack for getting the best out of marginal players, wasn't afraid to discipline even his best players and had an eye for talent. In the spring he had talked Hanlon into letting the Orioles keep an unknown 28-year-old rookie pitcher. "Ironman" Joe McGinnity wound up leading the league in wins with 28. McGraw not only managed well, he played the best baseball of his career. He batted .391, stole 71 bases and led the league in runs scored with 140 in 118 games.

The trade of Hughie caused an uproar in both Brooklyn and Baltimore. As he was everywhere, Hughie was a favorite of the Superbas fans
and they wanted him back. The Oriole fans, as much as they, too, loved
Hughie, saw the trade as proof they were second-class baseball citizens.
The newspapers were merciless on Hanlon. *The New York Evening Telegram*
said, "The Brooklyn management climbed to the housetop and protested
that never, no never, would there be any syndicate collusion between
Brooklyn and Baltimore. If this exchange of players is not a syndicate move,
pray, what is?"

After just two days, Hanlon rescinded the deal and Hughie went back
to Brooklyn. Before August was out, Hughie was back in Baltimore, but
for the most tragic of reasons— to help carry the casket of Minnie McGraw,
his best friend's wife, who died after surgery for acute appendicitis. As
Hughie's Elizabeth had been when she died nine months earlier, Minnie
was just 22. Back in Brooklyn, Hughie finished out the season as the regular first baseman. He batted .326 and scored 35 runs in the last 51 games.
The Superbas won 101 games, lost 47 and won the pennant by eight games
over the Beaneaters. Hughie's last word on the '99 season was about his
old buddy McGraw. "We won the pennant but McGraw showed splendid
managerial talent in this, his first attempt. He piloted Baltimore into third
place, which was getting the last ounce out of the material under his command."[15]

12

From Cornell to Brooklyn

Hughie stepped briskly through the swinging door, climbed onto the diving board, bounced once and dove — into the concrete floor of the Cornell University pool. "It was dark and not another soul was there," he said. "Without waiting to turn on the lights I stepped on the board and jumped. The caretaker had drained the tank during the afternoon to scrub the pool the next morning."[1]

Though Hughie was banged up, with two sprained wrists and a mild concussion, physically he recovered quickly. Mentally, he lived with the empty-pool dive for the rest of his baseball career. After the incident, when he got into confrontations with other players or managers, they often used the dive to mock Hughie and impugn his intelligence. In May of 1912 when he was managing the Tigers, Hughie got into an argument with White Sox pitcher Ed Walsh. Though Walsh, like Hughie, was a refuge from the Northeastern Pennsylvania anthracite mines, they often clashed on the field. This particular time, the shouting almost turned into a fist fight on the field when Sox coach Kid Gleason, who had been Hughie's teammate in '94 and '95 with the Orioles, interrupted and said: "You dived into an empty swimming pool. Last winter you dived out of an automobile onto a pile of rocks. That's twice you've tried to commit suicide but your head was too thick."[2] The bit about diving from an automobile was a reference to an automobile accident Hughie had during the 1911–12 off season.

Hughie had returned to Cornell in February of 1900 to continue his law studies and coach the baseball team. He didn't join the Giants until April 19 when the revamped National League opened its season minus four teams. As Hughie had feared when he fought against the trade, Louisville was one of the teams dropped. Cleveland, Washington and the Orioles

were the other three. It was a precipitous fall for the Orioles. Only two
seasons had passed since they ended their remarkable run of 1894–97, when
they reinvented baseball while winning almost 70 percent of their games.
Now the Orioles were no more, bought out by the league magnates for
$30,000 plus whatever they could sell the players for. McGraw was ped-
dled to St. Louis, along with Robby, but McGraw refused to go until he
was offered a package of salary and a bonus which totaled $9,500, the most
ever for a player.

The reduction of the league had put over 50 players out of work and
to protect the interests of the remaining players, a union was formed for
the first time since the Players League had folded after the 1890 season.
Hughie was elected secretary of the new union, the Players Protective Association. As he was, admittedly, nearing the end of his playing career, Hughie
made it known he wanted be a manager. The Phillies were interested in
him, but Hanlon refused to let him go for less than $7,500, more than the
Phillies could pay. In a letter to a friend back home, which wound up in
Sporting Life, he hinted at retirement. "I am capable of being a success as
a leader just as much as the man I have been under for the past seven years.
When the chance is open to me to show my worth in the managerial line
and he blocks it, it is almost — if not quite — time to call a halt."

But with no leverage, and with a law degree still at least a year away,
Hughie signed with the Superbas, but not before he fired another verbal
salvo at Hanlon. "If I am worth more than $7,500 to the Brooklyn team,
as Mr. Hanlon acknowledges, and it is essential to the success of his team
to have me why does he not show the appreciation of my true worth —
according to his own estimate — and pay me the same salary as Philadelphia or any of the other clubs is willing to pay me?"[3]

Then Hughie revealed a new wrinkle. When he had been in Philadelphia in '99 trying to rehabilitate his arm, he had been offered the job of
sports editor with one of the city's newspapers. But Hanlon and Brooklyn
secretary Abell and president Ebbets wouldn't budge. They wouldn't lower
the price for Hughie and didn't believe he would retire. Abell said Jennings
would play with Brooklyn or not at all and Ebbets said the Brooklyn club
"would not be forced into relinquishing a player."

In early April when Hughie went south with the Cornell team, he
stopped in Wilkes-Barre, where he told friends he had given up the fight,
for the time being anyway. "I can write when I can't play ball. I presume
I will be seen on the Brooklyn team this year."[4]

His presumption was correct. On April 19 he was in the opening day
lineup batting third, but playing first base. His shortstop days were over.
He was hit by a pitch and walked and scored a run as the Superbas opened

defense of their National League crown with a 3–2 win over the Giants at the Polo Grounds. On July 29, Hughie, as union secretary, met with 100 players in New York City and announced two demands: release of players who are not going to be used rather than farming them out and players to share in the purchase price when they are sold. "We are not out to fight the owners, but to resolve injustices in the contracts," Hughie said, knowing the demands were symbolic.[5] The players' only weapon would be a full-fledged players strike, but no one had the stomach for it.

Hughie played in 115 of the Giants' 142 games in 1900, all but two at first base. Though it was clear he was way off his game from the 90s, he contributed with a .272 average, 61 runs, 69 RBI, and 31 steals. He walked 31 times and was plunked a team-high 20 times, boosting his on-base percentage to .348. More important, for the fifth time in seven seasons, he was a National League champion. For the first time since the 1897 Temple Cup, a postseason championship series was staged. The best-of-seven series was arranged by the *Pittsburgh Chronicle-Telegraph* and all the games were played in Pittsburgh. The home-field advantage did the Pirates little good. The Superbas won four of the five games. Joe McGinnity pitched two shutouts for the Superbas. Hughie played every inning at first base, but batted just .183 with three hits.

Throughout the 1900 season the name Byron "Ban" Johnson had been on the lips of baseball players, fans and owners. Johnson was the visionary president of the minor Western League who believed he could establish teams in the East and make his league a major league on competitive par with the National League, which thought so little of Johnson's League that it routinely raided his players through a draft. When the National dropped four teams in 1900, Johnson started his assault. He changed the name of his league to the American League and on February 14 fired a preemptive shot at the N.L. by signing N.L. players who were out of work due to the dropping of the four teams and moving teams into the East in Boston, Philadelphia, and the abandoned Baltimore. But the league fell apart before a game was played and Johnson retreated back to the West. The N.L. gave Johnson another opening after the 1900 season. The National Agreement — which legitimized the N.L. as the only major league in "Organized Baseball" and which included several established minor leagues but not the Western League — expired. Seizing the chance, Johnson unilaterally declared his league a major league for the 1901 season. Johnson didn't just offer another major league, he offered an alternative major league, which banned alcohol, rowdy behavior by players and fans and demanded respect for female fans and umpires. His owners began offering contracts to National League players. The N.L.'s $2,400 salary ceiling and reserve clause made it easy to lure players. Over 100 NL players jumped to the AL in 1901 including Cy Young, Jesse Burkett, Ed Delahanty, and Napoleon Lajoie. Connie Mack, the owner of the A.L.'s Philadelphia Athletics, signed Lajoie to a $6,000 contract. Another lure was the A.L.'s promise to reserve players for only three years. Among all the action, rumors flew about Hughie. The *Chicago Daily Tribune* reported that Hughie was going to the A.L. as a manager, probably in Cleveland. President Johnson would not confirm or deny the report.[6] In December it was rumored that Buffalo would be the eighth team in the A.L. in 1901. Buffalo owner James Franklin entertained Hughie and made a flattering proposal for Hughie to be the first baseman/manager. He was offered $4,000, $1,000 more than he got in Brooklyn in 1900. But Buffalo did not get a team and nothing came of the other rumors. In January, Hughie declared he was through with the game. "I will never play professional baseball again. I have made arrangements to take a full three years law course at Cornell. When I leave Cornell I will begin practice with a well known New York firm who have made me an exceptional offer."[7]

In February, Hughie went back to Cornell. School officials offered him full tuition and a salary of $1,500 to stay through June 20, the end of the college baseball season. Hughie accepted, but as the winter wore on he realized he was not ready to give up the game. He wired Hanlon who, hoping to keep Hughie from jumping to the A.L. or carrying out his threat to quit, gave him leave from the Brooklyn team until June 20.

13

Philadelphia Freedom

The Philadelphia Phillies fans who came to Baker Bowl early on June 21, 1901, could hardly believe what they were seeing. As the new player made his way across the diamond to first base for practice, a murmur in the crowd swelled to a rousing cheer. Yes, that unmistakable shock of red hair and happy grin belonged to Hughie Jennings.

Wasn't he supposed to be down in Baltimore with the new American League Orioles and his best friend, Oriole manager John McGraw, or across town in Columbia Park with the A.L.'s Philadelphia Athletics, as Ban Johnson had ordered? What was he doing in Baker Bowl in the uniform of the Philadelphia Phillies?[1] The answers reached back to December, when the Players Protective Association met with the league owners in New York. Hughie and the Protective's lawyer, Judge Harry Taylor, with whom Hughie had been traded from Louisville to the old Orioles in '93, presented the players' demands. Among them was a demand for an end to the reserve clause. The owners refused to drop the clause, thereby calling the players' bluff to boycott the National League and jump to Johnson's American League. In early February, the Protective met again, this time in Cleveland, and reached an agreement with the American League that provided for a graded system of contracts of three, four and five years, after which players could be free agents. The A.L. also agreed that a player could not be traded or sold without his consent. With that, the war was on.

Hughie left Cleveland and reported to Cornell on February 10 to stay until June as agreed. At that point he was resigned to having to report to Hanlon and Brooklyn in June. But then, four days later, came the news that the American League was going to place a franchise in Baltimore in a brand-new 8,500-seat steel and concrete ballpark. The team's name would be the Orioles and its manager would be John McGraw. Hughie and McGraw exchanged wires and letters and made a deal. Hughie would report to Baltimore in June, not Brooklyn. What could make more sense, or be more fair, than for Hughie to return to Baltimore to be with his old friend John McGraw, and with a hefty salary raise? But Ban Johnson had another plan. In late April, Johnson went to Ithaca to talk to Hughie directly. Johnson led Hughie to believe McGraw had given him his release because he had already signed the allotted three N.L players, the limit the A.L owners had agreed to. Johnson told Hughie to report to the Philadelphia Athletics. By teaming Hughie with A's star Nap Lajoie, a fan favorite who had jumped to the A's from the N.L Phillies, Johnson hoped to draw fans away from the Phillies.[2] When McGraw heard what Johnson had done, he was incensed. He wired Hughie and told him to come to Baltimore as planned. As the date approached for Hughie to leave Cornell, McGraw went public with his anger.

> The assertion by President Johnson that the managers of the American League Clubs agreed to sign no National League men without permission from Johnson is rot. The agreement was for each club to sign no more than three National League men. This limit was raised to four and each team named its men. I went to Hot Springs believing this agreement would be lived up to, only to find that Chicago, Boston and Philadelphia were signing every National League man they could get. I found Baltimore was the only one getting left out, because it was living up to the agreement.
>
> This action about Jennings looks like a studied effort to worst the Baltimore Club to the gain of the Athletics and we will positively not allow it.
>
> Jennings wired me today. He will be here Wednesday and will stand by the Baltimore Club. We will play Jennings at first base and Johnson can take such action as he sees fit.
>
> Jennings has sent me copies of letters he sent to President Johnson and manager Connie Mack telling them Baltimore had first claim to his services. He has also written me that Johnson misrepresented the facts when he visited him some weeks ago. He asserts Johnson told him plainly that I had waived his claim and given consent to the Athletics.[3]

As promised, after stopping home to visit his daughter, Hughie went to Baltimore and reported to McGraw on June 19. Oriole president Sidney Frank was thrilled to have Hughie and wanted McGraw to put him in the lineup the next day against Milwaukee. But umpire Sheridan, under orders from Johnson to forfeit the game to Milwaukee if Jennings tried to play, would not allow it. Johnson decreed that Hughie would play with the Athletics or not at all in the American League.

"I am placed in a very disagreeable position," Hughie said. "If I defy President Johnson and play here I outlaw myself in the American League and if I disregard the option clause of the Brooklyn club, I outlaw myself from the National."[4]

Frank went over to Philadelphia to plead his case to Athletics manager Connie Mack, but Mack would not give Hughie up. Frank adamantly told Hughie he would pay him $3,000 to sit on the bench. Hughie was flattered, but said, "I would not accept a salary under those circumstances and besides I must think of the future. I do not want to ruin all prospects of playing again next year. I would not play in Philadelphia so long as McGraw holds me to my promise to him and it seems I will not be allowed to play here. So what else can I do but go to Brooklyn."[5]

The next day the Orioles, though not admitting the Athletics had any claim on Hughie, offered $5,000 to the A's to release him. They refused. That night, June 20, Hughie left for New York on the midnight train, or so everyone thought. The next afternoon he showed up in Baker Bowl as a Philadelphia Phillie, the Phillies having bought his release from Brooklyn for a reported $6,000. The *Philadelphia Inquirer* wasn't buying it. The deal had to have been made in advance, said the paper in a banner headline story. "Jennings seeks to excuse his breach of faith on the ground that he had promised McGraw to play in Baltimore and that because McGraw and Ban Johnson failed to come together, he (Jennings) was absolved from any obligation to the American League. Now as a matter of fact, there is every reason to believe that Jennings had not the slightest idea of playing with the Athletics or the Baltimore Club since June 8, if not before."[6]

As evidence, the paper pointed to a letter from Hanlon to the *Brooklyn Eagle* three weeks earlier in which Hanlon intimated he believed Hughie had some kind of understanding with the Phillies. The *Inquirer* was joined in its condemnation of Hughie by Johnson and other American League officials, managers and players, but Hughie was well satisfied with what he had done. "One would think that the American League had disposal of my services and that I had nothing whatever to say in the matter. In the first place, I was under reserve to Brooklyn and was in no way bound to the American League. Yet the American League, with no claim whatever on me, presumes to take away from me my right to sign where I please and assigns me to the Athletics. Because I preferred to go with McGraw all kinds of threats were made to me and McGraw. Naturally, I refused to be dictated to in that way and as I could not play with McGraw, accepted the most satisfactory berth that was offered me."[7]

That "most satisfactory berth" Hughie accepted was a contract for $3,300 for the rest of the season, transportation expenses and, it was speculated, a percentage of the $6,000 Brooklyn got for his release. Whatever the cost, the Phillies were happy to land Hughie on two levels. For one, it was a victory for the National League in the war with Ban Johnson and the American League. Secondly, Phillies owner Colonel John Rogers and manager Bill Shettsline saw Hughie as a winner. Though Hughie had hit only .275 with Brooklyn in '00, he scored 61 runs, drove in 69 and stole 31 bases in 115 games. Whatever his statistics, he was Hughie Jennings, captain of the famous Temple Cup Baltimore Orioles. He may have been beyond his prime as a hitter, and admittedly, his arm was shot, but he still had some baseball in him. He had just turned 30 that April. He knew everything there was to know about baseball. He could still run, was a sure-handed first baseman and a run creator. And he had that infectious positive personality. No Philadelphia team had won anything since the Philadelphia entry had won the American Association pennant in 1883, but Rogers felt the Phillies were close to winning in '01 and saw Hughie as the last piece to the puzzle. In '00 the Phillies had played .543 ball at 75–63 and had finished third, eight games behind the Brooklyn Trolley Dodgers and their first baseman, Hughie Jennings. But the Phillies' best player in '00, Lajoie, had jumped to the Athletics. The Phillies' remaining best players were Elmer Flick and "Big" Ed Delahanty. Flick led the National League in RBI in '00 and was second in batting, slugging and home runs. Delahanty, a four-time .400 hitter, had an off season by his standards, hitting .324, but he did lead the league in doubles. In his defense, Delahanty, a left fielder, had spent '00 playing out of position at first base to make room for James Slagle to play left. Slagle, a little lefty from Pennsylvania nicknamed the "Human Mosquito," had a fair season in '00, hitting .287 with 115 runs and 34 steals, but had no power and made a league-leading 29 errors. Shettsline was stuck with Slagle in left and Delahanty on first when the '01 season opened. But when Hughie arrived, Slagle, who was hitting just .202, was dealt to Boston. With Slagle gone, Delahanty moved back to left and Hughie became the regular first baseman.

The Phillies were 24–24 and in sixth place in the eight-team N.L when Hughie arrived, and they lost the first game he played. But then, with Hughie in the everyday lineup playing first and batting sixth, the Phillies suddenly got red-hot. Between June 23 and July 27, they won 21 games and lost nine and rose all the way to second place, just 2½ games behind Honus Wagner and the Pittsburgh Pirates. The Phillies cooled some, but stayed close to the Pirates through August. Hughie hit under .300 all season and contributed on the field only sporadically. Hughie's bigger contribution was just in being himself. So everyone around the league said. "It is strange what a wonderful effect one man can have on a team," wrote one scribe. "Look at Jennings at Philadelphia. He has gingered the former easy-going Phillies until they are hardly recognizable in their present style of play.

From a team of indifferent players and not a consideration in the pennant problem, Jennings has turned the Quakers into a hustling crowd that is making a hard bid for the bunting. Jennings is in the game with his feet, hands and head from the moment the umpire says play ball."[8]

Two days later, it was written that Hughie "inoculated the Phillies with a little jump virus" and "the surprise of the old league has been the showing of the Phillies. It must be admitted that Jennings' men are traveling a little ahead of their gait. Even the Philadelphia papers admit the greater part of the team's success is due to the influence of the hustling Hughey."[9]

There must have been something to the claim. Though the pitching staff was second in team ERA, the Phillies had as many regulars hit below .200 as it had, other than Hughie, legitimate stars. Second baseman Bill Hallman batted .184 and shortstop Monte Cross hit .197. Flick batted .336 and Delahanty was the only Phillie with over 100 RBI. Nonetheless, as late as September 7, the Phillies were well in the race. That afternoon, when the Phillies beat the Pirates 4–1 before 15,000 in Philadelphia, the biggest crowd of the season, they cut the Pirates lead to 3½ games. Hughie had two hits, including an RBI double. But the Pirates won the next two days and the Phillies' pennant hopes faded. On September 18, the Phillies went into Pittsburgh for a four-game series, needing to sweep to have a chance. Instead, they lost the first three. The Pirates clinched on September 27. Hughie asked for leave and Shettsline let him go. He finished 1901 with a .262 batting average, 38 runs and 39 RBI in 82 games, by far the least productive season of his career.

By October 3 he was back at Cornell, unencumbered by anything to do with major league baseball. Hughie had resigned as secretary of the Players Protective Association at their meeting in New York on June 23, saying his commitment to Cornell in the offseason wouldn't give him time to devote to the job. While that may have been true, Hughie was disgusted with the association. In July he predicted its demise. "The only evidence that we have that there is anything doing in the association is that someone has asked that the players attend a meeting in New York when next the Western teams visit the east. What will be done at this meeting I do not know. So far as I'm concerned the players will do just as well to let the organization die a natural death. It has served its purpose as well as it ever will. I'm inclined to believe that the next meeting will be a wake and the Players Protective Association will be the corpse."[10]

Hughie was a year off on his prediction. The Association lasted through the 1902 season, but collapsed when the National and American Leagues signed a peace treaty in the winter of '03. In the deal, the A.L.

accepted the reserve clause. The players lost all leverage. League jumping, salary bidding and franchise shifting came to an end.

Hughie stayed at Cornell from October until June of 1903 to finish his law studies. On June 10, he arrived in Philadelphia and was immediately put in the lineup, batting third and playing first base. He had two hits, scored one and batted in one of the Phillies two runs in a 4–2 loss to Chicago. But 1902 produced none of the 1901 magic for the Phillies. Instead of battling for the bunting as they had in '01, in '02 they battled to stay out of last place. On June 25, Hughie was hit on the left wrist by Christy Mathewson, his Pennsylvania coal-country neighbor and friend. Though the injury was described as a "shattered wrist" in newspaper accounts, an X-ray showed only one small bone in his right wrist had been broken. "The funny part of it is," Hughie said, "that I made up my mind two years ago never to get hit again and here I am with a broken wrist. It was one of Matty's funny slants that did it and I could not get out of the way."[11]

The *Brooklyn Eagle* used the occasion to reminisce about Hughie's days with the old Orioles. "So flagrant was Jennings' trick of allowing himself to be hit by a pitched ball that the N.L. passed a rule making it optional with the umpire to send a man to first on being hit, the official deciding whether the player got in the way purposely or not."

Hughie missed two weeks. By the time he got back in the lineup on July 7, the Phillies were 20 games out. If there was anything to play for, it was to stay out of the cellar, ahead of the New York Giants and their new manager, John McGraw. McGraw had jumped to the N.L. Giants from the A.L. Orioles during the 1902 season, lured by the first-ever $10,000 contract and the chance to be rid of Ban Johnson. After the '02 season, the Orioles followed McGraw to New York, where they became the Highlanders and later the Yankees. There wouldn't be another franchise shift for 50 years. On September 23, Hughie helped the cause with a 2-for-4 in a 3–1 win over Brooklyn and the Phillies were four up on the Giants in the loss column. In the end, the seventh-place Phillies were seven games better than the last-place Giants. The Phillies may have avoided last place, but over in Baltimore, the A.L. Orioles did not. Robby took over as manager after McGraw went to the Giants and watched helplessly as the Orioles stumbled to a 50–88 year in what would be their last major league season for over 50 years.

As Hughie took his position at first base on October 3, the last game of the regular '02 season, he likely didn't know it would be his last season as a regular player in the major leagues. He went 1-for-4 and had seven putouts as the Phillies lost to Brooklyn to finish 56–81, 7½ games ahead of the last-place Giants. Hughie batted .272 in 78 games. It was an inglorious end to the era of Hughie Jennings the player, the famous shortstop and captain of the old Orioles dynasty. But an even longer era of even more fame and greater glory lay ahead for Hughie Jennings the manager.

14

Back to Baltimore

"Think of Hugh Jennings in a minor league! Verily, times have changed," so wrote *The Sporting News* on July 11, 1903. And it was true. In July of 1903, Hughie Jennings was a minor leaguer, and indeed times had changed.

Back in April, Hughie had let it be known that he had been released by the Phillies and re-signed by Brooklyn. Hughie was in Washington D.C. with Cornell to play Georgetown University when he was asked if he expected to play in '03. "Some time ago I said I would retire from the game, but I suppose when the middle of June comes around I will don the togs and get back into the game again. I do not expect to again to play with the Philadelphias, for I really belong to the Brooklyns, and will, no doubt, join Mr. Hanlon's team when the college season ends."[1]

Hughie arrived in Brooklyn from Cornell on June 22 when the Superbas had played just two games in eight days because of rain. He was anxious to play, to try out his arm, but he languished in a hotel room as the deluge continued for two more days. Finally, on June 25, in the Superbas' 53rd game of the season, Hughie made his 1903 debut, replacing Jimmy Sheckard at first base in the second game of a doubleheader. By this time Hanlon had gotten over Hughie's defection to the Phillies in 1901 and Hughie had gotten over Hanlon's blocking of his managerial chance in 1900. Hanlon was glad to have his old Orioles' captain back and he had plans for Hughie. Playing first base for the Superbas was not part of the plan. There was no doubt Hughie was not the player he used to be, but perhaps he didn't deserve this sarcastic criticism in the *Washington Post*: "Hughey Jennings is still the greatest ball player on earth, according to the New York papers. Hughey played with the Phillies the last two seasons and one can't help but wonder where he kept his reputation during that time. It is said he will play the outfield for Brooklyn. He will probably have a small boy to carry the ball for him since it is doubtful he can throw it that far."[2]

On July 2, 1903, having played in just six games, Hughie's career as a major league player was over. But it was okay. Hughie was going home, to his adopted home at least, to be the manager of the Baltimore Orioles, or at least a team with that name. When the American League Orioles moved to New York and transformed into the Highlanders after the 1902 season, Baltimore had been left without a team. Hanlon, with Robby as his partner and manager, bought the Montreal franchise in the Eastern League and moved it into American League Park in Baltimore, which they had bought for $3,000 at a bankruptcy sale. It was a steal. With its concrete and steel grandstand, the park was estimated to be worth $15,000. Hanlon's plan was to put a team in Baltimore in the Eastern League and then ultimately in the National League. One idea floated was to have the American League Highlanders move to Brooklyn and the Trolley Dodgers to Baltimore.[3] In any case, as Hanlon now controlled Brooklyn as its field manager and Baltimore as its owner, he orchestrated a trade. Hughie, along with catcher Hugh Ahearn and outfielder Walt McCreedie, were sent to Baltimore for outfielder John Hayden, who was shipped back to Baltimore without ever playing a game in Brooklyn. Hughie replaced Robinson as manager. Robby was 39, but he was still a solid catcher and he happily handed the reins to Hughie.

"He was one of base ball's great receivers," Hughie wrote of Robby years later in his newspaper series. "He was intelligent and uncanny in the way he outguessed batters, and he could throw and he could hit. He was the oldest member of the Orioles and served as a sort of ballast. (This can be taken either way, seeing that Robby weighed more than 200 pounds and never succeeded in getting rid of any of it.)"[4]

Hughie was also offered part ownership in the Eastern League Orioles. He invested $3,600.[5] Hughie had always wanted to be a manager, even during his heyday as a player with the N.L. Orioles. After the 1895 season, he had tried to negotiate his release from the Orioles to accept an offer from Scranton, then in the Eastern League, for a one-third interest in the club and $300 per month as manager. When Hughie took over the Baltimore Eastern League team after the trade in '03, the other teams in the eight-team E.L. were Hartford, Worcester, Buffalo, Jersey City, Newark, Syracuse and Hartford. The new Orioles were a mishmash of career minor leaguers, veteran major league castoffs, young players on their way up and a couple of Hughie's coal country neighbors. Jim Mullin, a second baseman, though born in New York City, lived in Hughie's hometown, Avoca. Hughie bought him from Washington for $800. Mullin had played in 118 major league games before he was bought by Hughie, but he never got back to the majors.[6] There were two other coal country players on Hughie's

E.L. Orioles. Tom Jones, from Honesdale, a coal and railroad town 20 miles east of Scranton, went on to play eight major league seasons, including two for Hughie with the Tigers in 1909 and '10. Mike Mowery, from the southern Pennsylvania coal region town Brown's Mill, had a 14-season career as third baseman for four N.L. teams. There were no official major league affiliations with minor league teams in 1903. Under the terms of the National Agreement, players could be drafted from Eastern League teams to major league teams for $1,000. But as Hanlon owned the Orioles and managed Brooklyn, he treated the Orioles like a modern-day AAA team. For example, he assigned Tim Jordan from the Orioles to Brooklyn after the '05 season and he promptly led the N.L. in home runs in '06. There were deals struck with other teams, too, which resembled how the minor league system works today. In '05, Washington loaned outfielder Claude Rothgeb to the Orioles. The Nationals paid his salary while he played for the Orioles. President Noyes of the Washington club said, "He's subject to recall at anytime and he is getting the right sort of training from Hugh Jennings."[7]

The Orioles were near the bottom of the league standings when Hughie arrived in July of '03. By the end of the season, they had risen to fourth place and Hughie got a lot of the credit. The 1904 *Reach Guide* said the Orioles' fourth-place finish was "due to the spirited management of Hugh Jennings." The guide might have added "and to the spirited play of Hugh Jennings." Hughie played in 32 games at short and second and batted .328 with 26 runs and nine steals.[8] In 1904, Robby again managed the Orioles until Hughie finished his duties at Cornell. Over the Easter break, Hughie took Cornell on a southern trip, where they played games against the Atlanta Crackers of the Southern League, Mercer and Macon, and the Universities of North Carolina and Virginia.[9] Hughie caught up with the Orioles in early May and led them to a second-place finish, both as a manager and player. In 92 games, he batted .292 with 65 runs and 23 steals. After the '04 season, he went back to Cornell for another semester of studies. On February 5, Hugh Ambrose Jennings, Phi Delta Theta man, member of the Sphinx Head Senior Honorary Society, and former uneducated mule driver, was admitted to the Maryland bar.

The 1905 Eastern League season produced a fantastic pennant race which came down to the last day, September 24, when Jack Dunn's Providence Clam Diggers won out over Hughie's Orioles by one-half game. An unplayed game cost the Orioles the pennant. Providence finished 83–47, the Orioles, 82–47. "The hell of it is," Hughie said, "I had to lose to that wild-eyed Dunnie by the margin of a rain-out game."[10] Hughie, then 34, played in 56 games in '05, all at shortstop. After the '05 season, Hughie stayed in Baltimore through January where he took on his first case as a lawyer, unsuccessfully defending a black man accused of stealing a chicken. On February 1, he left for Ithaca and stopped in Scranton to see his little girl, who was in care of family and the nuns at Marywood Seminary in the city. He went on to Cornell for one last time for two solid months of law study. Asked about the prospects for the Orioles in '06 after their close miss in '05, Hughie couldn't resist taking a shot at Hanlon for taking his best players. "We'll have pretty much the same team as last year granting that Brooklyn returned the men whom it purchased, Jordan, Burchell and McNeil." Hughie used the word "purchased" sarcastically and knew full well he wasn't going to see those players again.

For the '06 season, Hughie was with the Orioles from the start. On Sunday, May 21, he took the Orioles to Allegheny, New York, to play an exhibition with the St. Bonaventure team. The official attendance was listed at 2,349, four times the average for an intercollegiate game. The fans surrounded the outfield, forcing the umpire to declare that a ball hit into the crowd would be an automatic double. This was nothing new to Hughie and the Orioles, but the collegians had never seen the crowd spill onto the field. St. Bonnie's pitcher, McNally, wasn't intimidated by the professional players. In an outing a week earlier, he had pitched six innings against Buffalo and allowed only four hits. The crowd expected Jennings to make an appearance as a player, and though he appeared in 75 games that season, he kept himself out of the game that day at St. Bonnie's. The Orioles managed to escape the ignominy of losing to collegians, but barely. The Orioles won it 4–3. The collegians collected seven hits, including two triples, and almost pulled the game out in the bottom of the ninth when they scored two and left the tying and winning runs on second and third.[11]

The depleted Orioles finished in third place in 1906. Hughie played in 75 games, and though he batted under .250, he made just 19 errors and led the league's shortstops in fielding percentage at .961. Hughie could still pick 'em and apparently, his arm had mended. All the same, his playing days were over once and for all. During '06, his fourth season managing the Orioles in the Eastern League, the losing, the raiding of his players by Hanlon, and the growing realization that Baltimore was not going to be a major league city again anytime soon, wore on Hughie. Sure, the 1905 pennant race had been exhilarating, but it was insignificant compared to what was going on in the major leagues. Hughie could only watch from relative obscurity as his old buddy McGraw, the highest-paid and highest-profiled player or manager in the game, managed the Giants to the best record in baseball. The 1905 baseball season was also a momentous one in the American League. The National and American and Leagues combined drew an astounding 5.8 million fans. The World Series between the National and American championship teams from two of the country's greatest cities, New York and Philadelphia, drew over 125,000 for five games. In 1904, because McGraw had refused to let the Giants play in the World Series, the A.L. was still viewed as a minor league in some quarters, but in '05 the A.L. was legitimized as a major league once and for all.

In '04, Giants' owner John T. Brush and McGraw scorned the American League, instead of playing in the A.L. champion in a World Series, as the Pirates had done in '03. Quoted in the *Sporting Life* that October of '04, Brush said, "There is nothing in the constitution or playing rules of the National League which requires its victorious club to submit its championship honors to a contest with a victorious club in a minor league."

McGraw likely regarded the American as a minor league, as well, but he had his own reason for not wanting to play the American League in a postseason series—his mutual hatred for American League president Ban Johnson. McGraw, also quoted in *Sporting Life* two weeks after Brush was, called the proposed series a "a haphazard box office game with Ban Johnson and Company."

Early in the '05 season the three-man National Commission—Johnson, N.L. president Harry Pulliam and commission chairman Garry Herrmann—agreed to stage a world's championship series between the leagues' champions. This time, McGraw and Brush agreed to go along with the postseason series. They had mellowed on the idea of a National League-American League postseason series for four reasons. One: McGraw was sensitive to the whispers that he was afraid to lose to the Americans. Two: the Giants had so dominated the National League in 1904–05, winning the pennant by 15 and 13 games, that by mid-September they were playing out the string. With nothing to look forward to, the fans stayed away in droves. Crowds of less than 1,000 were common in those late September games of '04 and '05. Three: the players were still angry that Brush and McGraw, who were making far more money than the players, didn't let them play in '04. And four: Brush, who made $100,000 on the team in '05 season, wanted to make even more.

In October, Hughie traveled between New York and Philadelphia and watched McGraw manage the Giants to a four games to one win over Connie Mack's A's in the second World Series. McGraw's success cemented Hughie's belief that he, too, belonged in the major leagues. In this belief he had an unusual ally—an umpire. Tim Horst was a tough character who had been a professional race walker and a boxing and wrestling official in New York City, before taking up umpiring baseball in the Penn State League in 1888. He signed on to umpire in the National League in 1891.

He worked the major leagues on and off for 13 seasons. He was called "Fearless Tim," "Terrible Tim" and "Sir Timothy." He was baseball's most respected and popular umpire in the 1890s. In 1892, he knocked out an abusive fan with his mask, in 1896, he dropped two Pirate players in a fight after a game, and in 1897, when a beer glass flew onto the field, he threw it back and knocked out a fan. He had many run-ins with McGraw, Hughie and the Orioles during those seasons, but didn't hold a grudge. After all, hard coal people watched out for each other, and Horst was the son of a mining family from Ashland, Pennsylvania. And Horst liked Hughie. He once said Hughey had "a grin that echoes."[12]

So Horst took it upon himself to help Hughie get a big league job. During the later part of the '06 season when he worked Highlanders games, he told owner Frank Farrell to hire Hughie as manager. Farrell made some inquiries which started a spate of rumors. It was reported that Hughie would most certainly succeed Jimmy Collins as manager of the Boston Americans in 1907.[13] In late August, Hughie was going to Detroit, a report that was quickly denied by Tigers president Frank Navin. "You can say positively that the Detroit club has not hired Hughey Jennings of Baltimore to manage the Detroit team next year," Navin said, in a published report on August 28.[14]

The *Post* wasn't buying it. On September 9, the paper reported, "Despite reports to the contrary it is learned today that Jennings will manager Tiger next season."

But Ban Johnson didn't want Hughie in his American League. He never forgave Hughie for refusing to report to the Athletics in '01, but it was more than that. "He's got that old Oriole stamp on him and he's too close to John McGraw," he told Navin. "We cleaned Oriole rowdiness out of this league and I won't have it brought back by Jennings."[15]

Hearing of this, Horst took the first train to Chicago, sought out Johnson and tried to convince him that Hughie would do more good for the American League than the harm he had done in 1901 and '02.[16] Horst may have had some impact on Johnson, but Johnson didn't relent until Detroit owner Bill Yawkey, a New York millionaire, threatened to pull his money out of the team. Given the go-ahead, Navin didn't wait for the end of the season. With the Tigers on their way to a sixth-place finish, and their fourth losing season in six, Navin was anxious for a change. In early September, he contacted Hanlon to negotiate Hughie's release. Hanlon wanted $5,000 and wouldn't budge. So, on September 16, the wily Navin, realizing that Hughie had played in 75 games with the Orioles in '06, drafted him as a player for $1,000.[17] At once he saved $4,000, stymied Hanlon, and thrust Hughie into the national spotlight. On October 1, after the Eastern

League season ended, Hughie took the Orioles to play an exhibition game with in Lehighton, the Pocono Mountain town where he had broken in as a professional ballplayer. There, he publicly announced he was going to manage the Detroit Tigers in 1907. Making the announcement in Lehighton was vintage Hughie. Never forget where you came from.

15

The "Ee-yah"

Herman "Germany" Schaefer lined a double into left field and Ty Cobb streaked home with the Detroit Tigers' first run of the 1907 season. In the third-base coaching box the team's new manager pulled up two handfuls of infield grass. With clenched fists raised over his head, he leaned his torso back, raised his right leg with bent knee, let loose with a piercing cry of "ee-yah" and threw the grass in the air like confetti. The fans howled with laughter and yelled back, trying to imitate the mysterious cry. Thus began a love affair between a baseball manager and baseball fans which was unequaled before and remains unequaled since.

During the early years of Hughie's 14-season tenure as Tiger manager, sportswriters, fans, managers and players around the country speculated wildly about the origin of Hughie's dance and signature yell. He gave contradictory hints about what it meant, but never revealed the true origin of the yell. A logical conclusion is that "ee-yah" was an outgrowth of Hughie's days as a mule driver in the mines. Mule drivers used voice commands to steer their mules, "giddap" for go, "whoa" for stop, "gee" for right turn, and "wah-haw" for left turn.[1] Hughie never confirmed or denied that his "ee-yah" was based on mule driving commands. Another theory held that the famous yell was a derivation of a native Hawaiian phrase "weeki-weeki" meaning "watch out" or "look out." The story goes Hughie learned the phrase from "Honolulu Johnny" Williams, a pitcher from Hawaii. But Williams played for the Tigers in 1914, long after "ee-yah" originated, and pitched in only four games, which were the extent of his major league career. A magazine story claimed the cry, and the dance-like gyrations that accompanied it, originated from a trip to the circus. "In his early youth Hughie attended a one-ring circus and was much impressed with a Cherokee Indian rain dance. In a side show, on the same occasion he witnessed a snake dance from the Far East. Hughie has combined these two dances with some original steps."[2]

111

Hughie, as did other managers, yelled common baseball phrases of the day while in the coaching box: "The old pepper," "a little ginger fizz," "don't weaken," "come on boys," "keep trying," "that's the eye," and "have a crack at it." But "atta-boy" and "ee-yah," were his trademarks. He embellished them with drawn-out syllables, grass throwing, and jigs and leg kicks. From time to time he threw in other intelligible sounds. The scribes had a ball describing Hughie's antics. "He gave an exhibition yesterday using a language foreign to locals. It is a mixture of Arabian slang and Swedish court tongue," wrote one.

"Eyah, eyah, eyah a shrill series of suppressed warhoops, a few of the dancing steps peculiar to the flying dervishes of Persia or a Cherokee rain dance will give a fair description of Jennings on the coaching lines," wrote another.

A New York sporting writer once wrote: "Manager Jennings executed a sailors hornpipe, a highland fling, and wound up with an Indian rain dance. He stood on one foot, then the other and showed alarming symptoms before the contest ended of standing on his head."[3]

Whether or not "ee-yah" was a hidden signal to the players was as mysterious as its origin. "Yow, skiatik. whee," wrote a Washington scribe. "Everyone of those Indian yells, South African cat calls and Siberian-Cossack cries means something to the Detroit players. The yells which keep the bleachers screaming with laughter are a code of signals. Frank Chance watched Jennings and the players like an eagle, but couldn't fathom the code."[4]

On the coaching lines with the Detroit Tigers in 1907–10 and with two fistfuls of plucked grass, Hughie is shown in this postcard about to let loose with the "ee-yah" cry that made him world famous.

Eddie Collins, the Athletics' Hall of Fame second baseman, also believed Hughie was up to something. "Judging from his results it's not illogical to suppose that 'ee-yah' contained some signs and secrets of team play such as steal, hit and run or sacrifice." [5] Hughie never denied that he was conveying secret signals, but Ty Cobb did.

> Many fans think Hughey gives his players orders through his famous "ee-yah" yell. That's not the case though. He gives signals the same as other coaches. I heard two players trying to "dope" out what "ee-yah" meant. "When he follows it up with a whistle that means hit-and-run," they said, and "he puts emphasis on the 'yah' for a sacrifice."
>
> Even if I told them that Jennings was not giving signals through "ee-yah" they would not have believed me. Some ball players are convinced there is something behind the cry and Jennings is perfectly willing for them to continue to think it, too. I do not know what "ee-yah" means. Jennings has also studied Spanish and used that with his pitchers so umpires and other players wouldn't know what it meant. The coaching of Jennings has a certain effect on his players. It kind of buoys them up and makes them dig in and work hard.
>
> We have made seven, eight, and nine runs in an inning many times. On successive days we had 10-run innings. Innings like that were due to Jennings' aggressive coaching.[6]

Whether "ee-yah" meant anything or where it came from will never be known, but we do know from Hughie and other sources that it started during Tiger spring games in Macon before the 1907 season. In explaining this, Hughie also gave life to still another story of where the cry came from and why he used it.

"I just started saying 'that's the way.' Those Tigers played so fast I had to keep yelling fast to keep up with them. Finally 'that's the way' was just one word, 'way-ah' then it became 'wee-ah.' "[7]

A newspaper story out of the Philadelphia area in 1909 theorized why Hughie became so wildly popular with fans throughout the American League. "If the businessman, the worker, who for a few hours of recreation goes to the game a while and forgets the batting averages of Ty Cobb and Honus Wagner and all other vain pursuits and makes a personal study of Jennings and his work he would go away refreshed to tackle the worries and problems of another day."[8]

Hughie's explanation may have ended speculation about how the cry started, but he sometimes told other stories. He even told the "Honolulu Johnny" story a few times. Keeping the fans and writers guessing was a shrewd idea. The more Hughie and his antics were written and talked about, the more the fans wanted to see him. Umpire Billy Evans, who played under Hughie at Cornell and doubled as a sportswriter, told a story that illustrates the point. "While on a streetcar in Washington D.C. the man next to me asked me about Jennings. He said he wasn't much of a baseball fan and this was his first major league game. 'Lately I haven't been able to pick up a paper without reading about Jennings and seeing a picture of him in some acrobatic pose. I want to see what this Jennings fellow really does.' Before the game I told Hughey about the incident and said 'give him a show, it would be a shame to disappoint this fellow seeing his first big league game.'"[9]

Evans needn't have worried. Hughie gave them a show all over the American League in 1907 and the fans, love him or hate him, came out to laugh at him or mock him. The Tigers were the biggest draw on the road in the league in 1907. Cobb's breakout season and the pennant race helped, but thousands of those new fans came out to see, and hear, Hughie. At home the Tigers drew 123,000 more than they had in 1906, though they still ranked seventh in the eight-team league. But not everybody loved Hughie's coaching lines shows. Horace Fogel, a Philadelphia writer, called on Ban Johnson to do something, calling Hughie's antics, "silly, destructive and an insult to American League fans." Johnson might have been expected to agree, but he didn't intervene. The ticket sales likely overshadowed his sense of discipline.[10] Johnson also saw that Hughie's "ee-yah" cry brought attention to the A.L. through endorsements. One, which ran in papers all over the East, pictured Hughie as a Tiger saying, "After a red hot finish to a ball game a pipe full of Tuxedo makes victory sweeter and defeat more endurable. Ee-yah for Tuxedo."

At times Hughie used props with his antics and got in trouble. On August 2, in the first game of a doubleheader in Washington, Hughie blew a tin whistle to distract the Nationals' pitcher, who was making his major league debut. His name was Walter Johnson. The whistle got Hughie a 10-day suspension. Sam Crawford told the story of what Hughie did to "Rube" Waddell, the hayseed pitcher who was considered a simpleton. "Hughey Jennings used to go to the dime store and buy little toys, like rubber snakes and jack-in-the-box. He'd get in the base coach's box and set them down on the grass and yell, 'Hey, Rube, look.' Rube would look over at the jack-in-the-box popping up and down and kind of grin, real-slow like, you know. Yeah we'd do anything to get him in a good mood and distract him from his pitching."[11]

Despite the Tigers' success on the field and at the gate in 1907, after the season one report said Hughie would not be giving a repeat performance in 1908. "Jennings is sick and tired of the yell. It bores him as much as 'skidoos' jars the average human being. He isn't going to use it anymore because it nettles him. Every kid in the streets shrieks it into his ears. Every man greets him with it. Every paper he picks up uses it as a prefix for his name. It haunts him day and night. He's through with it. He wants to forget it. 'I didn't yell that because the crowd wants to hear it. Now when anybody hears that noise it becomes a joke. It's been used so much the real meaning has been forgotten by the players. I won't use it because I want to say something that will be taken seriously and make them fight. 'Weehaw' is shop worn.'"[12]

But when the 1908 season began, Hughie was back in the coaching box plucking grass, dancing his jigs and crying "ee-yah." By 1917, Hughie's yell had become such a part of American culture that it was a rallying cry for American infantrymen in World War I. Soldiers in the European trenches "went over the top shouting the breaker boy's battle cry."[13]

16

Cobb

Charlie "Boss" Schmidt could hardly believe what he was seeing. From across the field at Warren Park in Macon, Georgia, he watched Ty Cobb push a woman to the ground, jump on her and choke her. Schmidt ran over and pulled Cobb off the woman. When Cobb fought back, Schmidt, a rugged 200-pound former boxer who reportedly had fought an exhibition with Jack Johnson, knocked him down and out with one punch. When Cobb opened his eyes seconds later, he saw his new manager standing over him. "You're gone from Detroit," Hughie Jennings said.[1]

It was March 16, 1907, and Hughie had known Cobb for only a week, when Cobb set upon the wife of Warren Park's black groundskeeper "Bungy" Davis that day. Davis had committed a grievous sin. He had clapped Cobb affectionately on the shoulder, tried to shake his hand and called him "Carrie." In Cobb's world a black man did not address a white man informally and certainly didn't touch him. Cobb slapped away the man's hand, knocked him down and kicked him. Davis ran and Cobb chased him toward the shack next to the field where Davis lived. When Davis's wife came out, Cobb set on her. He knocked her down and choked her.

Cobb thought Hughie should understand. After all, Cobb pleaded, in the South blacks knew their place. Incredibly, Cobb denied being a racist. Blacks worked on his farm and he treated them fairly, he said. While that was true, it was also true that Cobb, by his own admission, believed blacks were subservient and inferior. In 1908 he punched and knocked down a black street worker in Detroit, who had yelled at Cobb for walking in fresh street asphalt. Cobb paid to settle that incident and another, when he knocked a hotel chambermaid down some stairs after she cursed him for calling her a "nigger." Major league baseball was a racist organization in 1907, still 40 years away from integration, but Cobb's racism was beyond the pale. It wasn't just Cobb's virulent racism that prompted

Hughie, and Navin, to try to trade Cobb. It was the way he flew so quickly into a rage in front of everyone and attacked a woman. Schmidt, a Southerner himself from Arkansas, was no egalitarian, but beating a woman, of any race, was intolerable. The day after the attack Hughie sent wires all over trying to make a deal for Cobb. He offered him to Cleveland for 30-year-old Elmer Flick. But Cleveland manager Nap Lajoie wouldn't consider it. Flick, a career .300 hitter, had led the A.L. in batting in 1905. Even without the off-field baggage, Cobb, in Lajoie's view, wouldn't have been worth Flick. Only the New York Highlanders made an offer, Frank Delahanty even up for Cobb. In the emotional aftermath of the "Bungy Affair" Hughie had been determined to trade Cobb for whatever he could get. But Hughie could not bring himself to trade Cobb for Frank Delahanty, a .220 hitter so obscure that Hughie hadn't even known the Highlanders had him. After a fruitless week, Hughie softened his stance. A few teams offered to buy Cobb outright, but Hughie said no. "Cobb will not be dispersed of for cash. I'd just as soon exchange him for any equally as promising or valuable player."[2] There was no such player and Hughie, even if nobody else did, knew it.

While the trade talks were going on, Cobb, certain his days as a Tiger were done, went back to his home in Royston, Georgia, to wait. But when the outrage, and the trade talks, died down he reported back to camp in Augusta on March 23. The assessment of Cobb by the managers who refused to offer real value in a trade for him seems, in retrospect, curious for such experienced baseball men. But in March of 1907 none of the big league managers, except Hughie himself, knew what the Tigers had in Cobb. In two seasons as a big leaguer he had played in only 139 games combined, batted .293 and stolen 25 bases. Hughie saw something special in Cobb from the first day of camp. "I could see that Cobb was far from ordinary, but no man could guess how far removed he really was."[3]

The extraordinary Cobb had been 11 days short of his 19th birthday when he was called up to the Tigers from the Sally League Augusta Tourists on August 26, 1905. Three weeks earlier he had been called home to Royston after his father, William Cobb, had been shot to death by his wife Amanda, Ty's mother. William, who was supposed to have gone out of town on business, had returned in the dark of night, climbed onto the front porch roof and scratched on the bedroom window where Amanda slept. She shot him with both barrels of his own shotgun.

With his father freshly dead by his mother's hand and his mother awaiting trial on manslaughter charges for his baggage, Cobb arrived in Detroit at night after a 750-mile train trip. He had $75 in his pocket. No one met him at the station. A horse taxi took him to Ryan's Bed and Board,

A card showing Hughie Jennings and Ty Cobb and advertising Hassan cork tip cigarettes.

where he tried, and failed, to sleep in a room above a burlesque hall. The next morning, wearing rumpled clothes and a straw hat and carrying his four-fingered pancake glove and an ash bat, he caught another taxi to Bennett Park and reported to Tiger manager Bill Amour. Cobb debuted on August 30th with a double in his first at bat against Jack Chesboro. In his second game, when he was thrown out trying to steal second with a headfirst slide, Kid Elberfeld, the Highlanders' shortstop, ground Cobb's face in the ground with his knee on his neck. Little could he have known what a monster he was helping create. Though Armour had his supporters, one thing was certain, he didn't know what he had in Cobb. It would seem that he and Navin must have had some inkling of what was inside Cobb. Why else would they bring up an 18-year-old from a class C league? The answer was that injuries had put the Tigers in a personnel emergency and Cobb was one of their few options. By necessity, Amour played him in all 41 of the Tigers remaining games. He hit just .242 and stole only two bases.

During the 1905–06 off-season Cobb had just about given up on the Tigers when a contract for $1,500 for 1906 arrived in January. In spring camp the other Tigers— especially outfielders Sam Crawford, Matty McIntyre and Davy Jones— ostracized and tormented Cobb. They hated him because he was from the Deep South and because he was surly and unpleasant. They hated him because he was a Baptist who didn't socialize, joke, smoke, drink or play cards. But mostly they were afraid he would take a position away from one of them. They crowded him out of the batting cage, cut up his glove, broke his bats, nailed his shoes to the floor and left him without hot water in the hotel. When he found a note on his door

Hughie Jennings (left) with Ty Cobb, approximately 1919–20. Cobb was the source of much embarrassment for Hughie, but in the end Cobb counted Hughie among his new friends. (National Baseball Library and Archive photograph.)

warning him to leave, he bought a gun and slept with it. He left camp on March 30 to attend his mother's trial. She was quickly acquitted, but Cobb did not catch up with the team until April 7, prompting more complaints, especially from McIntyre. McIntyre went too far when he refused to help Cobb in the field. Playing left field, McIntyre let balls roll between himself and Cobb, who was playing center, and watched Cobb chase them. When he batted with Cobb on base, he purposely made outs and then admitted it to Amour, who finally did something. He suspended McIntyre and played Cobb regularly for a time. He played so well he acquired a following of fans, and a nickname, "The Georgia Peach," given to him by Joe Jackson of the *Detroit Free Press*.

But the abuse continued. No one would room with Cobb or talk to him unless to mock or insult him. Even Amour joined in. He called Cobb on every mistake and never gave him a bit of praise. There was a grounds equipment shack at Bennett Field, and Cobb took to hiding there before games. In July Cobb left the team. The official reason was "stomach illness," but Al Stump, in his book *Cobb*, said Cobb went through a mental breakdown and spent 45 days in a sanitarium. He returned to the team in

September. During the first game of a doubleheader in St. Louis on October 6, the next-to-last day of the season, Cobb finally exploded. He and McIntyre let a fly ball drop between them and the batter, George Stone, circled the bases for an inside-the-park home run. The pitcher, Ed Siever, blamed Cobb and challenged him to a fight in the hotel lobby. Cobb floored Siever with a right and pounded on him while he lay on the ground. Such was Cobb's fury, no one came to Siever's defense. Through it all Cobb managed to bat .315 in 98 games in 1906, fifth in the American League. The Tigers finished in sixth place (71–78).

Failing to trade Cobb after the "Bungy Affair" in March of '07 Hughie looked for a way to work with him and to get the other players to call a truce, if only for the sake of the team. He didn't expect he could make them like Cobb, but at least he hoped he could get them to get along on the field. Another fight between Schmidt and Cobb gave him his chance. Schmidt and Cobb got into it again on the field at Meridian, Mississippi, the day Cobb came back. With the Cobb-haters gathered around to cheer Schmidt, he beat Cobb bloody, splitting his lip and blackening his eyes. But Cobb refused to quit and earned some grudging respect by getting up each time Schmidt knocked him down. Though it was speculated that Hughie had framed Schmidt to beat up Cobb, Hughie always denied that. In any case, when Hughie heard about the fight he knew he had to do something quickly. He sent Cobb back to the hotel and called a meeting of the other players

"I informed them that Cobb was hot-tempered and easily aroused to anger and that there was only one thing to do and that was to forget the past and live in peace in the future. They all agreed. After the meeting I called aside Bill Donovan, Charley O'Leary, Bill Coughlin and Herman Schaefer and asked them to take Cobb to a show and try to convince him that the players were friendly to him. This they did and it straightened out matters for awhile. There were arguments after that at times, but no more fist fights between Cobb and other members of the team."[4]

Schaefer recalled the meeting this way: "He appealed to us in a funny way. We thought there was big call coming down, but instead he handed us out a bunch of salve that made us feel good. He pointed out that harmony meant more to us than it did to him. That he was old in the game, his reputation was made while we had ours to make. 'You can win that pennant,' he said, 'but you've got to have harmony. You've got to work with me. I want every man here to agree we will work together and stamp out this nonsense. Let's act like men and not schoolboys.'

"He had us all vowing we would be his lieutenants and keep each other in order. He told us stories of how they stood together in Baltimore.

From that day on there was a change. The fellows woke up to what harmony meant. With everybody on the team working to one end, Cobb and Schmidt were induced to shake hands and bury the hatchet. That's why the players consider Jennings great, not because of the famous 'ee-yah' and antics on the coaching lines, but it's these quiet talks behind the scenes. He makes men work with him and not just for him."[5]

That night Hughie had a heart-to-heart with Cobb. He tried to convince Cobb that his me-against-the-world attitude would only undermine Cobb's and the team's chance for success. Hughie took Cobb's side, up to a point, telling him that while he had plenty of reason to be angry with some of his teammates, he had to control his temper. Having forged an uneasy truce with Cobb the man, Hughie turned his attention to Cobb the player. From *Rounding Third*:

> It was apparent to me that any attempt to harness him was going to bring about trouble. He had never worn a saddle; he had never had a bit between his teeth, figuratively speaking. He did not care for either. That was plain to me. I pictured difficulties ahead but I decided to take my problem in hand and try to figure out some solutions. I finally concluded from my observations of him that Cobb was one of those rare individuals who can best teach themselves. He would learn quickest by being his own schoolmaster and I decided to appoint him that. I did not make my plans known to Cobb, ignoring him and letting him do as he pleased.
>
> A few weeks of this and Cobb appealed to a newspaper man traveling with the team. He said he could not understand why I instructed players and never said anything to him. It was a mystery to him why I ignored him completely. He thought I acted as if he were not a member of the club. Maybe I had in mind sending him to the minors or trading him. He was smarting under the inattention.
>
> I explained everything to the newspaperman, my observations, my conclusions and my resolutions. I was going to let Cobb handle himself, teach himself, guide himself.

Hughie was guilty of star treatment in his dealings with Cobb, but Hughie's appeasement of Cobb really was as much a strategy as it was a capitulation. After all, Cobb's talent was awe-inspiring and, after all, what else was to be done with him? Cobb wasn't motivated by personal glory. He wasn't motivated by team camaraderie. He was motivated by the raw desire to excel, to prove his manhood. Cobb didn't need to be cajoled. He didn't need to be led. He didn't need to be loved. He needed only to be the best. Cobb skipped most of the spring camps and games, but got himself in shape better than any spring conditioning regimen could. He got himself fired up to play better than any locker room speech could. Hughie let Cobb be Cobb because he knew nothing else would work. Cobb didn't get star treatment only because he was the brightest star, but also because he was the most untamable personality. Hughie knew Cobb needed at a visceral level to compete and win, but not so much at the team level. He was a good teammate only in that he produced more runs than any other player, but he was a poor teammate by any other measure. He had no interest in team games, but liked individual sports like golf and boxing. To Cobb baseball was more of an individual sport — in the batter's box, on the bases, in the field — than it was a team game. Hughie knew Cobb's obsession with winning at the personal level translated to wins at the team level. He treated Cobb in the way that would get the best statistical results. It wasn't that Cobb didn't want to win at the team level, he did, but not nearly obsessively as he did at the individual level. Hughie let Cobb be Cobb, because nothing else would work.

Cobb said as much years later. "He helped me become a pretty good ball player simply by letting me play my own way. I always believed that if left to my own devices and designs I could outthink the other fellow and Hughie agreed to give me freedom of action at the plate and on the bases. He would go through the formality of giving me signs, but it was our agreement that I could take them or leave them. I was permitted to try a lot of unorthodox things a manager with less gambling instinct would not have sanctioned. This lack of restraint and stenciled style enabled me, as vulgar fellows put it, to get away with murder."[6]

The other players didn't like Cobb's getting away with murder. From *Rounding Third:*

> Permitting Cobb to do as he pleased made my job most difficult. Cobb never attended morning practices. You can imagine how difficult it is to get other players to do something disagreeable to them, if one is excused from this duty. They naturally rebelled; they constantly wanted to know why they had to get up in the morning and come to the park and sweat and work, when Cobb did not have to do it. Trying to keep them in line and prevent them from sulking required rare diplomacy and I am afraid that my limit for diplomacy was a bit under the required standard on numerous occasions.
>
> Sometimes a player would not show up at morning practice. When he came to the park in the afternoon and I questioned him concerning his absence, he would answer: "Was Cobb here this morning? If he doesn't come, I don't see why I got to be here every day," or words to that effect. Of course, I might have compared Cobb's average with that of the offending player, but that would not have carried me far. Not only did Cobb fail to show up for morning practice, but he was almost always the last man to arrive in the afternoon. He rarely got to the park before 2 o'clock. Sometimes he got there just in time to get into

his uniform and appear on the field for the start of the game. Sometimes he did not get there before the game started and we had to use a substitute in center field for an inning or two. That made it more difficult. Cobb took liberties and privileges that no other player took or dared take, and my job became more and more embarrassing. My diplomatic resources were being constantly put to the test.

But with all this I could not kick with Cobb. He embarrassed me and caused me many unpleasant moments, but at the same time Cobb did play remarkable ball. He gave his last ounce.[7]

With a free hand to do as he wished, Cobb did the following against Cleveland on Opening Day, 1907: in the eighth inning, he drove a single past the second baseman, stole second, went to third when the catcher's throw got by Nap Lajoie at second, and then scored when the center fielder threw to third.

Tiger fans were in for a wild ride.

17

1907: The Year of the Tiger

King Louis XIV adjusted his beaver pelt hat as his carriage horses clomped through the streets of Paris, and his subjects swooned. The hats, as well as fur coats and shawls, became all the rage in Europe in the 1680s and beyond. When Polish trappers couldn't trap beavers fast enough, the French fur traders turned to the area in North America known as New France, where the tracts of virginal woodland were seemingly endless, where the pristine lakes were big as seas, where streams numbered in the thousands and beavers outnumbered people.

In 1701, to thwart competition from English trappers and traders, the French sent Antoine de la Mothe Cadillac to establish a settlement along a busy waterway, called "le Detroit" or the Strait. For the next six decades Detroit flourished under French rule. It became a British possession in 1760 as a spoil of the French and Indian War. After the War of 1812, the United States took over and established the Michigan Territory. In 1818 the United States government offered land for sale in Michigan and steamboat service started on Lake Erie. The Erie Canal, completed in 1825, linked the Hudson River, and thereby Boston, New York, and Pennsylvania to Lake Erie and Detroit. By 1836, Detroit was a regular port of call for 90 steamships and an estimated 200,000 homesteaders stopped and bought supplies on their way west. The city's population grew from about 850 in 1816, to 5,000 in 1830, to 9,192 counted in the 1840 census. Detroit got its first newspaper in 1829 and Michigan became a state in 1837.

In time English-speaking Americans came to outnumber the descendants of the French settlers. With prosperity came leisure time. To the transplanted Yankees, that meant time to play baseball. On August 8, 1859, the first game between organized teams was played between the Early Risers and the Detroits, teams of merchants and store clerks. The post-Civil War professional baseball boom spread to Detroit in 1879 when a professional team was organized to play at Recreation Park, where Grace Hospital is today. In 1881, the six-year old National League was looking for a Western team to replace Cincinnati, a N.L. charter franchise, which had folded. Detroit mayor William G. Thompson invested $20,000 of his own money and Detroit joined the N.L. in 1881 with Providence, Worcester, Massachusetts; Troy, New York; Buffalo, and Cleveland. Thompson's team — the address was listed as Mayor's Office, Detroit — was called simply the Detroits. On May 2 in 1881 when the Detroits took the field at Michigan and Trumbull in their red-trimmed light gray uniforms to play Buffalo, Detroit was a major league city. With bare-handed speedster Ned Hanlon in center field as their only star, the Wolverines finished 41–43 in the National League. In '82 Hanlon led the league in putouts, but the team got worse each season until they hit bottom at 28–84 in 1884. In 1887 Fredrick Stearns bought the team and bought a "Big Four" infield of his own from Buffalo— Dan Brouthers, Hardy Richardson, Jack Rowe and Jim "Deacon" White. Brouthers and Richardson hit 11 homers each to lead the league, outfielder Sam Thompson led the league in batting, .372; and RBI, 166, and the Wolverines won the '87 pennant with a 79–45 record and defeated St. Louis of the American Association in a 15-game cross-country playoff. But after the '88 season Stearns took the money and ran and the Wolverines folded.

By 1896, the year Charles King Brady drove the first automobile seen on Detroit streets, Detroit was back into baseball in Ban Johnson's Western League. In 1901, two years after Ranson Olds opened the city's first automobile factory, Detroit was major league again as a charter member of Johnson's American League. In its first six seasons in the American League Detroit complied a 403–457 record and finished with more wins than losses only twice. They also were near the bottom in attendance each season. They tried five different mangers in the six seasons. By August of '06 team president Frank Navin was sick of the losing, the small crowds and the managerial merry-go-round. He needed a manager who would bring a winning attitude, a crowd-pleasing personality, and a hope of longevity. He found Hugh Ambrose Jennings and brought him to the City of the Strait.

Hughie had been the Tigers' manager for just over a month in November of '06 when he made a bold prediction. "All the tidy Detroit team had needed for the last two years was a swell leader. They've got that now. I can already see the flag flying over our grounds. Yes sir, we'll finish first just as sure as Nick Altrock isn't as good looking as Harry Pulliam."[1] The prediction may have been out of character for the usually humble old coal cracker, but the touch of humor wasn't. Though Hughie was finished with college as a student, he found he couldn't stay away from coaching college ball in the offseason, as he had done for every season but one since '95. He spent February with the St. John's College team at Annapolis. Among the players was Wilbert "Robby" Robinson's son.[2]

The Tigers' spring camp was in Augusta in 1907, and Hughie wasn't happy with it. He was a big league manager now, and he expected big league accommodations. That meant Turkish baths, which their hotel in Augusta lacked. He wired Bill Coughlin, his captain, to take the veterans to Hot Springs until March 9, while Hughie, who belonged to the YMCA for all of his adult life, entered negotiations with the Augusta YMCA for the use of its baths.[3] Once the team was in camp, Hughie put them through a Hanlon-style regimen. They spent every hour of the day at practice when not in the baths or at their meals. One of the first things Hughie had done after accepting the Tigers job was make Bill Coughlin his captain. Coughlin was from Scranton, where he and Hughie were celebrities. Each December they were feted with an elaborate banquet in Scranton by the Coughlin-Jennings Club.

The 1907 Tigers were almost identical to the '06 Tigers, which had finished sixth with a 71–78 record, with one notable exception — Claude Rossman. The Tigers had bought the first baseman from Cleveland in December. He wasn't much of a fielder. His arm was so poor he could hardly get the ball to second base, but he had hit .308 for the Naps in '06, a pitchers' year, and had a reputation for hitting in the clutch. But he was not a player to take a second division team to the top of the league. Consequently, the scribes gave the Tigers little chance in '07. One wrote that Jennings' team "hardly looks like a champion aggregation. Hard bunch to handle. Petty grievances and spitework run rampant on the team, and even now there is little indication that such a strict chieftain as Jennings will be able to rout out the disturbing elements of the team. Until harmony is restored — and it does not look like Jennings will be able to do it — the Tigers can not be given a chance ahead of Washington. The infield is not a world beater, but the outfield is above the run if the trio is batting. Strong in pitchers and run by a wily resourceful field marshal, Bill Coughlin, who never overlooks a bet in a game."[4]

Hughie had 11 pitchers in camp, but brought only seven north. Of the seven, four — George Mullin, Ed Killian, Bill Donovan, and Ed Siever — would pitch all but 153 of the 1370 available innings in 1907. John Eubanks, Ed Willett, Elijah Jones pitched the 153 leftover innings. His catchers were Schmidt, Fred Payne and Jimmy Archer. Rossman was the first baseman;

Red Downs, Germany Schaefer, Charley O'Leary, Bobby Lowe, and Coughlin, the infielders; and Cobb, Ed Killian, Red Killefer, Sam Crawford, Davy
Jones, McIntyre, and Fred Payne, the outfielders. They were a cast of char-
acters worthy of their manager — Germany Schaefer, a comedian who once
batted with galoshes on his feet; the untamable Cobb; Charley Schmidt,
the erstwhile boxer who tried to tame him; Davy Jones, the quiet, but tem-
peramental outfielder; Bill Coughlin, the fearless 140-pound third baseman; and Charley O'Leary, the bantam shortstop with a chip on his
shoulder.[5]

Hughie's opening day lineup was: McIntyre, rf; Coughlin, 3b; Crawford, cf; Cobb, rf; Rossman, 1b; Schaefer, 2b; Schmidt; c; O'Leary, ss;
Mullin, p. Hughie put Crawford in center to separate McIntyre and Cobb,
who went to right. By mid-May McIntyre was on the bench in favor of
Davy Jones. On opening day, with the umpires in overcoats braced against
the 40-degree air, the Tigers won 2–0 at home, Bennett Park. It was the
first of 35 complete games for Mullin and the first of 92 victories by the
Tigers. Of their first 30 games, 26 were at home. The most notable game
of the homestead was a 6–5 extra-inning win over the Athletics on May
22. With the game tied in the 10th, Hughie showed his Mr. Hyde side by
going after his old Cornell friend, umpire Billy Evans. Evans called Schmidt
out for failing to touch third as he jogged home with what everyone
thought was the winning run. Hughie got in Evans' face and had to be
taken from the field by the police. Though the Tigers won in the 11th on
Coughlin's RBI single, Evans, too, was led from the field by police for his
own safety. Coincidentally, or not, Hughie's outburst came the day after
McGraw was tossed from a Giants game at the Polo Grounds after incit-
ing a near riot. Umpires Hank O'Day and Bob Emslie required police pro-
tection from the crowd, which was egged on by McGraw. It was one of
seven times McGraw was thrown out of games in '07.

The Tigers went 18–12 over their first 30 games and were in third
place, 2½ games behind the White Sox, on May 24 when they hit the road
for their first long swing through the East. Between May 29 and June 21
they played 19 road games. Fans in Chicago, Boston, New York, Washington and Philadelphia got their first dose of "Ee-yah" Jennings and the
suddenly phenomenal Ty Cobb. In one of the Chicago games Cobb scored
from second on a ball deep in the shortstop hole. He ran through Hughie's
frantic stop sign, taking such a wide turn that he hit Hughie with his hip
and knocked him down.[6] Though the Tigers won 11 of 19 on their first Eastern swing and were 28–20 overall when they headed home, they still weren't
being taken seriously as pennant contenders. After a 10–0 loss at Washington on June 14, the *Post* said "the Tigers looked like an amateur team."

But Hughie wrote it off as what it was, one game. "We crowded a whole season of poor work into one game. Every team is bound to have its off days and if we were to be beaten, I'm glad they did us up brown, for now that we have got rid of all those misplays, we will probably settle down. You have to expect these things in baseball. There are times when a team needed but one run to win but can't get it because everything the players try goes wrong. And then there are days when everything goes their way."[7]

He was proved right the next day when the Tigers scored a run in the ninth to tie and one in the 10th on a Cobb double to win 5–4. On a home-stand between July 3 and July 22, the Tigers won 14 of 18. On July 25 they overtook Cleveland for second place. At the end of July during a series in Boston, Hughie bought a tin whistle. During the next series in New York he used it on the coaching lines to disrupt the Highlander pitchers. On August 2 in the first game of a doubleheader in Washington, the Tigers faced a 19-year-old pitcher making his major-league debut. Hughie tried his best to rattle the green hurler with his new whistle, but the teenaged Walter Johnson held the Tigers to two runs on three hits over eight innings. When he was lifted for a pinch hitter in the eighth, Johnson and the Nationals were behind 2–1. Each team scored one in the ninth and the Tigers won 3–2. After the Tigers won the second game 9–6, they moved into a tie for first place with the White Sox, 1½ games ahead the Philadelphia A's. The scribes finally took the Tigers seriously and asked Hughie if he thought his team could stay in the race to the end.

"It's a long route to the end of the season. I cannot make any prediction as to the outcome of the race. My team is hustling, playing good ball and getting its share of good breaks. We all know that a team that does not have its share of luck cannot win and I must admit things have been going our way since we left home.

"One thing is certain. We will win very game we can, but we cannot expect to have as many good breaks as we have been getting. We may have a slump and we must get all we can while the sun shines. We have had a slump or two this season but always came out of them fighting for every inch. That's why I feel we have a chance."[8]

A.L. president Ban Johnson caught up with Hughie and his whistle after the August 2 doubleheader. He outlawed the whistle and hit Hughie with a 10-day suspension. When the Tigers arrived in Philadelphia on August 7 for the last series of their Eastern swing, the A's fans gave Hughie a car horn before the game. Once the game started, they produced thousands of tin whistles and tormented the Tigers' pitchers. The A's won two of three to pass the White Sox and pull to ½ game behind the Tigers. The

Tigers and A's traveled to Detroit on different sections of the same train and opened a three-game set at Bennett Park on August 12. The A's won the first two. The Tigers won the third game when "Wild Bill" Donovan beat Waddell, 9–2. The Highlanders came in next and beat the Tigers in the first three games of a four-game series. On Sunday, August 18, Hughie implored the Tiger fans to behave during the fourth game of the series. It was Detroit's first Sunday game at home since 1902, and the first at Bennett Field. Hughie's plea was heeded. The fans behaved and the Tigers rewarded them with a 13–6 win over New York. On September 1 the Tigers had a one-game lead over the A's but the schedule was against them. Of their last 35 games 26 were on the road, while the A's had 19 of their last 27 at home. But Hughie remained optimistic.

"The man who calculates the Tigers have no chance to win the pennant is dead wrong. Of course the long stretch of home games in Philadelphia will be a great advantage to the Athletics but they are going to get some awful battles in their yard from Chicago, Cleveland, and Detroit. If they can beat these first division clubs repeatedly they will certainly seal the Tigers doom, but I don't see it. It's possible, but not logical. There's a royal good chance of the bunting coming here."[9]

If there was a royal good chance, Cobb was the biggest reason. He continued to lead the league in most batting categories and he stayed out of trouble. But Hughie was a big reason, too, and owners around the league were becoming believers in the "Ee-yah" style. In Cleveland he was approached about managing the Naps while dining at the Union Club in Cleveland with Cornell friends. Club members connected to the Naps said Cleveland would pay more than Detroit. "As a matter of fact it would be hard for me to quit the Tigers, even if I wanted to, as I am signed to a players contract," Hughie answered.

Postponements forced the Tigers to play four doubleheaders on four consecutive days from September 12 to 15. In the second game on the 15th in St. Louis, umpire Billy Evans was hit in the head with a soda bottle thrown by a fan. He was carried from the field and taken to the hospital. Hughie sent flowers to hospital and had a friend in St. Louis wire word of the umpire's condition every day until Evans was released. The Tigers won only three of the eight games in the consecutive doubleheaders to fall behind the A's by percentage points. To shake things up Hughie sent Red Downs, who had been playing second base, back to Detroit and put Germany Schaefer in his place. It worked. The Tigers won five of six in New York and Boston. Schaefer made four double plays in the Boston series. They won in Boston without Donovan. He was sent ahead to Philly to rest up for the series everybody in baseball believed would decide the American League pennant. The Tigers arrived in Philadelphia for a three-game series on Friday, September 27. The A's were in first place with a winning percentage of .60584 and Tigers were second at .60583. The Tigers won the first game on Friday, 5–4. The Saturday game was rained out. As there was no Sunday ball in Philadelphia, a doubleheader was scheduled for Monday, setting the stage for what Hughie would always call "the most remarkable game ever played."

Columbia Park, at 29th Street and Columbia Avenue, had a capacity of 18,000, but over 20,000 jammed into the park while another 5,000 watched from windows and rooftops around the park. Standing room on roofs overlooking the park went for $2. Inside, the overflow of fans were parked behind ropes in deep center and held back with a rope by a line of police. It was agreed that hits into the fans would be doubles. The A's went ahead 7–1, but Hughie never considered lifting Donovan, even though he had pitched 10 innings on Friday. In the seventh Detroit scored four against spitballer Jimmie Dygert. Rube Waddell, who was scheduled to pitch the second game, came in and got out of the seventh. The game went to the ninth with the A's leading 8–6, but Cobb hit a two-run homer over the roped-off fans and over the fence to tie it. Eddie Plank relieved Waddell. In the top of the 12th the Tigers got a run. In the bottom Donovan, who had given up only one after the third inning, gave up a run on a wild pitch. In the 14th, with Donovan still in there, Harry Davis led off for the A's and hit one into the fans for an apparent double. There are varying accounts as to what happened next. One says Detroit center fielder Sam Crawford went into the crowd and came out with the ball and umpire Silk O'Loughlin called it an out. Another said O'Loughlin never claimed Crawford caught the ball, but rather called Davis out because one of the cops interfered with Crawford on the play. The other umpire, Tom Connolly, agreed there was interference. In any case a near riot ensued. The usually soft-spoken Mack entered the umpires' dressing room after the game to berate O'Loughlin and after that day never spoke to him again for the rest of his life.[10] Beyond all logic Donovan was still pitching when the game was called by darkness after 17 innings with the score 9–9. Strange as it was, and even though mathematically the A's could have still won the pennant, everyone believed the Tigers won the A.L. game that day in a game they didn't win. There were many subplots. Hughie recalled one in *Rounding Third*.

> During the game there was a disputed decision with the players crowding around the umpires. During the argument Donovan swung at Monte Cross, a shortstop, but out of the lineup that day and coaching at first base. Cross went down in a heap and a policeman rushed over

to arrest Donovan. But Schaefer's quick wit saved the situation. Grabbing the policeman he said, "What are you pinchin' him for? He didn't do nothin' it was this guy that hit him." Schaefer was pointing to Rossman, who was having a bad day. The policeman grabbed Rossman and lugged him off the field, poor Rossman not knowing what it was all about. That prevented us from losing. Donovan finished the game and held the Athletics safe. Another pitcher might have done it, but that is doubtful. Donovan was pitching air-tight ball at the time. Playing a tie was the break of the pennant race and threw the advantage to us.

The Tigers, in first place by ½ game, left for Washington for a four-game series. They beat Johnson again 5–3 in the first game on October 1. The next day they swept a doubleheader, 9–5 and 10–2. Cobb was 7-for-10 and scored two in each game. One of the hits was his 200th and it earned him a $500 bonus. Schaefer was 8-for-9 with five runs. While the Tigers won their doubleheader the A's lost one. Detroit had four games left and the A's, five. The A's only hope was to win all five while the Tigers lost two. Even so, Hughie wasn't taking anything for granted. "It's an uncertain game and as long as there is a chance to beat us we cannot feel secure. I'm proud of my team. It's a game, hustling ball club. It's not a one-man club. We had our slumps but came right back and beat the teams that figured to beat us. I do not claim any of the credit. The players deserve it. They have delivered the goods. I have had but little to do with it."

The *Post* disagreed with Hughie's self-depreciation: "Jennings has earned a place among the annals of baseball. He made a pennant winner out of a second division team. His energy, judgment and ability has brought about the change. It is a victory not for the Detroit team, but for Hughey Jennings."[11]

When the Tigers won again the next day, Hughie finally accepted the inevitable. "The pennant race became a case of Pike's Peak or bust. It looks like a clear case of Pike's Peak to us tonight, but I don't think there is any danger of our going busted in the remaining three days of the season."[12]

As the wins mounted on the road trip, the Detroit fans became feverish. Every day the crowds got bigger at the scoreboards around the city. During the October 2 doubleheader hundreds gathered in front of the Detroit Free Press building, where the score was posted by half innings. The Tigers were behind 3–1 and when a "3" was posted in the Tigers' half of the sixth, bedlam broke loose. Strangers embraced and pounded each other on the back. Men waved their hats and shouted until they were hoarse. Work came to a standstill, as similar scenes were played out in front of scoreboards all over the business district.

At least one fan got a little carried away that evening. In Battle Creek a drunken man was nearly shot as a burglar when he crawled through a cellar window to avoid waking his wife. It wasn't his wife who nearly shot him, but his neighbor. He had sneaked into the wrong house. He apologized for being out so late, saying he only wanted to find out what the score of the Detroit-Washington game was.[13]

During that series in Philadelphia, a shabbily dressed man had showed up in the hotel bar. He had been drinking and he told the players he was going to follow them down the home stretch. For a joke they referred him to Hughie. He grabbed Hughie just before he got on the bus for the park. Hughie couldn't resist talking to him as he had an Irish face, Irish brogue and better yet, red hair. Hughie figured the best way to get rid of him was to give him a ride to the park. On the bus the stranger pulled out a harmonica he called "the sweet potato" and played it. He took the players' minds of the importance of the game and helped them relax. They got him in the game. During the game he played his instrument and had the crowd laughing. When the A's came on or off the field between innings, he played a popular tune of the day "They Walked Right in Turned Around and Walked Right Out Again." When the Tigers ran the bases and scored he played "Didn't They Ramble?" The Tigers took a liking to him and slipped him some money, and he followed them to Washington and then to St. Louis for the final two games. After the last game Hughie and the boys took him to a men's store, outfitted him in fine style and gave him enough money to get to Chicago for the start of the World Series.[14]

The Tigers clinched on October 5 as Ed Siever beat the Browns 10–2. After a night of celebration, the Tigers dragged themselves Sportsman's Park on Sunday to play a doubleheader against the sixth-place Browns and were shocked at what awaited them. Browns fans greeted them like hometown heroes. When the first Tiger was spotted coming through the carriage gate onto the field for practice, the crowd stood and cheered until the entire team was on the field.

Meanwhile, back in Detroit, the celebration began the minute the game in St. Louis ended. A holiday was declared by order of City Council. Schools and workplaces emptied for a monster parade, a City Hall reception, and a banquet. Pictures of Hughie appeared in downtown storefronts. Committees on the official badge, flowers, and banquets were appointed at a meeting with the mayor. The official badge was of white satin, with a blue tiger head and the words: "Champs, 1907, We-a-a-ah."[15]

That night the celebration continued in a different manner. The *Chicago Tribune* described it this way: "Tonight bonfires blazed throughout the city and the fire department is taxed to the utmost. In the northern section of the city riotous rooters took possession of a vacant house and held an orgy all day until the neighbors summoned the police. Upon the arrival of the squad of patrolmen the rioters attempted to tear down the building welcoming the police with showers of bricks."[16]

Praise for Hughie poured in. "Jennings is now the reigning star of the baseball world," wrote the *Detroit News.* "In the past decade Comiskey, Connie Mack, Collins, McGraw and Fielder Jones have all been hailed as the greatest manager the game has produced, but this winter little will be heard of any of these, for their day has past a new hero holds the center of the stage. Jennings is entitled to the laurels that will be his for his achievement has been a remarkable one from every standpoint. Has done what McGraw did for the New York team and Collins for Boston in former years."[17]

In New York McGraw agreed with that assessment and took a shot at the N.L. "Hughey Jennings is the greatest man in baseball. It takes brains to be a successful ball player and still more to be a successful manger and the man who in his first year has made pennant winners of a team that represents the smallest city in the circuit has well earned that title. It was a bad day for me when we parted. I was with him all those years and together we developed the style of ball that the Detroit team has been playing and which won them the pennant and which would have won the pennant for the New Yorks if I hadn't been chased off the lines everyday by umpires acting under instruction of the office boy of the National League syndicate."[18] McGraw was tossed from seven games.

Whatever credit was due Hughie outside the lines for the Tigers' 27-game improvement and climb from sixth to first place from 1906–07, between the lines Cobb and Crawford were the key. Cobb led the A.L. in batting (.350), RBI (116), slugging percentage (.473), hits (212), stolen bases (49) and total bases (286). Cobb also finished tied for second in the A.L. in home runs (5) and third in the league in runs scored (97) and triples (15). Sam Crawford finished second behind Cobb in batting average (.323), slugging percentage (.460), and total bases (268). Batting ahead of Cobb, Crawford led the A.L. in runs (102). He was second in the league in doubles (34) and triples (17).

Three Tiger pitchers won twenty or more. Ed Killian went 25–13, Wild Bill Donovan was 25–4, and George Mullin finished at 20–20. Killian's 1.78 ERA was the second best in the American League, as were Mullin's 34 complete games and 357 innings pitched. The 25 wins by Donovan and Killian were second in the league.

18

The 1907 World Series

Before the first game of a doubleheader on the last day of the 1907 regular season, the St. Louis Browns' announcer called out the visiting Detroit Tigers' lineup through his megaphone. There was little reaction from the fans until they heard that a sore-armed 38-year-old who had not played in a major league game in four years was starting the game. Hearing the words: "Batting seventh and playing short stop, Hugh Jennings," the Browns fans reacted with wild prolonged cheers.

Hughie played short and second, batted 1-for-4 with a double and handled five chances in the field without an error in a 10–4 loss. The Tigers were also hammered in the second game, 10–3. After the games hundreds of the fans went onto the field and swarmed around Hughie to shake his hand or pat his back. The Tigers responded to the goodwill by singing a ditty that ends with the line "Don't give a darn for the whole state of Illinois."

Hughie was thrilled by the Browns' fans support. "It has been one of the happiest days of my life. The ovation to the team today when they went on the field and when they left was sweet to me and the boys. It shows the American public likes a game team no matter what city's name is writ on the shirt front."[1]

As it happened, the Tigers' world series opponents, the Chicago Cubs, were also in St. Louis that last day of 1907 the regular season. The Cubs, having long ago clinched the N.L. pennant they would win by 17 games, were playing out the string against the Cardinals at Robison Field. They split a doubleheader, winning 7–1 and losing 1–0. The win was their 107th of the season. Despite inhabiting the same city for the weekend, the Tigers and Cubs avoided each other. They stayed at in different hotels and, with the World Series set to begin in two days, both left St. Louis that evening and went straight to Chicago, but on separate sections of he same train. The train reached Chicago in the morning. The Cubs got to go to their homes for lunch, while the Tigers checked into the Lexington hotel. After lunch both teams got into their uniforms and went to the grounds for a shared practice at the invitation of Cubs' owner Charley Murphy.

The next morning in the Auditorium Annex in Chicago the National Commission — Chairman August Herrmann, Ban Johnson and Harry Pulliam — met with Chance and Hughie; umpires Jack Sheridan and Hank O'Day; and Germany Schaefer, representing the players for both teams. They hammered out details, going over the rules for the managers, players, umpires and scorers. When Herrmann said the series would be played under the John T. Brush rules put into effect for the 1905 series, which allowed for the ballplayers to share the receipts of the first four games, Schaefer asked if tie games were considered legal games. Herrmann said that though tie games had to be replayed, they were legal as far as records and gate receipts were concerned. That's just what Schaefer wanted to hear. In what turned out to be a prophetic statement, he said the players wanted receipts from five games if one of the first four turned out to be a tie. Since there had never been a tie game in any of the three previous World Series, Herrmann and the commission, after a brief huddle, agreed. Ticket prices were set. The Cubs would charge $2 for box seats, $1.50 for grandstand and $1 for general admission standing room. The Tigers, with a much smaller capacity park, were allowed to charge $2.50, $2 and $1. Herrmann read the articles of agreement and asked for questions. Hughie asked to speak, was given the floor and said, "Mr. Chairman, will there be an objection to the use of an inoffensive tin whistle in the world championship series." Though Herrmann was well aware of the much publicized whistle incident, he said he personally did not have objection to use of what he called "the famous little noise maker," but left the decision up the umpires. Herrmann then asked Hughie for a demonstration. But Hank O'Day, the National league umpire, didn't want to hear it. "The coaching rules will be strictly enforced," he said, "and there will be no tin whistles used."

"Well," said Hughie with a laugh, knowing full well his whistle would be banned, "I just wanted to have the thing settled." It was typical Hughie, injecting a moment of levity when things turned serious.[2]

Game one was set for 2:30 p.m. at the West Side Grounds at the corner of Lincoln and Polk Streets. The Metropolitan elevated railroad had special trains leaving from Douglas or Garfield Stations. The Ogden Avenue or Harrison Street surface lines also led to the game. Interest in the 1907 series was international. Charley Murphy was busy taking care of a delegation from Cuba. Rooms around the park were rented out by fans hoping to get a place at the front of the ticket line. Rue the fan who stayed too late at the hotel bar and slept in. Lines formed before daylight and by 9 a.m., 8,000 fans stretched down the streets around the park, hoping for a chance to buy grandstand or general admission tickets. The box seats had sold out in advance. When the gates opened at 11, the gatekeepers could hardly handle the flow. Though attendance would be officially listed at 24,377, it was more than that as many fans without tickets simply squeezed in with the crowd, while cops were busy swinging batons at young men scaling the fences.

Hughie seemed unaffected by all the hoopla. As the players came out of their rooms at the Lexington on the morning of the first game, Hughie suggested they avoid reading the papers until after the game. Columns in the Chicago papers were giving short shrift to the Tigers' chances against Cub pitching, suggesting that Cobb was a flash in the pan and that the Cub pitchers would keep him in check. Many Tiger rooters from Detroit milled around the Lexington lobby hoping the catch glimpses of their heroes. Hughie appeared and was his usual smiling self. He had a laugh and a handshake for everyone. Detroit writer Malcolm Bingay was there and spoke to Al Day, the Tigers' trainer the previous season, who said the Tigers looked beat from the rigors of the pennant race. "They show signs of the strain they have suffered," he said. "They look like prizefighters do when they have gone through hard training." Schaefer gave credence to Day's claims. He had spent much of the previous night with trainer McMahon working on his legs, which were prone to the old Charley Horse.

In the newspapers, Cubs' player/manager Frank Chance said he was confident. He believed the Cubs were better drilled and would take the series with little trouble. Hughie, of course, had a different take, which had little to do directly with baseball. "We have six Irishmen on this team and that means we will fight to the last and I cannot say more than that."

Hughie made the obvious choice for his game one starter, tabbing his ace "Wild" Bill Donovan, but not because he was Irish. The 190-pound right hander from upstate New York had led the league in winning percentage at 25–4, completing 27 of 32 starts with a 2.19 ERA. He had a full four days' rest, having last pitched October 3 in a 3–1 win over the Senators. Chance, on the other hand, had a tougher decision. His best pitcher, Mordecai Brown, widely considered to be the best pitcher in the N.L., had a sore arm. The injury was officially, and oddly, described as muscle stiffness caused by a cold. More likely, Brown, like most pitchers of the day, was simply overworked. The Tigers were without their lead left-handed starter, Ed Killian. Like Brown, his arm was weak from overwork, and like Brown, he was not expected to play in either of the first two games. As the series opened it was believed that Brown, who had a 1.39 ERA for the season, winning 20 of 27 starts, would not pitch until the third game, if at all. Not having to face Brown was not much of an advantage for the Tigers considering that the named starter, Orval Overall, had won 23 games with a 1.70 ERA and led the league in shutouts with eight. Overall, a 6'-2", 215- pounder from California, was well rested. Charlie Murphy's prediction that he would be the "Christy Mathewson of the 1907 series" would prove to be prophetic.

It was clear and warm in Chicago for the series opener. Though the game was scheduled for 2:30 it was 2:42 by the time the Tigers' leadoff batter, Davy Jones, stepped into the box and took the first pitch from Overall. The start had been delayed by a ceremony recognizing Ty Cobb as the American League batting champion. A St. Louis jeweler presented Cobb with a diamond-studded gold medal and then broke into a lengthy oration undeterred by the shouts of "play ball" and shut up" from the crowd. The Tigers didn't score in the first, and as Donovan left the bench for the mound to start the bottom of the first Hughie said, "All you've got to do, Bill, is pitch like you've been pitching all season."[3]

For eight innings Donavan did just that. Holding the Cubs to just one run, he took a 3–1 lead into the ninth. The Cubs scored their run in the fourth when Chance walked, Steinfedlt sacrificed and Kling singled. The Tigers cut off another run in the inning when they nailed Kling trying to steal home on the back end of a double steal, with Johnny Evers stealing second. The Evers steal was one of 11 in the game, seven by the Cubs. The Tigers scored three in the top of the eighth. Jones singled to right and stole second. Joe Tinker booted Schaefer's grounder, putting runners on first and third. Schaefer stole second on the next pitch. Crawford singled, knocking in Jones and Schaefer, and went to third on Frank Schulte's throwing error. Rossman hit a sacrifice fly to center, scoring Crawford with the third run, giving the Tigers the 3–1 lead. Donovan put the Cubs down in order in the eighth.

The Tigers did not score in their half of the ninth, but they had the Cubs down to their last three outs. Chance led off with a single and Donovan plunked Harry Steinfeldt in the ribs. Tinker tried to bunt them over but popped it to Rossman for the first out. Coughlin booted an Evers groundball to load the bases. When Schulte grounded out, Chance scored to make it 3–2 and Kling went to third. It was a tradeoff the Tigers were happy with. There were two outs. Tinker was next and he had struck out three times. Chance sent Del Howard up to pinch hit. Donovan reared back with everything he had left and fired two fast balls. Howard looked overmatched and watched them go by for strikes. The Tigers were one strike away. They got the strike, swinging on a curve, but didn't get the out. The ball went through Schmidt, Kling raced home to tie the game and Evers went to third. Evers then tried to steal home, and the game, but Schmidt held on to the pitch and angrily pounced on Evers like a football player for the third out, but the damage had been done. The teams remained in a deadlock through three more innings. The game was called because of darkness after 12, tied 3–3. As per the agreement, the players got a share of the gate, but the game would have to be replayed. Though the series was still 0–0, the tie was a moral victory for the Cubs. The Tigers had Overall and the Cubs beaten in game one in Chicago and let it get away. Hughie's Tigers would pay dearly.

There was cursing and shouting heard through the walls of the Tiger clubhouse after the game. Donovan grumbled that he had struck out 12, but still couldn't get a win. Schmidt was a easy target for blame and some players did so, but Hughie said nothing and Cobb pointed the finger at himself for going 0–5. The Tigers weren't the only ones unhappy with the tie. Some who were there swore the pitch Howard swung at actually hit his uniform. Others were sure it had hit Howard's bat. Then there were those who, knowing about the deal to let the players share in the gate from a tie game, were convinced Schmidt missed the third strike purposely. Ban Johnson was livid and actually considered the fans' conspiracy theory. After all it had been only the night before that Schaefer had posed the then seemingly innocent question, "Is a tie game a legal game?"

Whatever his reservations, Johnson and the commission officially declared Schaefer's timely question a coincidence, but immediately declared that beginning in '08 the players share of the World Series would come from the first four games played no matter what happened. The morning of the second game, Hughie worried about a hangover from the tie that had been so agonizingly close to a win. "I don't want to hear about it anymore," he said. "We didn't win it. We didn't lose it."

Whether or not the tie had any affect on the Tigers on the field the rest of the series isn't known but the affect the Cub pitchers had on the Tigers is a matter of record. Given a reprieve, the Cubs and their stingy pitchers proceeded to make short shrift of the Tigers. Detroit scored just one run in each of the next four games and was unceremoniously swept.

For game two, before 21,901 paid, Hughie started George Mullin, his fourth-best pitcher. Mullin was 20–20 with a 2.59 ERA and had given up a league highs in hits, 303, and walks, 138. Hughie made a catching change, too, starting Frank Payne. Hughie benched Schmidt less for the passed ball than for his erratic throwing. The Cubs had stolen seven bases, though they were twice caught trying to steal home. Chance pitched Jack Pfiester, a lefty. A triple by Rossman and a single by Payne gave the Tigers a 1–0 lead in the second, but the lead was short-lived. In their half of the second the Cubs tied it on a bases-loaded, no out walk to Tinker. But Mullin got out of the jam, and earned a round of applause from the Cub fans for doing so, by striking out Pfiester and Jimmy Slagle and getting Jimmy Sheckard to ground out. In the top of the fourth the Tigers were run out of a possible rally by, of all players, Cobb. Cobb led off the fourth with a single for his first hit of the series. Rossman then dropped a ball in front of Schulte in right, but Cobb either didn't see it or badly misjudged it. Though Hughie screamed at Cobb to take second, Cobb, apparently judging that Schulte would catch it on the fly, went halfway and stopped. When it hit the ground Cobb raced for second, but Schulte's throw beat him and it went for a 9–6 forceout. Instead of runners at first and third with no outs, the Tigers had a runner on first with one out. Coughlin and Slagle flew out to end the inning. In their half of the fourth the Cubs scored two, and Pfiester made them stand up for a 3–1 win. In the sixth inning Hughie upped his antics in the coaching box. O'Day and Sheridan put up with Hughie's prancing, yelling, and grass-tossing, but threw him out of the coaching box in the sixth for arguing calls. First he jawed at Sheridan when Schaefer was called out trying to steal second, and then he went after O'Day when Crawford was called out on a swinging strike, which Hughie was sure was not a swing. Many fans mistakenly believed Hughie had been thrown out of the game, but that wasn't the case. He was tossed from the coaching box and watched the Tigers' last three at-bats from the dugout.

The next morning at the hotel, Hughie had a Detroit paper brought to him and read he had an ally in Chicago White Sox manager Charles Comiskey. Comiskey threw aside any pretense of objectivity, sided with Hughie and blasted the umpires. "I'm for Hughey and I hope his Tigers win," he told Malcolm Bingay. "When the umpires representing the national commission threw Hughie off the coaching lines they did a rank injustice. He had only protested two decisions that were raw ones. He had a right to protest. It was an outrage to send him to the bench."

Hughie said the Cubs were nothing but lucky and the Tigers had simply failed to, as his old friend Wee Willie Keeler used to say, "hit 'em where they ain't." Hughie put it this way, "when an infield plays all out of position and just happens to get the ball, I don't call that good baseball."

As to his banishment from the coaching box, Hughie was cautious. "I don't care to make any statement on the work of the umpires. I thought Schaefer had stolen second and I knew that Crawford was called out on a third strike when he did not swing. But that is past. Today is another thing. They beat us on the bases, but they did not play good ball. They were lucky in breaking up our hit and run plays. Frank Chance toward the end of the game last night was a sadly worried man. He had more reason to be than I had, I thought."

Hughie had Ed Killian, a 25-game winner available for game three, but went with Ed Siever. The light-hitting Cubs got to Siever early for seven hits in four innings and by the time Hughie brought Killian in it was 4–0. That was more than enough for Ed Reulbach. He gave up only one run and six hits in the 5–1 win.

Hughie and Yawkey were defiantly confident in the face of a 2–0 deficit and had reason to be. The Cubs had outscored them only 29–24 in the three games. The Tigers had come from behind in games all season, they forged winning streaks just when it looked like they were going into a slump and they were going home where they had a played .650 ball. Cobb and Crawford were the American League's top two hitters at .350 and .323 and Hughie expected them to break out at home in game three, a rematch of the game one pitchers, the Cubs' Orval Overall and the Tigers' Donovan. Hughie expected Wild Bill to pitch at least as well as he had in game one.

Only 13,114 paid at the gate for game three, off almost 10,000 from game one. The no-shows were mostly Tiger fans who had come over from Detroit prepared to stay for two days, but not for the third day necessitated by the game one tie. October 8, the day of the tie game, was a Tuesday, meaning the three-day stretch of games in Chicago fell right in the middle of the work week. Fans in the Chicago area who couldn't get to game three devised ways to follow the game. Cub fanatics from Blue Island, a Chicago suburb, kept abreast of things by air. The Blue Island mayor and city clerk, accompanied by a pigeon racer named Robert Kruger, brought 40 pigeons to the game and turned them loose at 10-minute intervals with game updates.

With the travel day lost to the tie game over 1,000 people — the teams, fans, and baseball dignitaries— had to catch trains to Detroit for game four, just hours after game three. An added train left at 9:30 carrying Charles Comiskey and Joe Farrell and their entourage and hundreds of Cub rooters. The regular 10 o'clock Chicago-to-Detroit run had two sections: the Cubs and Tigers and the baseball dignitaries in first section, and the Detroit fans who had stuck out the three days in Detroit in the second section.

Though Hughie and the Tigers had had a rough time of it in Chicago, blowing the chance to win the tie game and scoring only two runs in the two losses, there was a consolation — money. Thanks to the 59,392 fans who had paid to see the first three games, the players' purse was bulging with $38,774. That was already $5,373 more than the Cubs and Pirates had shared in '06, with receipts from two more games yet to be added. Chicago offered another consolation for Hughie — love. As National Leaguers, the Chicago fans knew of Hughie only by reputation before the series began, but after three games watching and listening to Hughie in the coaching box, they were enamored. They adopted "ee-yah" as their own. The marched to the games to it, many waving both Cub and Tiger banners, sang it in the bars after the games and at the train station as they boarded for Detroit.

Hughie may have remained confident down two games to none, but based on the reception the Tigers got when the train reached Detroit, the Tiger rooters weren't. Only a handful showed up at the station. Some of the Detroit fans on the train tried to make up for the lack of welcoming rooters. Yelling "ee-yah," they led the team in an impromptu parade up Jefferson Avenue. Meanwhile Chance, Overall and Slagle disembarked and immediately hailed cabs and went to pay their respects to Detroit Mayor Thompson before checking in at the Cadillac hotel, and then going to Bennett Park for game four.

Just before the game, the weather turned cold and rainy. This was bad news, as Donavan had a reputation as a warm-weather pitcher. Despite the cool weather, 11,306 paid to see the game that afternoon. While that was a decent crowd by Detroit standards (the Tigers had averaged only 3900 per game during the season), it wasn't a lot compared to the Chicago crowds, nor was it what Yawkey and Navin hoped for in the first-ever modern World Series game in Detroit history. They had made preparations to accommodate 18,000. But it wasn't just the cold weather and the Tigers being in a 2–0 hole that kept attendance down. A ticket sales mismanagement scandal also kept fans away. Tiger management did not limit the number of tickets individuals could buy in advance. Scalpers bought hundreds of them in blocks.

There was a silver lining in the ticket mismanagement cloud. When the anticipated crowds didn't show up, or simply refused to pay the $5 to $15 the scalpers were demanding, the scalpers had to sell the tickets for what they could get or be stuck with them. As game time approached, tickets with a $2.50 face value were sold for as little as 25 cents. Several scalpers were arrested. One of them, Harry Weitzman, talked to the *Detroit News*. "I don't blame the public because I'm losing hundreds of dollars. It is not composed of suckers. I could have pulled out all right if I kept on as I started just dealing a few tickets, but when I took on a big bunch, I lost."

Most of the fans who did show packed themselves into grandstands bundled against the cold and rain, leaving 2000 empty seats. Only a few stood along the outfield ropes. A few hundred took out their anger by patronizing the wildcat bleachers. At home plate just before the game, the

Tigers fans showed their appreciation for Hughie with gifts. He was presented with a diamond-studded watch and a life-size floral Tiger. Chance laughed when he saw the Tiger brought out and yelled to Hughie. "What are you going to do with that, Hughey? Eat it?"

"No, we'll ram it down your throats," Hughie snapped.

That didn't happen, but Wild Bill did hit Chance on the hand with a pitch in the first inning, breaking his finger. Chance merely had the finger tied up to the next one, took his base and promptly stole second. For four innings, Donovan held up his end of the deal despite the weather, holding the Cubs to three harmless hits. In the bottom of the fourth, Cobb cracked a line shot to center and serenaded by Hughie's cries of "atta boy" and "go Tyrus," he raced to third with a triple. Rossman singled him home to give the Tigers a 1–0 lead heading into the fifth. Then disaster struck in the form of a 15-minute rain delay after the Cubs' first batter in the fifth, Evers, reached on a throwing error by O'Leary. When the game resumed, Donovan walked Schulte on four pitches. After a sacrifice bunt by Tinker moved Evers and Schulte to second and third, Overall, who was not a good-hitting pitcher, suddenly was. He lined a hard single to right center, scoring both runners for a 2–1 Cub lead. In the seventh the Cubs sent the soaked Tigers fans toward the exits with four runs to make it 6–1.

Tigers fans despaired over the difficulty of coming back from a 3–0 deficit. Only 7,370 showed up for game five. But Hughie said the right thing. "So far they have beaten us, but nobody can claim we have quit, and a break in the luck which has been against us would send us in on even terms again. The Cubs have taken three straight, why can't the Tigers do it? Victory today and tomorrow would put a might different phase on the fight, wouldn't it?"

Chance, whose mangled fingers kept him out of the lineup, had a different take, of course. "We want all four games in a row. We want to prove we have the best all around team in America."

When the gates opened the crowd trickled in and Chance walked along the grandstand talking to the early arrivals, telling them this would be their last chance to see a game this year. When the Cubs scored a run in the first inning the early edition of the *News*, on the stands before the game ended, printed this 30-point headline on the front page: "Chicago Gets Run in the First Inning" with two subheads under it: "Looks Almost Impossible Now for Tigers to Land a Corner on Base Ball Glory" and "Player Are Fagged Out."

In the parlance of the day, that meant the Tigers were tired and it was true. Or at least it looked that way to most observers. The Cubs looked faster and more motivated. Having been upset in '06 by the crosstown

"Hitless Wonders" White Sox they played like a team determined to assert their dominance, even if it cost their boss money, which it did. Game six was scheduled for the next day, Sunday, in Chicago and Murphy was expecting 25,000 to pay for the thrill of seeing their Cubs clinch in their home city. Mordecai Brown put an end to that dream. His arm finally rested, he got the start in game five and easily shut down the Tigers with a seven-hit shutout, striking out four and walking but one. The Cubs got single runs in the first and second innings, won 2–0 and clinched the series. While the Tigers had scored 118 more runs than the Cubs had during the season, the Cub pitchers led the major leagues in earned run average at 1.73 and gave up 142 fewer runs than the Tiger pitchers had. In the series Pfiester, Reulbach, Overall and Brown threw 43 scoreless innings out of 48 and shut down the American League's top two average hitters, Cobb and Sam Crawford. Cobb managed only a .200 average in the Series after batting .350 in the regular season; Crawford hit .238 after a .323 season. Meanwhile, Steinfeldt and Evers batted .471 and .350 respectively for the Cubs, numbers the Tigers had hoped to get from Cobb and Crawford. In addition the Cubs ran wild against the Tigers, stealing seven bases in game one and finishing the Series with 18. Hughie kept up his spirit to the final out, prancing in the coaching box and hollering his "atta boys" and "ee-yahs" and when it was over he was positive. "Another year is coming," he told the players. "And we'll be up there again. Next time we will be world champions. As it is there are honors enough."

There was money, too, to the ease the pain of losing. Tigers management had made $16,000 on the series and Yawkey and Navin announced that they were giving $15,000 of it to Hughie to divide among the players in addition to their 40 percent share, as losers, of the players' pool. This brought the total share for Jennings and the players to $1,945.96, meaning the Cubs' shares were only $197 more than the Tigers'. Murphy, the Cubs' owner, tried to remedy that by having an exhibition game in Chicago the next day with the Cubs playing a local amateur team, the Zeepoes. But the fans weren't buying. Only 3,200 turned out, adding just $1,600 to the Cubs' pool. Outside the park one enterprising entrepreneur took advantage of Hughie's popularity. Hawking postcards depicting a Tiger in a coffin, he yelled, "Get the latest so-fin-eer. Only five cents. The Tiger is dead his last words were 'ee-yah.'"

Back in Detroit on Monday night, Hughie and a group of his friends from Philadelphia who had been in Detroit for the series took the Woodward street car to the train station, where Hughie was going to see them off. Hughie rode on the rear platform and was spotted by a group of fans. Some 500 of them swarmed the trolley and pulled it off the wire. They refused to let it proceed until Hughie made a speech. At the Central Michigan Station, Hughie was again surrounded and had to give a little speech. Once his friends left, he walked over to the Penobscot Inn for dinner. He sneaked in the back and took a secluded table in a corner. But, he was found out and the diners, waiters and orchestra rose and gave him a rousing ovation. Of course they cried for a speech. Hughie tried to decline, but several of the diners dragged Hughie from his chair and put him up on a table, knocking away plates and glasses.

To the Detroit citizens who mobbed Hughie everywhere he went in the days after the World Series, Hughie was not the manager who lost the world championship in four games. He was the manager who tamed Ty Cobb, the manager who led the Tigers stunning rise from sixth place in 1906 to an American League pennant in 1907. To the Detroit fans Hughie Jennings was the manager who resurrected Detroit baseball. But the fans loved Hughie as much for his personality and style as they did for what he had done for the Tigers and Detroit. His fiery us-against-the-world persona, perpetual optimism, and fierce work ethic made him the perfect ambassador for Detroit, the second-smallest major league city, and a city which just a generation earlier was still considered a remote fur outpost, a place to stop on the way to someplace else.

Thrown on the table in the Penobscot Inn that evening, Hughie thanked the adoring fans for their support and asked for more of it for next season. "Ee-yahs" rang throughout the dinning room. When things quieted down, he sneaked out without dinner and walked home. The next night Hughie and the Tigers were guests of honor at the Detroit Opera House for the opening performance of the play, "The Man of the Hour." Hughie stayed in Detroit until Thursday, then left for Baltimore for a reunion of the Old Orioles. From there he went to a sanitarium, what we would call a resort today, in West Virginia for some rest.[4]

As the fans did, Yawkey and Navin had reasons to love Hughie — some 120,000 of them. With Hughie at the helm guiding Cobb's emergence as a star and the team's 90 wins, attendance at Tiger games grew by 123,036, or 41 percent, from 174,043 in '06 to 297,079 in '07. Work on Bennett Park began on Monday, just two days after the last World Series game. The plan was to extend the raised grandstand to the ground and extend the Trumbull Avenue bleachers the length of the field. The renovations increased seating capacity from 8,000 to 14,000 and standing room from 18,000 to 20,000.

The Tigers did not change the name of the park, but if they had, no one would have objected to "The House that Jennings Built."

19

The Greatest Race Ever

Hughie didn't like the severe look on Navin's face, and when his boss pulled him aside in the lobby of the Annex in Chicago at the American League meeting in December of 1907, Hughie feared the worst. Were the rumors he'd been hearing true? Had Ban Johnson changed his mind, after all, and decided to drop Detroit from the American League?

Back in October after the World Series, Johnson, influenced by the poor World Series attendance and a ticket-scandal backlash, threatened to drop Detroit from the league and replace it with Buffalo. Johnson reasoned that if Detroit wouldn't support a winner, what would happen if they started losing again? But once Navin reminded Johnson of the Tigers' 120,000 increase in regular-season attendance from 1906 to 1907, and promised to deliver an expanded ballpark, Johnson appeared to relent. On October 31 the *Sporting News* reported the news in a story headlined, "Status Settled. Detroit Will Not Lose Major Franchise."

The news wasn't about the demise of the Tigers, but rather about the bottom line. Johnson had given Navin a reprieve, though not a permanent one, and expenses had to be cut. "We have to cancel the old contract," Navin said handing Hughie an envelope. "We don't want to take advantage of you, but I wish you would look it over and see whether you are willing to stand the cut."[1]

When Hughie read the contract he was left speechless and confused, until Navin burst into laughter. The contract called for a hefty raise. The raise was not, as one published report put it, "sufficient to pay the fine imposed on Standard Oil by Judge Landis, it was nevertheless a liberal one." (Earlier in 1907 District Judge Kenesaw Mountain Landis, the future first commissioner of baseball, fined Standard Oil $29.2 million for accepting railroad freight rebates.) Terms of Hughie's contract for 1908 were never disclosed, but one estimate put it at $9,000, which would have made Hughie the A.L.'s second-highest-paid manager after Connie Mack.[2]

Navin showed even more faith in the future of baseball in Detroit when he bought half the franchise from Yawkey for $40,000 in January. Yawkey, who was planning to move to New York City, showed great faith in Navin by loaning him the down payment and naming him president with him full control. Yawkey remained a silent half partner until his death 28 years later. After the A.L. meeting Hughie went home. He was admitted to the Pennsylvania Bar and joined his brother's law firm in Scranton. In late February he went back to Detroit where he met up with Mullin, Donovan, Siever, Killian, Summers, Rossman, Coughlin and backup catcher Fred Payne. They left for Hot Springs at 8:25 on February 28. As they boarded the train Hughie told the writers, "everybody is happy. Our chance for the pennant is as good as $5 gold pieces during a financial stringency."[3]

They picked up Schaefer and O'Leary in Chicago and met the rest of the team in Little Rock. Cobb was a no-show. He and Navin had been wrangling over a contract since November and were getting nowhere. By the time camp opened on March 2, Navin said publicly that Cobb would not be a Tiger this year. Privately, they continued to negotiate. Hughie wanted Cobb in camp at any price and pressured Navin to give in. Cobb was demanding a three-year deal at $5,000 per, and an injury clause that would guarantee his salary if he was injured and couldn't play. Navin was willing to pay $5,000 for 1908, but was adamant against a three-year deal and the injury clause. When Hughie was asked about Cobb, he had a stock answer. "I haven't the slightest idea what Cobb is to receive in the way of salary this year or next. But I do know I am the manager of the team and that there must be a change for the sake of discipline."[4]

On March 21, Cobb went to Detroit and met with ex-mayor George Codd, a close friend of his and of Navin. Codd convinced Cobb to drop the three-year demand and the injury clause. He signed for $5,000 and an $800 bonus if he led the league in batting. Even signed, Cobb still took 10 days to report to Little Rock, arriving on March 31. Asked about the contract he said, "I believe that in two years all players will demand they be guaranteed salary when injured. If half the truth was told of how players are docked for time they spend in the hospital after receiving injuries it wouldn't look good for the team owners."[5]

During the trip north Hughie came up with an innovation. He arranged two games at every stop, a game for the regulars in the city and a game in the country for younger players. But the plan didn't work, at least not to the extent that it gave Hughie peace of mind about his pitching staff. He had brought 10 new pitchers to camp, but wound up keeping only three, Ed Summers, George Suggs, and George Winter. Of them only

Summers—a 6'-2", 180 pound rookie from Indianapolis—would have an impact in 1908.

In Chicago for their 1908 season opener against the White Sox on April 14, Hughie must have laughed when he saw this headline on page 12 of the *Chicago Tribune*: "W-e-e-e-a-ah" and "Stri-ike Tuh" at White Sox Park Today.

From the story: "Manager Jennings smilingly attempting to appear gloomy. 'Exhibition games, in which real practice is obtained, have been denied so often of late that my men are far from ready. We are hoping for the best, but we will need some luck to help us get a majority of the games from the White Sox. My pitchers are working fairly well, but I would like to have them a lot better than they are.'"[6]

Hughie was right. The Tigers were far from ready. They lost five of their first six and by May 9 they were 6–11 and tied for last place. They didn't reach .500 until May 23 when they were 14–14. But they fell back under on June 9 at 22–23. Even at that they were only 2½ games back of the White Sox, Naps, and Browns, who were all tied for first place. A hot streak put the Tigers at 32–25 on June 23, but then they lost three straight to the Browns at home to fall 4½ back. So it went all season. The Tigers, Naps, White Sox and Browns stayed within a few games of each other in the most exciting pennant race in the eight-year history of the American League. On road trips the Tigers were the biggest draw in the American League. In New York on May 17, 20,000 fans lined the field and saw everything they came to see—Cobb on the run, Hughie on the warpath and a Yankee win. In the second inning with a runner on first and Cobb on second, Coughlin hit to short and the Yankees tried for a double play. Coughlin beat the throw at first. Cobb tried to score from second, but was called out at home when it looked like he had slide around the tag. Hughie howled at umpire Horst and was tossed from the game. The Yankees won 7–6.

A few days later in Washington, Hughie was asked about the incident and got himself suspended for this remark published in the *Washington Post*. "Horst is umpiring miserable ball and made a lot of mistakes against us. There is no chance for a visiting team to get a close decision against New York and when I told him so he put me off the grounds."

The *Post* came to his defense, suggesting there was a double standard. "Jennings was suspended for 10 days for giving out an interview in Washington regarding the incompetence of a certain umpire. Johnson is trying to protect umps, but Connie Mack called Silk O'Loughlin a crook after the 17-inning game last year and gave several interviews saying O'Loughlin could not be honest, yet no action was taken against Mack."

Cobb continued to cause Hughie problems off the field, too. On June

6 workers were spreading asphalt on the street in front of the Pontchartrain Hotel where Cobb lived. When Cobb came out he stepped on the fresh
pavement. One of the paving workers, a black man named Fred Collins,
told Cobb to watch where he was walking. Cobb knocked Collins down,
and went on his way to Bennett Park, where the Tigers had a 2:30 game
against Boston. Collins was injured and called the police. Just before the
game several Detroit cops came to the Detroit bench and called Cobb aside.
They were about to arrest him, when a hundred fans rushed onto the field
and surrounded the police and Cobb. The cops decided to wait until after
the game to make the arrest. In court, a sympathetic magistrate ordered
Cobb to pay Collins $75, but gave him a suspended sentence with no fine.[7]

Any goodwill Cobb had gained with his teammates by getting the
team to the World Series in '07 was lost with the holdout, the Collins incident and by Cobb's marriage. On August 3 Cobb left the team flat without notice and went back to Georgia to marry 17-year-old Charlotte
"Charlie" Lombard. He stayed away six days and missed four games. When
he returned Hughie put him back in the lineup and Cobb had a triple, single and stolen base in a 5–2 win at Washington. Hughie would have liked
to discipline Cobb by benching him or suspending him, but what was he
to do? He was in a pennant race and Cobb was the best player, even if he
was an arrogant son-of-a-bitch.[8]

For a week in August fans who came out to see Hughie in the coaching box were disappointed. They didn't get to hear an "ee-yah" or an "atta-
boy." Speculation was that Ban Johnson had ordered Hughie to curtail his
act, but that wasn't the case. Hughie had laryngitis and couldn't speak
above a whisper. On August 22 it was reported that Frank Farrell, the owner
of New York A.L. club, offered Navin $25,000 for Hughie. Navin refused
to even talk. Hughie lodged away that $25,000 figure for future reference,
but played dumb publicly. "I am perfectly satisfied with my berth with the
Detroit club and while I know nothing of any offer being made for me, I
have no intention of leaving Detroit."[9]

Besides, Hughie had fish to fry in '08 without worrying about the
future. On September 1 the standings looked like this:

Detroit Tigers	68–49		
St. Louis Browns	67–51	.567	1.5
Chicago White Sox	67–52	.563	2.0
Cleveland Naps	67–53	.558	2.5

But after losing three straight to Boston, on September 24 the Tigers
were 79–61 and in third, place two games behind the Naps and White Sox.

Then over the next eight days they won 10 straight at home, including two doubleheaders. In the ninth of the 10 consecutive wins, on October 2, the Tigers were losing 6–5 in the ninth. The Tigers had a runner on third and Cobb on first. Rossman hit a drive to left. Cobb, as the winning run, was stopped at third by one of the umpires, who thought the ball had gone into the crowd for a double. Cobb argued that it had not, but Hughie grabbed him and practically carried him home. Later he reminded Cobb to, "score first, argue later." The other umpire ruled the ball in play and the Tigers won 7–6 to remain in first place by one-half game.[10]

The next day Cleveland lost, 3–2, to the White Sox, while the Tigers rolled to their 10th straight win, as Wild Bill Donovan shut out the Browns, 6–0. After the game the Tigers boarded the train for Chicago for a season-ending three-game series. In the morning the standings looked like this.

Detroit Tigers	89–61	
Cleveland Naps	88–63	1½
Chicago White Sox	86–63	2½

The White Sox won the first game. Never before had so many fans watched baseball in one city. While Some 22,000 saw the White Sox-Tigers game, 30,247, the largest crowd ever at Chicago's West Side Grounds, saw the Cubs beat the Pirates in their last regular-season game. The next day, October 5, the Sox won again, as spitballer Ed Walsh got his 40th win, 6–1. The American League pennant race was forced to the final day. Walsh, who was born and lived just five miles from Hughie in anthracite country, wound up leading the league in games (66), IP (464), K's (269), complete games (42), saves (6), shutouts (11), and winning percentage (.727). His ERA was 1.42.

Heading into the final game on October 6 the three teams stood this way:

Detroit Tigers	89–63	
Chicago White Sox	88–63	½
Cleveland Naps	89–64	½

The Naps lost one game of a doubleheader and were eliminated, leaving the Tigers and White Sox to decide the pennant between them. Fans lined up early in the morning to get into the park. The gates were opened at noon, and by 2 p.m. every available space was filled and the gates were closed. The 22,000 fans came armed with noise makers of all kinds, but the Tigers silenced them early. Cobb hit a 2-run triple in a 4-run first and that was more than enough for Donovan. He pitched the game of his life, a two-hit shutout with 10 strikeouts. The Tigers won 7–0 and were A.L. champs again. Walsh pitched in relief, his 14th appearance in the Sox' last 17 games. Unplayed games figured in the race. In those days tied or postponed games which could not be made up during the season were not rescheduled.

"Horns and squawkers, drums and blazing torches waved aloft, with Hugh Jennings's familiar cry of 'wee-ah' on every tongue," was how one scribe described the scene in Detroit after the Tigers clinched. The mayor called the pennant race the most gallant fight in the history of baseball and issued a proclamation: "Resolved that we on behalf of the people of Detroit extend to manager Hugh Jennings and the team hearty congratulations." The resolution asked that city merchants and citizens decorate their businesses and homes for the World Series. A city clerk delivered a certified copy of the resolution to Hughie the next day. The team arrived in the morning and was greeted at Michigan Central station by several thousand. Donovan was carried on the shoulders of the fans. A brass band played and automobiles waited to take the players to the Hotel Pontchartrain for a party. The fans and band marched behind.[11]

Meanwhile over in the N.L. the pennant race was yet to be decided. When the Cubs beat the Pirates in their last game the Pirates were eliminated. But the Giants still had three games to play in Boston and were 1½ games behind the Cubs. The Giants swept the series and the N.L. season ended with the Giants and the Cubs each 98–55. A playoff game, of sorts, was held the next day in New York. It wasn't strictly a playoff game. It was a replay of the infamous "Merkle's Blunder" game of September 23. Fred Merkle had been a runner at first and had failed to touch second when the winning run scored. He was declared out, negating the run, but the N.L. later ordered the game to be replayed.

The replay was the most anticipated game in the history of the sport. By one estimate nearly 250,000 fans showed up at the Polo Grounds. The gates were closed at 1:30 for the 3:00 game after over 30,000 fans were packed in. Firemen with high-pressure hoses knocked down fans who tried to scale the walls. Nearly 40,000 fans watched from Coogan's Bluff, telephone poles and other vantage points. Two fans were killed when they fell from a pillar on the elevated subway platform. McGraw started Christy Mathewson, the league's best pitcher. But Mathewson, who had already pitched 380 innings in 56 games, lost, 4–2.

Hughie was disappointed that his old friend, John McGraw, and the Giants had lost. He had been looking forward to matching wits with "Mac," as he called him, in the World Series. And he relished the idea of playing on the big stage in New York, before several hundred of his most fervent fans from the Scranton area, who were sure to make the easy trip to New York. Disappointed as he was, Hughie consoled himself with the chance at revenge against the Cubs for the crushing defeat in the 1907 series.

Downtown Detroit was decorated in Michigan blue and yellow for the series opener on October 10. There were tigers in every window display, many sitting alongside teddy bears with black patches over their eyes and black mourning bands on their arms. Men wore yellow neckties and ladies yellow chrysanthemums. One fan from Chicago said, "the only civil answer you could get from a policeman was 'wee-ah.'"[12]

But there would be no revenge. In a series which had strange similarities to the '07 series, the Cubs won four games to one. As they had in '07, the Cubs rallied in the ninth to snatch away victory from the Tigers in game one. This time the game ended not in a tie, but in a 10–6 Cub win after the Tigers led 6–5 in the ninth. Steady rain and cold kept attendance down to 10,812. By the end there were two inches of mud on the base paths. Two of the Cubs' wins were by scores identical to '07 series scores, including the deciding game which the Cubs again won 2–0. Only 6,210 witnessed the final game in Detroit, the smallest crowd in Series history. The Tigers' shares came to $870.66 per player. Hughie got the same. Unlike 1907, when Hughie had declared the Cubs had been more lucky than good, after the '08 series he conceded they were the better team. "Frank Chance has a wonderful team, one of the greatest that ever played ball. I congratulate him and his followers. He has a team of game, heady ballplayers. Chicago won because the Cubs outplayed us. There are no regrets for me to offer. We were beaten and beaten fairly."[13]

20

Three Straight Pennants

The 40-year-old first baseman stepped into the batter's box and promptly cracked a base hit into center field and the fans in Boston's Huntington Avenue Grounds roared their approval. It didn't matter that the batter was playing for the visiting team. After all, he was the gingeriest, pepperiest man in baseball. He was the happy-go-lucky, three-time A.L. champion manager of the Detroit Tigers. He was the grass-pulling, jig-dancing Hughie "Ee-yah" Jennings. For the fans around the A.L., watching his coaching-line shows was always the treat, but for the fans in Boston on October 1, 1909, seeing the Old Orioles legend play was a treat of a life-time. It was only his third appearance as a player in a major league game since 1902. Hughie put himself in the lineup the day after the Tigers had clinched the 1909 A.L. pennant, their third consecutive. The Tigers clinched when Chicago beat the Philadelphia A's in a doubleheader a day earlier. After Hughie learned that, he shipped eight of his stars—Cobb, Crawford, Moriarity, Stanage; and pitchers Mullin, Donovan, Killian and Summers— back to Detroit to rest up for the World Series.

Hughie played first base and had two hits, scored a run, made seven putouts and one assist and was in on two double plays. It didn't matter that the Red Sox won 9–6. Hughie's grin "echoed," as umpire Tim Horst had once described it, all afternoon. O'Leary was one player who didn't get the day off but he didn't complain. "He wouldn't let me join the boys on a day off. I had to play the whole game, but I got my fun watching Hughey."[1]

The 1909 pennant race provided little of the drama of the previous two. The Tigers led most of the way. At one point in July they led by eight games. They stumbled once, when they lost six of nine between August 7 and 18, and dropped 1½ back of the Athletics. Among the losses were three to the Athletics on Saturday, Monday, and Tuesday, August 7, 9, and 10. There was no game on the 8th because Sunday ball was still illegal in Pennsylvania. Hughie defied the law. He took the Tigers to play Scranton on Sunday, a 110-mile trip. As he was the city's favorite son, Scranton officials made no attempt to enforce the Sunday ban. Thousands of fans surrounded the field to watch the Tigers win 12–11. Cobb pitched four innings and Jennings played first base for two innings.

Beginning on the 19th, the Tigers went on a 14-game winning streak, all at home, which included a three-game sweep of the A's. By the time they lost again on September 3, they were up by six games. They won an A.L. record 98 games and won the pennant by 3½ games. But the season had been filled with enough unusual games and happenings to overcome the lack of a pennant race. Cobb got in big trouble, Coughlin got released, Schaefer got traded and Hughie uncovered a spy ring. For having the guts to change the whole infield from a two-time pennant winning club, Hughie got more credit than ever for the Tigers' success, and his popularity around the league and the country soared.

In 1909 The Tigers became the first team in the A.L to play before 1,000,000 fans. In Philadelphia they drew over 100,000 for three games. One of those three games, on September 18, drew 35,409, the largest paid baseball attendance to date. The Tigers drew 490,490 at home, a franchise record. Cobb was a huge draw, as he played as though he belonged in a higher league. He led the A.L. in batting average, runs, hits home runs, RBI, stolen bases, slugging percentage and on-base percentage. But Hughie was a big part of the draw, too. His face was in every cigar store in Detroit, and he endorsed various products in newspaper ads. In an ad for a shoe company he was pictured in his famous raised-leg pose above this: "The greatest baseball manger the world has ever known. Why? Because he's full of ginger, life, snap, everything that makes for success. That's why Baumgartner Shoes, Baumgartner Wearables of all kinds are winners over all competitors."

In an ad for Boston Garters he was pictured in a cartoon drawing in shorts and wearing garters holding up a pair of black socks. In an ad for Coca-Cola he is again pictured in his famous raised-leg pose. "Gentlemen: The hardest thing a ball player has to contend with is thirst. If you try to satisfy it with water you will get leggy or lose your ginger or it makes you sick. And alcohol is fatal to good ball. I drink Coca-Cola and hardily recommend it to all athletes." He also pitched for Gillette razors.

Releasing Coughlin, his starting third baseman in 1907 and '08, was one of the hardest things Hughie ever had to do. Coughlin was originally from Wilkes-Barre and was an off-season Scranton resident and friend of Hughie's. That made it hard enough, but that wasn't the worst of it. Coughlin was also a former breaker boy who had lost a finger sorting the Black

Diamonds. But Coughlin's playing tested Hughie's loyalty. He had turned 30 the previous season in 1908 and his hitting was anemic. When Hughie benched him on September 24 Coughlin was hitting .215. Of his 87 hits, only six were better than singles. His fielding had fallen off. Forced to play in the World Series due to injuries, he went 1–8. Hughie toyed with the idea of making him a paid coach in 1909, a role he had taken on informally under Hughie for three seasons. But a deal could not be worked out. Coughlin went back to the minors were he was a successful manager at Williamsport and Wilkes-Barre. He and Hughie remained friends. Hughie had Navin buy George Moriarity from the Yankees to replace Coughlin. Moriarity, a 6'-0" and 180 pound 24-year-old from Miami, batted .283 in '09.

When the Tigers repeated in 1908 not everyone was aboard Hughie's bandwagon. His jealous critics said he owed his success to the team his predecessor had built and to the individual play of Cobb, Sam Crawford and Schaefer. In some quarters more praise went to Schaefer than Jennings. But Hughie changed that perception in 1909. Replacing Coughlin was just the beginning of the changes in the Tiger infield. By the end of the season the entire infield from the 1907 and '08 pennant-winning teams was gone. In mid-August the Tigers went to Washington for a series with the Nationals and left Germany Schaefer behind in exchange for Jim Delahanty, younger brother of the legendary Phillies slugger Ed Delahanty. Hughie liked Schaefer, he reminded him of himself and the Old Orioles and he had a sense of humor. He once appeared in the batter's box with an umbrella and rubber boots because the umpire wouldn't call a game during a rainstorm. But Hughie thought, correctly, he could get more run production out of Delahanty, who was a better hitter.

"The trade is of mutual benefit. Schaefer can play outfield and is hitting better. He's an excellent base runner and natural leader."[2] It was true that Schaefer was hitting better. He had hit .258 in '08, the highest mark in his career. For Delahanty, the Tigers were his seventh team in nine seasons. Hughie also traded his first baseman, Claude Rossman, to St. Louis for Tom Jones and replaced O'Leary at short with rookie Donnie Bush. Hughie had bought Bush, a 5'-4" 22-year-old fielding wizard, from Indianapolis of the Interstate League late in September of '08. He played in 20 games in '08 and showed enough to win the job for '09. He played in all 157 games in '09 and led the league in assists, bases on balls and sacrifice hits. Legendary sports writer and author Ring Lardner led the praise of Hughie. "Hughey Jennings did something decidedly uncommon when he led his team to its third straight pennant this season. Instead of standing pat, as most managers have done with a championship team, he finished with three infielders who had nothing to do with the victory of one year ago and a fourth who had played in only a small percentage of the games."[3]

Writing in the *Washington Post*, Ed Grillo said Hughie deserved more money. "Jennings should demand a salary greater than has ever been paid a manager. If Washington signed McClure for $10,000 after eight years without success Jennings can easily figure he is worth three times that to Detroit." Hughie took note of Grillo's suggestion and used it in negotiations with Navin after the '09 World Series

Hughie believed that honest communication among him and the players was a key to success. "I have established a system of harmony and at the same time mutual criticism on our team. During the last invasion of the East we had about 10 meetings. We talk about what has been done, what has to be done and what ought not be done. The value of the meetings is unquestioned and they serve to make the team work together. On the other hand too much harmony is a bad thing. I train my men to take criticism from their fellow players as well as give it. I know a stupid play will bring unfavorable comment upon them and I find that keeps them on edge."[4]

On September 4 in Cleveland, at 2 o'clock in the morning, Cobb got in a fight with George Standsfield, the black watchman at the Hotel Euclid. The watchman had a club and Cobb pulled a knife. Both men were bloodied in the fight. Cobb was cut in the cheek and on the head. Standsfield was hospitalized. Cobb bandaged himself and played all 18 innings of a doubleheader that afternoon. Fans and players were aghast at seeing Cobb play with blood seeping from the bandages about his face and head. A warrant was issued for Cobb's arrest for aggravated assault and intent to kill. In the morning the police went to arrest him. They waited outside by the car the Tigers were supposed to leave in, but Hughie sneaked Cobb out a back service entrance and through side streets to the train station, where the Tigers left for St. Louis.[5]

Cobb avoided Ohio the rest of the season and during the World Series. He did a lot of train-hopping through Canada. During one trip between Pittsburgh and Detroit during the World Series, an uncle drove him through Ohio, while Cobb hid in the back seat under a blanket.[6] In the days after the incident, Cobb received 13 letters containing death threats, some of which were deemed credible. One letter from Philadelphia read, "I'll be on a roof across from the park with a rifle in the third inning and I'll put a bullet in your heart." In the hotel the night before the first game of a series in Philadelphia in mid-September, Hughie tried to talk Cobb out of playing, but the Peach wouldn't consider it. Cobb survived the series thanks to the 50 armed cops who circled him in right field. This was the series which drew 100,000, and included the record crowd of over 30,000 for the Saturday game.

In September, Hughie exposed a Highlander sign-stealing scheme with the help of Washington manager Joe Cantillon. The Highlanders put a piece of wood on the outfield fence that was a slightly different shade of green than the rest of the fence. Manager George Stallings stationed a player behind a hole in the outfield fence with a pair of binoculars. The player read the catchers' signals, and by moving the piece of wood tipped off the batters. If it moved to the right, a curve was coming and if it moved to the left, a fastball. A quick shake meant a pitchout. In September, the Tigers were in Washington. A Washington newspaperman who was wise to the Highlanders' scheme told Cantillon about it. Before the Tigers left Washington, Cantillon pulled Hughie aside and told him what was going on in New York.[7]

In New York Hughie kept quiet until he sent men out behind the fence and caught the guy dead to rights. The spy ran away so quickly he left behind a bottle of beer and a half-eaten sandwich. After the scheme was exposed, Detroit then took three of four from the Highlanders, their only losses in their final 16 games. Hughie threatened to go to Ban Johnson. It took his old Oriole buddy, Wee Willie Keeler, then with the Highlanders, to calm him down. Once the incident got around the league, some players speculated that the Highlanders had laid down to keep Hughie from going to Johnson.[8]

A 1909 card for Piedmont cigarettes, showing Hughie Jennings.

The Tigers' opponents in the 1909 World Series were the Pittsburgh Pirates, who had played .723 ball (110–42) in winning the N.L. pennant by seven games, while outscoring their opponents 701–448. The Pirate stars were Honus Wagner, who won his seventh N.L. batting title in 1909, and player/manager Fred Clarke. The big three pitchers were Howie Camnitz, Vic Willis and Lefty Leifield, who won 25, 22, and 19 games respectively, none of whom would win a game in the series. But 27-year-old Babe Adams, who had been 12–3 during the regular season, bailed the big three out.

The Tigers arrived in Pittsburgh on October 7, the day before the first game, in two parts. One, which included Hughie, came from a charity exhibition game in New York. The other part came from Detroit including Crawford, Mullin, and Cobb. Cobb, still wanted in Ohio, had to take a circuitous route through Canada, Buffalo and Lake Erie. The Tigers went through a two-hour workout and checked in at the Colonial Annex Hotel. Before the game Hughie proclaimed the Tigers had to win, if only because of luck. "The third time is the charm, so you see we are due to win for we lost in the other two series."

Forbes Field, the Pirates' new million-dollar park, with its triple-decked grandstand, could accommodate only one-third of the fanatics who stormed the gates. Lines formed beginning at 8 p.m. the night before. Fans brought cots or slept on sidewalks in hopes of getting one of 12,000 general admission tickets. Streetcars dropped fans three blocks away at the end of the line, which eventually extended a mile. Scalpers demanded $10–20 for tickets with a face value of $1.50 and $2. While some fans bit, thousands of the overpriced tickets went unsold. Even so, a Series-record 29,265 fans got in for game one. Among them were 2,500 Detroit rooters, including Mayor Philip Breitmeyer and Michigan governor Fred Warner, and a surprisingly large, and loud, group of female fans. They could be heard above the din of Pirate rooters cheering "One! Two! Three! Four! Five! Six! Seven! We-ah!"[9]

Bookies installed the Pirates as 3–1 favorites, but there were few takers. Action was greater for even money that Wagner would outhit Cobb. No one was surprised at the outcome of game one, a 4–1 Pirate win on a six-hitter by Adams. The Tigers now had a 1–9–1 record in Series games. Going into game two, fans were beginning to wonder if the A.L. wasn't just a glorified minor league. Many expected a sweep by the Pirates. But Hughie was confident. "No sir, the Pirates have not got us bluffed. Watch us today and see if we look like scared men. I don't like to make excuses but I think the Pirates got all the breaks yesterday."[10]

Game two set another attendance record, as over 31,000 saw Donovan even the series with a five-hitter, 7–2. Pittsburgh scored both in the first inning, but Donovan faced only one over the minimum over the last five innings. Cobb stole home in a three-run third. After a day off, the Series resumed at Bennett Park in Detroit on October 11. Navin had temporary circus bleachers erected, and was able to accommodate 18,277, a Detroit record. Among the fans was one Dr. Fredrick Cook, who was then being celebrated as the discoverer of the North Pole. Hughie met him and they shook hands before the game. Cook claimed to have reached the pole on April 21, 1908, and earned millions selling tales of his adventures. He was later debunked, convicted of fraud, and sent to prison.[11]

The Pirates scored five in the first inning off Summers, the knuckle-baller who had won 19 during the season. Down 6–0, the Tigers scored four in the seventh, sending the fans in the temporary bleachers into a frenzy. They stormed the field and had to be driven back by police before the game could resume. The key play was a sacrifice fly in the top of the seventh. Cobb threw a strike home for what looked like the third out, but Bobby Byrne's slide managed to elude the tag by Schmidt. Wagner followed with his third hit, scoring Tommy Leach. Wagner also stole three bases as the Pirates won 8–6. Tiger fans may have thought "uh-oh, here we go again," but the next day, George Mullin pitched one of the best games of his career, shutting out the Pirates 5–0 on four hits to even the series 2–2. He struck out 10, including Clarke and Wagner in the third inning with two men on. It was damp, windy and cold with light snow. By the end of the game the temperature was below freezing. Scores of women brought in blankets from their automobiles and carriages.

Back at Forbes Field for game five, Adams allowed only six hits— Crawford touched him for a single, double and home run — and Clarke hit a three-run homer as Pittsburgh prevailed, 8–4, to take a 3–2 lead in the series. That night Hughie was the honored guest of the Pittsburgh alumni chapter of Phi Delta Theta at a smoker at the Fort Pitt Hotel. Phi Delta Theta was Hughie's fraternity at Cornell.[12]

Back in Detroit the next day it was a do-or-die game for the Tigers. Hughie took a chance on Mullin on just a day's rest and it worked. After getting tagged for three runs in the first, he settled down, and the Tigers won 5–4 to force a deciding seventh game for the first time in Series history. The Tigers got the home field for the seventh game on a coin flip. Clarke went with Adams as his pitcher and Hughie went with Donovan. He passed over Ed Willett, who had started 34 regular-season games but made only one relief appearance in the series, and Ed Killian, 19 regular-season starts, who was not used at all in the series. Though Donovan had pitched a complete game in game two, he was weak from a bout with malaria and had started only 17 games in the regular season. Donovan lived up to his Wild Bill nickname. After hitting the first batter with a pitch, he proceeded to walk six batters in the first two innings. After three innings, Donovan was gone and Adams was holding a 2–0 lead. Hughie had fresh arms on the bench, but brought Mullin back. He was spent and it showed. The Pirates got to him for five more and won easily, 8–0.

The *Pittsburgh Press* was the first to pounce on Hughie for starting Donovan. "Manager Hughey Jennings made a big mistake when he decided on the veteran Donovan to oppose Adams. Donovan made good his sobriquet of 'Wild Bill' before the first inning was over."

An hour after the final game Hughie met Pirate manager Clarke in the writers' room and Hughie congratulated him. Clarke said, "I know what it's like to be a loser in a series like this and I appreciate your congratulations." They talked the entire series over. Hughie admitted he may have made a mistake going with Donovan.

"We were beaten," Hughie said. "But I feel my team is, nevertheless, worthy of credit for its game fight. I blame our defeat on the weather conditions more than anything else. Had it been warm in any of the last four days Bill Donovan would surely have won his game. He insisted on pitching everyday, even though it was cold, but it was evident after he had gone a few innings that he could not warm up to his work. Mullin did great work, but a man, even though he is big and strong, cannot expect to work everyday and that was why I was willing to pitch Donovan today, for I felt confident George could not deliver and this was not a game for one of the youngsters."[13]

Baseball had never seen anything like the 1909 World Series. Attendance was 145,807. Winners' receipts were $1,825.22. The Tigers, as losers, got $ 1,274.76 each. Navin was furious with Hughie for how he handled the pitchers in the Series, and was going to insist on no raise for Hughie in 1910. Hughie didn't take the news well. "I have accomplished something no other American League manager has ever done. I have won three consecutive flags and I consider that a feat worth paying for. Jimmy McAleer is to get $10,000 next year for managing Washington. If leading a tailender is worth $10,000, then my job ought to be worth $15,000 and that is what I intend to ask. If I don't get it I'll quit baseball."[14]

But on October 24, Hughie signed a contract for 1910 with a base salary of $10,000, to be supplemented with a percentage of profits. "The terms are perfectly satisfactory to me," Hughie said. "We agreed to them with no difficulty."

The *Washington Post* speculated that Hughie would do all right in 1910. "Hughey is figuring on an income of about $30,000 next year, if the Tigers reach the World Series and something less if they don't. Official figures place the net earnings of the club for the '08 season at $166,000. The World Series brought the club's earnings up to $200,000. Just what Jennings' salary is is not given, but it is known that with his percentage of profits and world series money he has received $41,599 for the three seasons and will want his salary doubled. He draws a percentage of earnings but doesn't own stock. Ban Johnson is on record as having written to Detroit club that Jennings is a detriment to the league. Meaning perhaps it is not in the best interest of the A.L. to have a city like Detroit win pennants."[15]

Detroit would not win another pennant for 24 years, long after Hughie Jennings was gone from Detroit and from this Earth.

21

A Wreck and
a Wedding

Because he was up late reading in his father's farmhouse near the Lehigh Creek in the Pocono Mountains of Pennsylvania On December 1, 1911, George Boyle saved the life of Hughie Jennings, famous ballplayer. It was nearly midnight when a metallic crash and screams pierced the usual stark quiet around the farm. Boyle threw down his book, ran to the porch and looked down the road toward the bridge. In the moonlight he could make out the form of an automobile bottom-up in the creek. He roused his father and brother and they ran to the scene. There they found Mr. and Mrs Holden, newlyweds from Scranton, who had been passengers in the back seat, trying to pull the driver from the wreck. The Boyles helped the Holdens get the badly injured man up the bank of the creek and pointed the Holdens toward the farmhouse. As the newlyweds helped Hughie Jennings to the house, the Boyles went back to the car, where a third passenger was trapped. With brute strength the Boyles raised the car enough to pull Father Lynett out. The Catholic pastor from Matamoras, a nearby town, was barely conscious and unable to walk. The Boyles carried him to the farmhouse. Hughie was able to stagger to the house aided by the Holdens but collapsed into unconsciousness on the farmhouse floor. One of the Boyle sons pedaled his bike three miles to the nearest telephone in Gouldsboro and called to Scranton for a doctor. The Holdens and Boyles tended to the injured men as best they could and waited. In Scranton, Dr. Webb and Father Malone of St. Patrick's Cathedral, where Hughie had been married that January, hired a car and set out for the farmhouse, arriving at three in the morning. While Dr. Webb attended to Hughie and Father Lynett, Father Malone gave them Last Rites, a Catholic rite for the dying.

Hughie was nearly killed in his automobile in December of 1911. He was driving when the car left a bridge and flipped on its roof in Lehigh Creek, in the Pocono Mountains of Pennsylvania, as shown in this postcard.

Another messenger was sent to Gouldsboro to contact the Lackawanna Railroad, which agreed to hold the milk and accommodation train so the injured men could be taken to Scranton in the baggage car. At 5 a.m. Hughie's brother and law partner, William, and Hughie's brother in law, Charles O'Boyle, arrived at the farmhouse in another car. William looked down at Hughie and said, "It's me, Will. Do you know me?" Hughie, who was drifting in and out of consciousness, fluttered his eyes and nodded his head. The men were wrapped in blankets, laid on the back seats of the cars and taken to the train station. By the time the train reached Scranton the rumor had spread that Hughie was dead. A crowd formed and pressed against the train as it arrived. Special agents pushed the crowd back as men of the Lackawanna first-aid brigade pushed through to help carry the victims. Father Lynett was put in an ambulance and Hughie into a glass-enclosed six-seated carriage. A half-hour later word came from the hospital that Father Lynett had a broken right leg, left arm and four broken ribs. Hughie had a broken left wrist, a fractured skull, a concussion and numerous cuts and contusions on his head and face. A day later, stories about the wreck appeared in major newspapers across the country. It was conjectured that mechanical failure had caused the crash, or that it was driver error.

The latter was likely the case. Hughie wasn't much of an automobile driver, and if he hadn't been a Detroiter seven months a year, it's likely he might not have owned the car that wound up in Lehigh Creek in 1911. But as one of Detroit's leading citizens, and a man of some means at that, he could hardly ignore the horseless carriage. Ford had introduced his Model T in 1908, the year after Hughie came to Detroit, and between '07 and 1910, automobile ownership in America increased 100 times. But a Model T, designed for the common man, would not do for Hughie Jennings, one of the two or three highest-paid and best known men in baseball. After the 1910 season, perhaps to console himself for missing the World Series for the first time in three years, Hughie bought one of the first E-M-F model "30" Touring cars ever built.[1] The company was founded in 1908 and named for the owners, Everitt, Metzger, Flanders. Deservedly, or not, the E-M-F engendered nicknames such as "Every Mechanical Fault," "Every Morning Fix-It," "Every Mechanic's Friend" and "Eternally Missing Fire." Even so, E-M-Fs were considered luxury cars for high-class citizens at a cost of $1,250. A similar Ford was $780. Ford eventually outproduced and undercut E-M-F, and the company was absorbed by Studebaker.[2]

After the 1910 season Hughie drove the car to New York, before going home to Scranton, and told a story in *Rounding Third* about an incident which happened along the way.

> Buyers say they don't want to buy cars for speed. That's the strange thing about buyers. I know that was my own attitude when I bought my first car. On my recent trip from Detroit to New York in my E-M-F touring car I had the particular phase of human nature illustrated. I noticed ahead a car of the same make as my own, but as it contained a boy and an old lady, evidently the young driver's grandma, I didn't doubt I would be given the road without an effort.
>
> I tooted twice and the car pulled out to the right to let me by. I was just abreast and nodding my thanks, when the old lady tapped the boy driver and said something to him. He smiled and cut loose. For two miles we ran neck-and-neck. How long we would have raced that way, I don't know, but we met a thrashing machine on the road and one of us had to yield. I pride myself on my nerve and determined to bluff my opponents, but I was out bluffed by the old lady. She never blinked an eye but still tapping the boy on the arm told him to go to it. I decided it would be well to observe the rule ladies first and jammed on the brakes.
>
> The last I saw of the old lady she was looking back beckoning me to come up and laughing fit to kill. Yea, I bet when grandma and grandpa went to buy that car they both argued they didn't want a racer, but just a quiet tempered one that would take them there and back, but I'll bet they arrived before folks were expecting them.[3]

The story casts doubt on Hughie's claim that he was doing 15 miles per hour when he drove the car into the creek that night and illustrates that he was lucky to be alive. In fact, thousands of people across the country thought he wouldn't be alive for long. The *Washington Post* reported that Hughie's chance of recovering was "a little better than even." A headline in the *Boston Globe* read: "Hugh Jennings Dying, Minister, Too, After Automobile Wreck."

The *Newark Daily Advocate* reported a rumor that even if Hughie did survive, his head injuries were permanent and his mind was wandering. The newspaper sent a wire out and quickly came an answer from Dr. Webb saying there was no clot on Hughie's brain and that he would be back attending to business in 30 days. Hughie defied the odds, and by December 5 was able to sit up in bed and have visitors. Wrapped in a blanket of Indian colors and with "his right eye closed and the flesh around it rounded out in a lump as big as a tomato and not unlike it in color," Hughie explained what happened to the *Scranton Times*.

> Over in Pike County is a game preserve of 1400 acres owned by three brothers named Holden. They were Catholics and particular friends of Father Lynett. I was over there hunting a week ago last Friday and had my machine along. One of the tires went bad and the front axle went a little out of plumb. I left the machine in a garage at Port Jervis for repair and went home by train. Last Friday I went after it.
>
> That morning David Holden, the youngest of the three brothers who own the preserve, was married by Father Lynett. When I got ready to start back to Scranton it was agreed that Mr. Holden and his bride and Father Lynett would make the trip. We got to Gouldsboro about nine o'clock when the machine showed a leak in the gas line and we had to lay over in Gouldsboro to get it fixed.
>
> We were three miles or so this side of Gouldsboro. I was not overly familiar with the road and I should say we were making 15 miles an hour when I saw we were striking a sharp curve and I slowed down. The curve takes a double twist like a capital "S." Before I knew of the second twist, up went one wheel and over we went. I gripped the steering wheel harder hoping to get back to terra firma and the next thing I was sputtering water from my mouth. I couldn't tell if we had fallen one inch or tumbled down a mine shaft. I don't remember the fall. I can remember wriggling to get my face out of the water, as I lay under the machine. It happened in a flash and gave me no time to think, except to utter a prayer.

Hughie also described his first look at himself after the wreck.

> I waited until all the nurses had left me in my cradle. I tiptoed to the looking glass across the room. I couldn't laugh. I couldn't even smile. There I stood with my mouth grown together. I had a King William taped on my lip. It stretched across the lip then turned at right angles

on both sides of my face up into my hair. My nose was cast, broken you know, One eye was closed and the other was open just enough so that I could take a squint in the glass." (A King William is a cigar.)

A week after the crash, On December 7, Navin came to Scranton and said, "I'm here to congratulate him on escaping death and get his name on a contract for 1912." Navin said he would pay Hughie so much he couldn't afford to die and reportedly offered him $18,000 per year for two or three years. Hughie signed right there in the hospital. Ned Hanlon, Hughie's manager with the Old Orioles, also visited Hughie in the hospital, as did boxer James "Gentleman Jim" Corbett. Hanlon said he wasn't surprised Hughie recovered. "He's got a good head in more ways than one and had hard bumps before. Knowing him as I do I felt all along that if there was a chance Hughey would come across."[4]

Hughie was hospitalized until December 17. When he was discharged he said he was done with automobiles. "No don't send any taxicabs to take me home. Get a pair of slow horses and a rig."[5]

Hughie's last words as he left the hospital were for Father Lynett, whose injuries turned out to be worse than initially believed. His broken ribs caused an injury to his lung. Tears welled up in Hughie's eyes. "Poor Father Lynett," Hughie said, "the poor fellow. I wish I could take the bruises he has. And yet he is such a patient man, such a good man, that if he wasn't with me I'm sure I'd have been killed."[6]

Hughie's remarkable recovery wasn't only a result of his physical toughness and undying positive outlook. It had been spurred on, too, because had something new in his life to live for, a wife. She was a Scranton girl, Nora O'Boyle, a school teacher at Scranton Central High School. Hughie met her in Philadelphia during the 1909 season. She was with a Scranton group which had taken a train excursion to Philadelphia to see Hughie pilot the Tigers.

"He was looking at the grandstand for friends when his spotted a dark-eyed young lady. She waved and shouted 'Hurrah for Detroit.' The Tigers got walloped that day and the players said it was Hughie's fault, that he acted like a man who was dreaming in the coaching box. Hughie admitted he was paying attention to the grandstand more than the field that day. He knew she was the one, he said."[7]

The next season, 1910, the Tigers were in Philadelphia in May, and Nora was again in attendance, this time with her father. After the game Hughie took Miss O'Boyle and her father to dinner and asked for her hand. His first wife, Elizabeth, had been gone for 12 years and it was time. Hughie and his fiancee set a date for January 9. At least that was the date they made public. Hughie's plan was to have the wedding a day later to, as he put it, "foil the rice throwers." Somehow the press got wind on the plan. On January 1 Joe Grillo wrote in his baseball gossip column in the *Washington Post*, "the secret is out here so he can go back to the original arrangement."

With the secret out, the wedding was a sensation in Scranton. St. Patrick's Cathedral and the sidewalks around it were packed. As Hughie put it, "ground rules were necessary."[8]

The ceremony was performed by the Rt. Rev. Edmond P. Prendergast, auxiliary bishop of Philadelphia, a cousin of the bride. John F. Murtaugh, state senator from Elmira, New York, and a college friend of Hughie's, was best man. Nora wore a broadcloth with pearl trimmings and long veil bedecked with orange blossoms. Her sister, Amelia O'Boyle, was bridesmaid. Rev M.F. Crane of Avoca, who had baptized Hughie; and the Rev. J.M. Mal-one, the rector of the cathedral who would 11

A 1910 card advertising Sweet Corporal cigarettes ("The Standard for Years") on one side and showing Hughie Jennings in his Detroit days on the other.

months later read Hughie his last rites after the car wreck, assisted the bishop. The Very Reverend Father Alexander, the vice-superior of St. Bonaventure, was there. Hughie gave his wife a diamond pendant, his best man a set of gold cuff links set with diamonds, and his ushers gold scarf pins. "On the way out Mr. Jennings' face beamed with the perennial smile which is one of his strongest marks of identification."[9]

The newlyweds left Scranton on the 1:55 train for Buffalo, where they stayed one day. "It will not be out of place to see the falls, so we'll go there." Hughie said. After seeing the falls they stopped in Chicago and El Paso, and finally in Los Angeles, where they honeymooned until late February. On February 25, 1911, they arrived back in Scranton, just in time to leave for the Tigers' training camp Monroe, Louisiana.[10] Fans who came to the training camp games in 1911 hoping to get to see one of Hughie's coaching-box shows were disappointed. He came down with a sore throat and his voice faded to a whisper. He was hospitalized and had an operation to relieve a growth in his ear. The doctor blamed a substance in the ear which affected the tubercular glands, and through them the throat. Nora stayed by his side as he missed a week of camp.

For Hughie the year 1911, which had started promisingly with a marriage in January and ended disastrously with a car wreck in December, had been unremarkable in between. Though the Tigers improved slightly from 1910, when they finished the A.L. season in third place, 18 games behind the Athletics, they still finished 13 games behind the Athletics in 1911.

On March 10, 1912, Hughie, still on the mend from the wreck, limped into training camp at Monroe, Louisiana, on a cane. His wrist and arm were so badly battered he couldn't whistle because he couldn't turn his hand enough to get his fingers to lips. And with only one good leg, he couldn't do his trademark kicks. Worst of all, he couldn't do what he did best, swing the fungo bat. Known as the best fungo hitter alive, he could hit a fungo as accurately as a throw. "My hand ought to come around," he said, "and I am sure that my leg will be all right after I take a few baths and run the track."[11]

In 1912 for the third consecutive season, Hughie started a training camp without an A.L. championship to defend. On August 20, 1911, with 40 games left, the Tigers had been five games behind the Athletics, but a series of injuries decimated the lineup and they went 20-20 over the last 40 games. Cobb was the only bright spot. His 1911 statistics were simply startling. He scored his 100th run in the Tigers 94th game. By season's end he had scored a league-leading 147 in 146 games. He also led the A.L. in batting (.420), slugging (.621), RBI (144), hits (248), doubles (47), triples (24), and steals (83).

Two seasons out of the pennant race was enough for Hughie. He was used to winning. Since 1894 he had been a player or manager on eight major league pennant-winning teams. With 30 players in camp, including 13 pitchers, Hughie was optimistic that the Tigers could get back on top in 1912. He was convinced the 20-20 finish in '11 had been an aberration. Instead it was a trend. The Tigers played .451 ball in '12 (69-84) and dropped all the way to sixth place. The 1912 season would have been totally forgettable, if it not for two things, a new park and a remarkable game on May 18 at Shibe Park in Philadelphia. After the 1911 season it was clear that 16-year-old Bennett Park was no longer worthy of Detroit. The "Paris of the West," with its tree-lined Grand Boulevard of magnificent homes claimed the world's greatest industrialist, Henry Ford; greatest architect, Albert Kahn; ballplayer, Ty Cobb, and baseball manager, Hughie Jennings. Now the city would have a ballpark in keeping with its greatness. A concrete-and-steel ballpark was built at "The Corner," as the site at the corner of Michigan and Trumbull Avenues was called, at a cost of $300,000. The city fathers suggested Navin name the place after himself. It later would be renamed Tiger Stadium. The signature feature of the park was a

125-foot flagpole in fair territory in dead center field. The park opened on April 20. More than 25,000 fans crammed into the park, which was designed to hold 23,000 in its yellow seats. Cobb put on a show, stealing home for the first of a record seven times that season. Cobb later made a couple of running catches in center field, as the Tigers won, 6-5. It was one of the few bright moments of the season. The Tigers finished below .500 and in sixth place for the second consecutive season.

A 1911 card for Piedmont cigarettes with a jubilant Jennings.

The series of events which led to the May 18 game at Shibe Park in Philadelphia, one of the most infamous games in baseball history, began three days earlier in New York. On May 15 in New York, Cobb came out to the park early for batting practice and immediately was heckled by a fan. This was nothing new and Cobb ignored him. But the fan, Claude Lueker, kept it up throughout the game. He called Cobb a moron and other nastier things. Cobb put up with the personal insults, but when Lueker said things about his sister and mother, Cobb went wild. Cobb said the comments which put him over the edge were "Your sister screws niggers" and "Your mother is a whore."[12] Lueker also reportedly called Cobb's mother a murderer.

Hughie, who later called Lueker's comments "opprobrious epithets", knew Cobb as well as anyone, and when he saw the expression on his face, he knew the heckler was in trouble. Cobb, followed by several of his teammates, jumped over the rail, pushed his way through the fans to Lueker, grabbed him by the neck and threw him down. As Cobb punched and kicked Lueker the fans around yelled, "Stop, he has no hands!" But Cobb continued kicking and punching and yelled, "I don't care if he has no legs."

It was true. Lueker had lost eight of his fingers in an industrial accident and was defenseless in a fight, not that he would have had any chance with three hands against the enraged Cobb. Cobb's teammates kept the fans from intervening and let Cobb pummel and kick Lueker. After at least a dozen punches and kicks, fearing Cobb would kill Lueker, his teammates pulled Cobb away. Lueker said he wanted Cobb arrested on the spot. Instead the police led Lueker away.

Two days later, Ban Johnson suspended Cobb indefinitely. When the

Tiger players heard about the suspension, they rallied around Cobb. Hughie was shocked at the players' emotional reaction. It was true that most of Cobb's teammates hated him, but they felt that Lueker's calling Cobb's mother a husband-killer and a whore was a bit much. It was more than they would have put up with themselves. Besides, they felt they had to take a stand against rowdy fans.

The Tiger players decided to strike to show their solidarity with Cobb. They were backed by three Detroit judges and a minister, who publicly denounced Johnson and several labor unions, which threatened a baseball boycott. After a rainout on May 17, they were due to play the Philadelphia Athletics in Philadelphia on May 18. To a man, the Tigers said they would not play unless Cobb played. Several sent Johnson telegrams to that effect. Johnson wouldn't be bluffed. He wired Navin that the Tigers would be fined $5,000 by the League if they didn't field a team.

Navin caught a train to Philadelphia sat down with Hughie and they came up with an idea. With the help of Aloysius Travers, the 20-year-old assistant manager of the St. Joseph's College team, Hughie rounded up a team of local amateurs. The plan was for the amateurs to take the field in Tiger uniforms if the Tigers refused to play, then have the game postponed on some pretext, thereby avoiding the $5,000 fine. With the assembled amateurs in the stands, Cobb and the Tigers put on their uniforms and practiced before the game as usual. When some of the A's said the Tigers were bluffing and would take the field when the umpire said "play ball," Jim Delahanty went to the A's bench and offered to bet $5,000 that no regular member of the Tigers would play unless Cobb played. Delahanty meant it as a challenge for the A's to join him and the Tigers. But Mack convinced the A's it was an internal matter with the Tigers and the A's didn't strike.

As game time approached, umpire Bill Dinneen told Cobb he was under orders. Cobb would not be allowed to play. Cobb walked off the field and the Tigers followed. Hughie pleaded with his men to play, but they were adamant. Cobb was moved by their support. "I play with the most loyal team in the world," he said. The Tigers went into the clubhouse and handed over their uniforms to the amateurs. Even then, Hughie held out hope that a fiasco could be avoided. But Mack, noting that 20,000 fans were in the stands, insisted there be a game.

So it was that Travers, Jim McGarr, Pat Meany, Jack Coffey, Hap Ward, Billy Maharg, Dan McGarvey, Bill Leinhauser and Ed Irvin put on Tiger uniforms. Two Detroit scouts, Joe Sugden, 41, and Jim "Deacon" McGuire, 48, completed the lineup, and scored the only two runs for Detroit. The Athletics won 24–2, the biggest rout in baseball history. The only recruit to hit for Detroit was Irvin, who hit two triples in three at bats and closed his major league career with a 2.000 slugging average. Only one of the players ever played in another major league game. Billy Maharg batted once for the Phils in 1916 and later turned to gambling. He was an accused conspirator in the Black Sox scandal of 1919. Travers pitched a complete game in his only major league game, giving up 26 hits and 24 runs in eight innings. He went back to St. Joseph's College and later became a Catholic priest.

The next day Ban Johnson laid down the law with Navin. The Tigers would either play Washington on May 20 or they would never play again in the American League. The threat worked. Cobb agreed to go back to work and the team followed him. The incident cost the Tigers twice what it cost Cobb. They were fined $100 for striking, while Cobb was fined $50 and suspended for 10 days.

The last batter in the top of the ninth inning of the remarkable game was cheered lustily by they fans who remained. Pinch hitter Hughie Jennings took a called third strike.[13]

22

Hugh Jennings, Esq.

James Donavan, Jr. took a mighty cut and hit a deep fly down the left field line, which carried out of the ballpark in Scranton, Pennsylvania. When it came down it was a foul ball — and a "fowl" ball as well. The ball crashed into a coop owned by Thomas Royce and killed his blooded rooster. Royce, claiming the rooster was worth $500, hired a lawyer, filed suit against the teenaged Donavan and his father, James Donavan, Sr., and demanded a jury trial. At the trial the Donavans' lawyer, Rufus Clarke, asserted the killing of the chicken was an unavoidable accident in a youth baseball game and that the great American pastime must not be trammeled and handicapped by absurd lawsuits. Then he turned his anger toward Royce's lawyer lamenting that, "the Scranton public saw, with pain and surprise, so eminent a baseball leader as Mr. Jennings arrayed against the interest of his own vocation."

Hughie rose and defended himself, as well as Royce's claim of injury. "The attorney for the defense holds the stand I have taken in this particular case indicates disloyalty to the great profession through which I have made my livelihood. Far be it from me."

Hughie went on to claim that the object of the game was to hit fair, not foul balls. The jury deliberated seven minutes and awarded Royce his full claim plus $250 for Hughie.[1]

Hughie had settled in Scranton from Novembers through Februarys after marrying Nora and buying a house on Vine Street, and joined his brother's law firm. In a sensational front-page murder case, Hughie and his brother were retained to defend a pair of brothers from Poland who were accused, along with three other immigrants, of beating a man to death for proposing marriage to a woman one of the men coveted. Hughie was removed from that case by the car wreck in 1911. His brother successfully arranged a plea bargain for the brothers in exchange for testimony against the other three, who were convicted. Working cases with his brother at their law offices was only part of Hughie's burgeoning off-season life. He was one of the founders of the Old Forge-Duryea Bank in Scranton and a director of the Traders Bank. He joined the Elks, Kiwanis, Irish-American Society, Red Cross, Chamber of Commerce, and Knights of Columbus. He became an icon in Scranton, a booming city which, as one of the earliest large cities in the country to have an electric trolley system, boasted of itself as "The Electric City." He was in demand as a speaker, addressing groups as diverse as the local Democrats and prison inmates.

Hughie Jennings when he practiced with his brother in Scranton in the early 1920s.

Hughie was wealthy by the standards of the day and was generous with his money. During coal strikes and at Christmastime he would get lists of destitute families from local parish priests and personally drop off care packages of food and clothing at the addresses. He also helped put his brothers through college and secretly aided down-and-out old ballplayers.[2] He was also known to use his automobile to transport miners to and from work. He paid attention to the city's youth, too. He often stopped at Scranton high schools to instruct boys on baseball.

When Hughie signed with the Tigers for the first time in 1907, his friends in Scranton started a Jennings-Coughlin Club. They organized train excursions to see the Tigers in New York and Philadelphia. Each winter, before Hughie and Coughlin went back to baseball, the club threw a lavish sendoff party. After several years Hughie picked up the tab and threw the party for the club. They dined on blue points, green turtle soup, and lake trout. They smoked Cuban cigars and listened to an Italian orchestra and an Irish tenor. Hughie offered a toast. "It gives me great pleasure," Hughie said, "to take the entertainment away from the members tonight and show you a little of the appreciation I hold for your kindness to me and Mr. Coughlin."[3] The party, as it did each year, went well into the next day. The morning after was once described this way: "Some who attend may bee seen with dress suits the next afternoon, but Hughie always puts on the brakes before he ever reaches such a stage in the proceedings."[4]

For winter conditioning, Hughie went to Pittston almost every afternoon and played handball at the YMCA with Bucky Harris. Pittston, the city of Hughie's birth and Harris' hometown, was a hotbed of handball. Some of the best players in the East came there to play, Hughie and Harris among them. They once beat the New York City champions, Gorman and Wynne.[5] Hughie also stopped in Pittston at night from time to time to watch Harris and his brother Merle play basketball at the Armory. In 1916 he signed Harris to his first professional baseball contract after a basketball game in Pittston.

As busy as he was, Hughie found time for pure fun in the off-season, too. When weather allowed, he played golf with his wife for 10 cents a hole. They played as if a championship depended on every shot. The story goes that Nora made a decent living at it.[6] College football was a favorite pastime. One October he took in a Penn-Brown football game with his old college buddy, umpire Billy Evans. According to Evans, Hughie made a startling admission during the game.

"I got my coaching style from watching cheerleaders," he told Evans. "It struck me that if one man could create such a feeling among thousands at a football game, a sort of cheerleader in a baseball game ought to make nine players enthuse."[7]

Hughie could count on a regular dose of fun every October when John McGraw hosted his annual reunion of the old Orioles. At least it was usually fun, as the year they got their old bat boy to drive them around to the city's night spots in a carriage. But at the 1913 affair, after a night of heavy drinking, McGraw blamed Robby, a Giants' coach, for the Giants' loss to the A's in the World Series earlier in the month. McGraw said Robby made too many coaching mistakes in the Series. Robby in turn blamed McGraw, and McGraw fired him on the spot. Eyewitnesses say Robby doused McGraw with a glass of beer and walked out. They didn't speak to each other for 17 years. Six days later Robby started a legendary 18 years as manager of the Brooklyn Dodgers.

After the 1912 season Hughie signed on to do a Vaudeville tour with Ben Smith, a famous blackface comedian, actor and singer. The musical skit, titled "The New Mascot," centered around a black boy, played by Smith, hired by Hughie to carry the Tigers' bats from the train station to the ballpark clubhouse. In the skit the black boy carried the bats to the park, but wouldn't go inside because he is afraid of Tigers. It was left to Hughie, in a straw hat and street clothes, to explain they were ballplayers, not Tigers. Hughie also told humorous baseball stories during the skit. In one, a player from the Sun Flower league tries out for the Tigers and Hughie tells him to go out in right. The kid freezes and says, "Excuse me, Mr. Jennings, I've never been to the Detroit grounds before, which one is right?"

In another bit, Smith, in blackface, comes out of the park and says, "There's a fellow in there that says he's from Georgia and doesn't like me because of my color." Hughie answers: "Oh, that's all right. He's a fine fellow and gentleman. That's Ty Cobb." Incredible as it may seem today, this passed for humor 95 years ago. At the end Hughie would pull out a mat of grass and demonstrate the Tiger signal system saying, "when I pull out one blade it's the signal for the batter to get a base hit. When I pull out two and throw one away it's a signal for sacrifice."

"What do you do when you want a home run?" Smith would ask, and Hughie would pull out a handfuls of grass and do his "ee-yah" dance and yell. For the finale, Hughie would join Smith in the chorus of "That's How I Need You."

The show opened in Detroit and played all over the Midwest and East. It appeared at Hammerstein's in New York City on a bill with 16 other acts and at F.F. Proctor's Theater on Broadway. It also played Scranton and Wilkes-Barre. A review in the Wilkes-Barre paper, perhaps kindly, made scant mention of Hughie's contribution. "While it is not the best act on the bill by any manner or means it is a novelty that is sure to become extremely popular throughout the big time circuit over which it is being booked. Ben Smith, well-known black face comedian and minstrel man, is the mascot and the fun revolves around the little ploy of engaging the colored boy. Mr. Smith has the best tenor voice Wilkes-Barre has ever heard. He has chosen the sweetest melodies that it has been our good fortune to hear in many a day. Mr. Jennings interprets some of the signals he gives from the coaching box."

In Scranton Hughie left the stage "amid a bedlam of applause and a bale of floral tributes." After the show closed in Toronto in February, Hughie said he was through with acting, and for once in his life admitted a lack of confidence. "This theatrical game is too hard work and too worrying. I suppose those who have made it their life's work do not suffer the strain that one like myself undergoes. It has me worrying all the time for fear that I will go wrong with my lines and break up the act or that I will fail to be well received by the audience."[8]

A review in the Indianapolis Star on December 25, 1912, suggested that Hughie would be wise to keep his day jobs. "Having seen his stunt we do not hesitate to say Hughey is some attorney and as a manager of a ball club he is a bear."

As Hughie became entrenched in Detroit through the 1910s, his popularity on the streets there soared just as it did in Scranton. In Detroit, unlike the humorless and paranoid Cobb, Hughie was a man of the people. Among Hughie's legions of fans in Detroit was a blind man nicknamed "Dud" who had a confectionery store on Porter Street which Hughie frequented. Dud summed up Hughie's impact on thousands of the city's citizens: "Rooting for the home team was the greatest pleasure in my life after the Jennings regime started."[9]

In Detroit Hughie lived in Glynn Court near a sandlot ballfield. Every day he went to the corner store for the late editions of the daily papers, where the sandlot boys who knew his routine waited for him. Hughie always stopped and chatted with them and encouraged them to keep trying to be good ballplayers and good boys. "First, he would say, be clean. Hughie dwelt on that clean idea. He didn't mean just physically, but mentally and morally as well. He wanted to be hard on the boys and tell them about the roughness of life in baseball, but it was difficult for one of his sweet disposition to be hard. The kids who met him in the corner would go away with passes for the game the next afternoon, but what was much more valuable they went away with some of Jennings' philosophy, which was a sweet and comforting philosophy."[10]

Perhaps the best testimony to Hughie's popularity in Detroit was that he was used in a successful scam. A swindler circulated around the upper-crust social events of Detroit one year, representing himself as a committee to collect funds to purchase a home for Jennings. Fans who shelled out checks included Michigan's 1st District United States House of Representatives Congressman, Edwin Denby, who later served as Secretary of the Navy. He lost $50 in the scam.[11] Apparently Hughie was as popular in the smoke-filled back rooms of Detroit as he was on the streets. Members of administration of the city of Detroit tried to add Hughie to the city's staff so he could be a permanent resident. They backed him as a candidate for the post of City Corporation Counsel. Said one city father, "It will take him little more time to direct the games at Bennett Park than it will the other city employees to watch him."[12]

Hughie wasn't just beloved in Scranton and Detroit. Everywhere the Tigers went he was feted with dinners by Cornell Alumni Associations, Kiwanis clubs and bar associations. YMCAs in every A.L. city laid out the red carpet for him. The years did not diminish his appeal in Baltimore, either. In 1914, Hughie had been out of Baltimore for 12 years, but he was still selling clothes in newspaper ads there for John H. Emerson Tailor, one of the city's leading tailors.

The ads read: "When Mother nature's groundskeeper Mr. Jack Frost locks up the baseball parks for the winter — he locks up Hughie Jennings, too. But in Hughie's place appears the honorable and dignified Hugh Jennings of Scranton PA — attorney at law, businessman, real estate owner, capitalist and Royal Tailored Man. The world respects Hughie as one of the greatest diamond generals it has ever seen. Which is, brethren, the main reason why Herr Jennings is a Royal Tailored Man. He carries the million dollar look because he has earned it. Big men like Hughie Jennings do not wear the best merchant tailoring just to look pretty. The wear made-to-order clothes because such clothes are genuine, sincere and in keeping with high standards of individuality."

During World War I, as he watched young ballplayers go into the army, it ate at Hughie that, given his age and physical history, he couldn't go with them. To compensate, he used his celebrity to help the war effort in small ways. In 1917, when the proceeds of a Detroit-Washington game were pledged to the war effort, Hughie sold tickets from a truck on downtown streets the night before. Hughie, Christy Mathewson, and Ty Cobb signed a ball which was auctioned off at a minor league game in Muskogee, Oklahoma, and brought $405 for the Red Cross.[13] But when Cobb, who had a draft deferment as the father of two children aged two and eight, joined the Army after the abbreviated 1918 season, Hughie had to find a way to go "Over There."

On September 17, 1918, he applied for a berth as athletic instructor with the Over Seas Service of the Knights of Columbus. During the war, the Knights, a Catholic service organization, served a role similar to the USO today. They set up "huts" at camps in the USA and in Europe, anywhere there were soldiers. They provided recreation and spiritual activities for the soldiers. Each hut was staffed by a K of C secretary and a chaplain. Hughie and other baseball men — Johnny Evers, Jack Hendricks, Bill McCabe and Jack Noonan among them — went to Europe to work with the soldiers in athletics. "When the secretaries of athletic reputation arrived overseas and commenced organizing sport exhibitions and competitions among the men, the effect was electrical. It is estimated that, everyday, 5,000 games of baseball were played by men of the A. E. F. with equipment provided by the Knights."[14]

On October 17 a collision in North Channel between two troop transports, the Otranto and Kashmir, cost 346 lives. In Wisconsin the *Sheboygan Press* reported that Hughie had been on board the Otranto on his way across to begin work as a member of the Knights of Columbus field force. It turned out not to be true. On October 12, 1918, in a letter to a friend, Hughie had written that he had been accepted, applied for his passport and didn't expect to be in France before November 1. Hughie's service, such as it was, came full circle on September 14, 1919, when he met General Perishing before a Detroit-Washington game in D.C.

23

The Tigers Are Tamed

Fittingly, Harry Coveleski delivered the pitch. After all, he had been rescued from the minor league scrap heap by Hughie Jennings. And after all, he and Hughie had a bond of loyalty only a pair of coal crackers from Pennsylvania hard coal country would understand. So it was fitting that Harry Coveleski threw the pitch that marked the beginning of the end of Hughie's reign in Detroit. Bill Carrigan, the Boston Red Sox manager, having inserted himself as a pinch-hitter, hit the pitch. It rolled sharply to Donie Bush at shortstop, a perfect double-play ball. Bush collected it cleanly and threw to Ralph Young at second base. The ball dropped from Young's glove onto the dirt of Fenway Park's infield as Duffy Lewis crossed the plate with the winning run. It was September 18, 1915, and the run Lewis scored gave the Red Sox a 1–0, 12-inning victory over the Detroit Tigers. It was the Red Sox' second consecutive defeat of the Tigers. When the Red Sox won again the next day, the Tigers' A.L. pennant hopes were effectively ended for the season that Hughie would call "my biggest disappointment in Detroit."[1]

No wonder, as Hughie won 100 games in 1915, the most in his 14-season tenure, yet finished second to the Red Sox, who won 101. The September 18 game had to be the most frustrating game of Hughie's most disappointing season. A Boston record crowd of 37,528 overflowed the grandstand and ringed the outfield. The Tigers loaded the bases twice with no outs and failed to score. In one of those bases-loaded situations, Cobb batted with no outs and hit back to the mound for a pitcher-to-catcher fielder's choice. In the ninth inning, a score was thwarted when Tris Speaker shouldered his way into the midst of the fans to catch a drive by Cobb. The failure of 1915 stung bitterly because Hughie had hopes that a pennant in 1915 would erase the failures of the previous five seasons, when the Tigers had finished third, second, sixth, sixth and fourth following their three A.L. championships in 1907, '08, and '09. Though the failure to win in 1915 helped doom Hughie in Detroit in the long run, in the short run it preserved his job. Hughie lasted five more seasons after 1915, in part because he teased Navin with just enough winning to offer hope for each succeeding season. There were other reasons Hughie survived. The two-year deal he signed from his hospital bed after the 1911 car wreck got him through 1913. The 100 wins in 1915 got him a further extension. But Navin retained Hughie for other reasons, too. For one, he did it to defy Ban Johnson, who continually pressured him to get rid of Hughie. For another, Hughie was flat out an effective manager, as evidenced by the fact that team presidents around the league were ready to hire Hughie away. Then, too, Navin was making money. In 1916 the Tigers drew almost 700,000 fans at home, almost 200,000 above the previous record. Still, in retrospect, it's amazing Hughie lasted as long as he did in Detroit. As early as 1911 there had been calls for his head among some factions in Detroit, and all along through the seasons there were attempts to hire him away.

In October 1911, it was announced that a famous shortstop was to be named manager of the Reds. In July 1912, it was rumored Hughie was headed to Boston to manage the Doves for a five-figure salary and an interest in the club. A report in the *Atlanta Constitution* said he was seriously considering it. An offer from president Noyes of the Washington Nationals, which included stock in the club, was not just a rumor. Hughie admitted the offer had been made and that he was interested. "I would like to get an interest in the local club and manage the team here. I have been treated royally in Detroit and well satisfied there. But I would have some of my own money in the club here and that is naturally the one thing that a fellow who has been in baseball for over 20 years strives for."[2]

In June 1912, it was speculated that Hughie would be fired after the season and replaced with Donovan. Hughie's $18,000 salary was one of the highest in the game, and Navin seemed to believe he wasn't getting enough bang for his buck. In a newspaper interview Navin said, "I am not at all satisfied with the way things are going. Jennings appears to have lost hold on his men. They seem to have no confidence in his judgment. Our pitchers have been handled poorly and the team has showed little science. In fact, under Jennings we have always won by the ability of the players, rather than by strategy. As Jennings is under contract we won't make any change right now. We want to give him a chance, anyhow. What we do next year depends on the showing of the Tigers between now and October."[3]

Curiously, despite all he had said, before the season was out, Navin signed Hughie to a two-year extension with a raise that made him the highest-paid manager in the American League through 1915. It was speculated that Navin and Yawkey gave Hughie the extension to rebel against

Ban Johnson. They resented being dictated to by Johnson, who wanted Hughie out for, as Johnson saw it, backing the players in the Cobb strike game and for openly rooting for McGraw's Giants in the 1911 World Series.

Hughie Jennings coaches for the Tigers around 1915. (National Baseball Library and Archive photograph.)

Over the next few seasons, even as the Tigers fell into the second division, league presidents continued to covet Hughie. In December 1914, Colonel Jacob Ruppert bought the Yankees for $450,000 and immediately said he wanted Hughie to manage. In 1915 Harry Sinclair, the backer of a New York team in the new rival Federal League, offered Hughie the manager's job. He said Hughie wasn't bound legally to Detroit for 1915 and was just the man for his team.

"There nothing to report," Navin said. "Jennings will be with the Detroit team next season and for many seasons to come, I hope."[4]

Though they would not seriously compete for the pennant, the Tigers did manage winning seasons in 1916, '17, and again in '19 when they went 80–60 and finished just eight games out. *Free Press* baseball writer Harry Bullion wrote that the Tigers were "man for man on paper as powerful as any collection of athletes in the league." Bullion had a case. Cobb had led the American League in batting in 1919 with a .384 average, and left fielder Bobby Veach was second at .355. Right fielder Ira Flagstead wasn't far behind at .331. Pitcher Hooks Dauss won 21 games. The Tigers were second in the A.L. in runs scored and team batting and first in team slugging percentage. So there was optimism in camp in 1920. After camp Hughie took the Tigers on a demanding barnstorming tour across the south with the Boston Braves. Day after day they played each other on backwater diamonds, dodging rain and hailstorms at every stop.[5] If Hughie's plan was to get the team ready for a grueling pennant race, it failed miserably. The Tigers and Hughie took a fall unprecedented in the history of the game. Beginning with a 3–2 extra inning loss to the White Sox in Chicago on opening day, the Tigers lost 13 consecutive games over 19 days. They didn't win until May 3, when they defeated Cleveland 5–1. It didn't matter that Cobb batted .158 during the streak, Hughie got the blame and his fate was sealed. By the end of the season the Tigers were in seventh place with a 61–93 record, 37 games behind the pennant-winning Indians. The losing changed Hughie. He became a poor loser. He looked for goats. He assigned blame. He retired his "ee-yah" and "atta-boy" cries and his jigs. The ever-present smile faded. Worst of all, for the first time in his life, he drank heavily. As Cobb put it, "he tried to find some solace in the bottle."[6]

On October 5, two days after the 1920 season mercifully ended, Hughie was called to a Chicago courtroom by Assistant State Atty. Replogle to testify in an investigation of game fixing in the 1919 World Series. Hughie didn't have any intimate knowledge of the alleged fix, but was called as an expert witness to explain how a seemingly slight error might have a deciding effect on the outcome of a game.[7] After his testimony he went back to Detroit, and on October 15 resigned as manager of the Detroit Tigers. He resigned, he said, because it would be beneficial to both him and the Tigers. He immediately left for Scranton and said he was going to practice law.

24

Hughie the Giant

On July 19, 1927, there was a commotion behind the Giants' dugout in the Polo Grounds. It started with a stir of recognition in the stands. A few fans began chanting the old ballplayer's name. A few more joined in and then hundreds took up the chant. Finally, with the help of his wife, the old ballplayer rose from his seat. Thin from illness and limping along on a cane, Hughie Jennings came down out of the grandstand and joined John McGraw on the field to a tumultuous ovation from 25,000 fans, among them thousands of injured war veterans. It was John McGraw Day. He was being honored for his 25 years, 10 pennants and three World Series titles with the Giants, but the Little Napoleon didn't mind sharing the spotlight with his best old buddy.

McGraw Day had started with a baseball game between teams of Broadway actors, Eddie Cantor and one Julius "Groucho" Marx among them. Mayor James Walker gave McGraw a mammoth silver loving cup with his image in an old Oriole uniform engraved on it. Famed aviators Commander Richard Byrd and Clarence Chamberlain, the first pilots to fly to the North Pole, Commissioner Landis, and boxer James Corbett all were cheered wildly.

"But," said the *New York Times*, "the greatest ovation was for a man who was not in the circle of celebrities, who did nor even appear on the program. He was Hughey Jennings, lifetime pal of John McGraw who out-Byrded Byrd in the size of his ovation. The freckled, smiling, battle-scarred veteran limping out to shake hands with McGraw struck the high sentimental note of the jubilee."[1]

After leaving Detroit seven years earlier, despite his claim that he was going home to practice law, Hughie had signed with the Giants before October was out.[2] McGraw called the position assistant manager and it was not just a title. Hughie's duties included opening training camps, scouting players, coaching third base and acting as manager when McGraw was sick or tossed by an umpire, both frequent occurrences. Hughie also reprised his role as the "ee-yah" man. "Jennings will earn his salt by manufacturing Giant pep. Jennings' job at present at least is to sing out his colorful 'ee-yahs,' pick grass and lavishly spill the Jennings brand of pep."[3]

Before his first home opener in a Giant uniform, Hughie and McGraw entertained the fans by playing short and third in warmups and taking batting practice. Baseball was fun again. Winning didn't hurt. Hughie's timing in arriving in New York was impeccable. The Giants hadn't won a pennant since 1917, but coinciding with Hughie's arrival they won four consecutive National League pennants and two World Series titles from 1921–24. The total of Hughie's full shares, two winners and two losers, came to $17,732.

The job came with social perks, too. In August of '21 Suzanne Lenglen, a French tennis star, came to a game at the Polo Grounds and "redoubtable Hughey" did the honors for the day. He showed her around the grounds, made the introductions and presented her with an autographed baseball as they were followed around by a "battery of motion picture men." She was said to be amazed by the speed of the ball and players.[4]

Hughie came to New York one year after Babe Ruth. Though he was friendly enough with the Babe that Ruth once invited him to go moose hunting, Hughie saw Ruth as the death of "scientific baseball" and didn't like it. He grudgingly gave the Babe his due saying, "never saw a batter like him and never expect to see another."[5]

The Giants played the Yankees in the Series each of Hughie's first three years. Hughie called the first game of the '23 Series of the best he was ever involved in. Casey Stengel won it with an inside-the-park home run with two outs in the bottom of the ninth, as Hughie frantically waved him home. In the seventh, first baseman George "High Pockets" Kelly made a sensational stop of a grounder by Ruth and threw a runner out at the plate. Hughie declared Kelly's play the best he had ever seen.[6]

Though neither Hughie nor McGraw ever disclosed the nature of the negotiations which brought Hughie to New York, it is likely they had talked about such a deal for years before. They regularly got together at least twice a year to celebrate their birthdays, which were five days apart in April, and for the Old Orioles' reunions in October. But they also spent time together during spring camps when Hughie was still with the Tigers. In 1916 and 1917 Hughie moved the Tiger camp to Waxahachie, Texas, 34 miles from the Giants' camp in Dallas. In 1917, Hughie and McGraw agreed to a spring tour between the Giants and Tigers. Traveling with an entourage of 75 people on special train of a half dozen Pullmans, they played a series of games in Dallas, Fort Worth, Oklahoma City, Tulsa,

Wichita, Manhattan, Kansas; and Kansas City. In Manhattan, at Kansas State Agricultural College, 2500 students paid World Series prices of $2 per ticket. Cobb, who was feuding with McGraw, refused to play, but an even more famous athlete did. Jim Thorpe played right field for the Giants in the last seven games.[7]

After the 1919 season, Hughie's next to last in Detroit, he and Nora went to Cuba with McGraw and his second wife, Blanche. Hughie and Nora and the McGraws expanded their relationship in New York. After the 1923 season the couples sailed to Europe. They saw the usual sights and toured a battlefield of the recent war. Hughie and Nora went to Rome and were received by Pope Pius XI. On a Paris street Hughie and McGraw ran into Moe Berg. As a rookie in '23 Berg had appeared in just 49 games. Berg was stunned when McGraw recognized him. "Listen kid," Hughie said. "He not only knows your name, he knows how to pitch to you, too."[8] On their return from Europe McGraw talked enthusiastically about organizing a baseball tour after the 1924 season.

In 1924 the Giants training camp was in Sarasota, Florida. Seven players and 10 newspapermen left on a special train from Penn Station on February 20. Pickups were made in Philadelphia and Baltimore. When the train got to Florida, Hughie was waiting for them. McGraw, who had business interests in Havana, was in Cuba again on a working vacation. Hughie ran the camp until McGraw arrived on March 1. Hughie ran the Giants again for five weeks in June and July of 1924, when McGraw went home to rest his knee. While Hughie was running the team, he made one notable move, putting rookie Hack Wilson in center field when Billy Southworth broke his hand. McGraw's leg, which was first injured in 1902, was put in a plaster cast and he was ordered to stay off it. When the Giants were on the road McGraw accepted his condition, but when they came home he couldn't take it anymore. He rented a room in a building overlooking center field. From there he watched the games and kept in touch with Hughie on a special phone hooked directly to the dugout. The scribes had a field day.

"I don't do as much directing as the papers have intimated," McGraw insisted. "Many stories have appeared saying I use a pair of field glasses and a private telephone to run the team from my window. That's not exactly true. I don't use field glasses. If I did I'd be accused of tipping pitches. I limit my moves to once in a while changing batters. I sent Bill Terry to bat for Frank Snyder the other day. Otherwise Hughey runs the team."[9]

In the 1924 World Series the Giants faced the Cinderellas of the A.L., the Washington Senators and their "Boy Wonder" manager, Stanley Ray-

HUGH JENNINGS
NEW YORK GIANTS – COACH   1922

Top: A 1991 card showing Hughie Jennings as coach of the New York Giants in 1922 and boasting of his 1945 Hall of Fame induction. *Bottom:* Hughie as he appeared when he was the New York Giants assistant manager for his longtime friend John McGraw from 1920–25. (National Baseball Library and Archive photograph.)

mond "Bucky" Harris, off-season handball partner of Hughie Jennings. Harris, 24, was the youngest manager in major league baseball. He was also the full-time second baseman. For Hughie, competing against Harris, who called him "Big Daddy," was like trying to beat his own son. Harris had been a breaker boy in the same breaker where Hughie had worked years earlier. Hughie and Harris's father Tom had been batterymates on an amateur team in Pittston. Bucky once said that It was only because of Hughie that Bucky's mother let him pursue a career in baseball. "She saw how far Jennings had gone," Harris once said. "And she encouraged me to keep on when she saw what the game meant to me."[10]

On the eve of the 1924 Series, Bucky Harris wrote a breakdown of the teams for the Washington Post. After going through the teams position by position he wrote, "There is however one other department that should be mentioned. That is coaching. The Giants have one of the greatest coaches who ever did duty in a base line — Hughie Jennings. In my mind he is a man any major league magnate could use as a manager. I got my first big league training from Jennings, my mentor. He took me south with the Detroit club in 1916. I never thought I'd meet him in opposition in the world series."

Though Hughie never found losing acceptable, losing to the Senators in the 1924 World Series wasn't the worst of it. Seeing his prodigy, Harris, play and manage so well at such a tender age was easy to take. Harris hit .333 in the series with two home runs and played like a demon at second base. And, too,

Hughie, for one of the few times in his life, was miffed at McGraw. McGraw had blamed him in the press for the 8–7 loss in game four. Hughie, coaching third, had sent a home runner who was tagged out. Within 24 hours of the seventh game of the final out of the '24 world series Hughie, McGraw and two teams of players which included Casey Stengal, Johnny Evers and several members of the Chicago White Sox sailed for Europe on the Canadian Pacific liner *Mount Royal*. The teams were scheduled to demonstrate baseball in England, Ireland, Scotland, France, and Italy, but disbanded because of poor turnouts before they reached the end. The English writers were merciless. "An inning by the dullest professional cricketer who has ever dawdled through the leaden hours on an English cricket ground had infinite variety when compared to the thwackings of a baseball star," was one example. In Dublin only 20 showed up for a game played in the rain. In France they were met a group of school children who were surprised that the ballplayers from New York weren't really "Giants." At most stops Hughie's antics amused the crowd more than anything. The French joined Hughie in his "atta-boy" and "ee-yah" yells. The *New York Times* noted that "the rooting of the Frenchmen evoked much laughter."[11]

Only two games on the tour drew decent crowds, both in England. In Liverpool more than 10,000 saw the White Sox beat the Giants 16–12. "Hughey taught a section of youth to 'atta-boy' until Everton Field began to sound like the Polo Grounds. He amused the Duchess of York when she saw him dancing waving, and plucking in his usual style."[12]

In London 7,000 attended, most of them to see, not baseball, but the King and Prince of Wales.[13] On November 20, after the tour disbanded early, Hughie took Johnny Evers on a side trip to Rome to meet the Pope. McGraw reportedly lost $20,000 on the trip and had to admit that baseball was never going to catch on Europe.[14]

Though the Giants had put together a 10-game winning streak under Hughie when McGraw was out during the '24 season, Hughie was a reluctant manager. He'd had his share of glory. He was 53 in 1924 and looked and felt older. He didn't miss the stress and scrutiny that came with running a major league ball team and which, in New York, was 10 times what it had been in Detroit. On the other hand, being the assistant suited him perfectly. For one thing, it paid well. Though the terms of Hughie's deal were never made public, given that the Giants had the highest payroll in the N.L. and that McGraw made $40,000, $20,000 for Hughie was not out of the question. Just as important, the assistant job was relatively stress-free, and gave him time to spend with Nora. They rented a house in New Rochelle. It was 45 minutes from Broadway and near a golf course and a beach. Nora made breakfast every morning when the Giants were home. Baked apples and cream were a favorite. In the afternoon she drove him to Polo Grounds and stayed for every game. Back home in the evenings she prepared dinner, then brought Hughie a cigar and a paper as he rocked on the front porch. If he needed her to, she would talk about the Giants as well as any male ballplayer or coach.[15] The local constabulary appreciated having Hughie as a resident. In July, Hughie was presented with a police badge by his friends on the New Rochelle police force. Police commissioner Enright is made the presentation and the Keith Boys' Band entertained.[16] This was the life for Hughie, but in 1925 it was interrupted.

McGraw spent most of the summer of '25 with his eyes swollen nearly shut and his nose running with blood due to a severe sinus problem.[17] Hughie found himself managing the team for half the season. In July the Giants held a slim lead over the Pittsburgh Pirates. The teams stayed within a game or two each other into early August, but then the Giants lost six of eight. On September 14 the Giants left for their last road trip five games back. McGraw was too sick to go and it fell to Hughie to lead the Giants to their fifth consecutive N.L pennant. But nine days later, when the Giants lost a doubleheader in St. Louis while the Pirates won their ninth straight, the race was over.

Hughie took it hard. He felt he had let his old friend down. But there was something else amiss. During the final weeks of the season he was not himself. He was moody, distracted and quick to anger. He still hit fungoes and ran a lap with the players at the end of each practice, but barely made it. At end of season he realized he had "a lack of pep" but he hid it. His wife finally figured out something was wrong when he said he didn't want to play 18 holes.[18] His condition was exacerbated by the news that greeted him when he got back to New York. Matty was dead. Christy Mathewson, the dashing Bucknell graduate who was the idol of the baseball world, died on October 8, the day before the World Series was to begin. Mathewson was a coal country product from Factoryville, 10 miles north of Scranton. McGraw, for whom Mathewson had pitched for 14 seasons,

HUGHIE JENNINGS

Hughie Jennings

was a pall bearer. The funeral was in Lewisburg, Pennsylvania. Hughie attended on his way home to Scranton. Mathewson, who had been gassed in World War One, died of tuberculosis.

Little did Hughie know that he had the disease, too.

25

The Long Decline

Afraid of what he might find when he got to the room, John McGraw walked down the hall of the Winyah Sanitarium in Asheville, North Carolina, with great trepidation. How relieved he must have been when Hughie Jennings met him at the door and without so much as a hello asked, "How do the boys look?" But McGraw, who had come to Asheville from Augusta after rain washed out the sixth game of an exhibition series between the Giants and Washington, didn't want to talk baseball right away. He looked his old friend over and said, "You're 15 pounds heavier. Where do they get that stuff that you are about gone?"[1]

For several days Hughie had been looking forward to seeing McGraw. Since the Old Oriole days they had always celebrated their birthdays together. It was April 9 in 1926 when McGraw walked in the room, and that was close enough. Hughie's birthday was April 2nd and McGraw's was the 7th. They drank a birthday toast and posed for a local photographer. They talked about Hughie's series of newspaper articles. The book-length series, which was called *Rounding Third*, was being syndicated in several newspapers, including the Bridgeport Telegram and Los Angeles Times. When Hughie again asked about the Giants. McGraw asked him, "when can I depend on you joining us."

A mist seemed to form in Hughie's eyes and he said, "I promised my wife I'd stay here until the doctors say I can leave."[2]

McGraw was just one of a string of visitors Hughie had in Asheville that April. When the Yankees and the Brooklyn Robins played an exhibition game in Asheville the ballplayers, Babe Ruth among them, went to see Hughie. He met the Yankees' new pair of infielders, Mark Koenig and Tony Lazzeri, and predicted that if they came through for Huggins, the Yankees would win the A.L. On April 9 Norman E. Brown, the sports editor of the *Central Press Syndicate*, visited. "I visited him for three reasons," Brown wrote in a syndicated story. "Because of my respect for him as a baseball man, because of my personal friendship and to learn the exact truth of his illness. He is not near death. He is not confined to bed. He is not prohibited from seeing visitors. Except for a cough he seemed healthy. He spends his time reading, writing letters, and napping on the porch and talking to his daily visitors. He takes automobile rides through the Carolina hills with his wife driving."

While Brown was with Hughie, Cobb walked in the room unannounced. He and Hughie talked baseball and Hughie wanted the complete rundown on the Tigers. Cobb had succeeded Hughie as manager of the Tigers. Nodding to Hughie, Cobb turned to Brown and said, "he let me grow up."

Winyah Sanitarium was known as a tubercular hospital, but when McGraw rejoined the Giants in Washington on April 11, he issued a flat denial that Hughie had tuberculosis or was even seriously ill. "I can't understand how such a report gained a foothold, it's an injustice to circulate such rumors. The day before I arrived at Asheville a report was published that he was critically ill. Is a man critically ill when he sits up and talks for an hour and a half? The truth is he had a breakdown following a complication of illnesses, including influenza and four ulcerated teeth. He has gained 10 pounds and expects to be out by May 1. He is making so much progress, the doctor visits him only once a week. I don't know when he'll be back with the Giants, but I told him he must not come back until he is completely recovered. His own health comes first."[3]

In a local paper, after the McGraw visit, Hughie countered rumors that he was sinking rapidly. "Never felt better since my arrival here. That report is false. In fact any visitors will be welcome to see me up to noon today." In the same story Nora also disapproved of reports sent out that husband was failing rapidly.[4]

It's likely that everyone, including Hughie and his wife, were being overly optimistic about his condition. When Hughie had gone home to Scranton after Matty's funeral the previous October he went to his family doctor, who diagnosed a nervous breakdown and sent him Asheville for complete rest, with orders for no visitors or activity. In February doctors said they would not be responsible if he insisted on going to the Giants' camp at Saratoga.[5] In March the *New York Times* reported that Hughie would be discharged within eight weeks. By the time finally did leave on June 12, he'd been in Winyah for a solid eight months. Even then he didn't go back to his busy life in Scranton. He and Nora rented a cottage at Mount Pocono, where he continued to rest. The most he did was motor to Scranton for a bank directors' meeting once a week. The 1926 baseball season came and went, and though Hughie was still under contract with the Giants he received not a dime from the club. Even worse, the club owners, Francis X. McQuade and Charles Stoneham, never visited him or so much as sent him a note. In December Hughie lashed out at the Giants.

"The day I suffered a nervous breakdown caused principally because I overexerted myself in an effort to give the Giants every ounce of my energy in 1924 and 1925 when McGraw was ill, Judge Francis X. McQuade and Charles Stoneham owners of the Giants absolutely deserted me. They cut me off the payroll and from that day to this never directly asked me by wire, letter, or word of mouth how I felt. They are ingrates and I am through with the Giants, as much as I would like to go back to my real friend John McGraw who stuck with me all the way through. True, the treatment I received from the Giant officials, excepting McGraw, is a matter between me and them and I hesitated to tell the public. But apparently from the queries I have received from newspapers and friends throughout the country the public would like to know."[6]

Stoneham responded by releasing copies of letters which showed that as late as October 26 of 1926 the Giants had offered to rehire Jennings as assistant manager for 1927. There was no denial, however, that Jennings was cut off the payroll in '26. Stoneham denied the Giants had treated Hughie shabbily. "Jennings had always been treated fairly by the New York Giants. In four of his five years with us he was paid a good salary, the largest paid an assistant manager by any big league club. He received four full world series shares. His job was kept open for him all last season and it was offered to him again a few weeks ago. We greatly regret the attitude taken by Mr. Jennings. If he feels that he has been neglected we assure him that such neglect was not intentional. Mr. McGraw, who represents our club in its relations with the players and coaches, has kept in touch with Mr. Jennings and has endeavored to express out great solicitations as to his welfare."

Hughie stood by what he said. He said that McGraw never brought greetings from the Giants, nor would he. "Stoneham's statement that he sent McGraw is ridiculous. Ridiculous because McGraw thinks so little of McQuade and Stoneham that he only speaks to them when he has to."[7]

The Giants took a public relations hit over the feud with Hughie, but as Hughie was in no condition to accept the Giants' offer to return to his assistant manager position, it died down after the New Year. Little was heard from Hughie during the first half of 1927. He continued to divide his time between Scranton and Mount Pocono and limited his activities to attending bank meetings and visiting his daughter Grace, who had married Dr. T.P. McWilliams, a prominent Scranton dentist, and his granddaughter, also named Grace.

Jennings with his granddaughter Grace McWilliams, circa 1920. Grace was about three years old. Today she is in her 80s. She still lives in Scranton where she is the mother of the city's mayor, Chris Doherty. (Courtesy Tom Doherty.)

In June of 1927 McGraw took the Giants to Olean, New York, to play the St. Bonaventure team as the main event in the dedication for the school's new athletic field. That Hughie wasn't there said much about his health. When McGraw learned the field was to be named "McGraw Field," he insisted he wouldn't accept the honor unless the name was changed.

"It would be an injustice to me, to the baseball world, and the college and what is most important to Hughey himself. The most pleasant experiences of my life were in the company of my friend here on these same grounds, which you would dedicate in my name today in the absence of my chum, an invalid. I consider it not only inappropriate but unfitting to call this McGraw field. Furthermore in the good name of Hughey I will not consent to it."[8]

Then, to a rousing ovation, he suggested the field be named "McGraw-Jennings Field." The Reverend Thomas Plassman, president of the college, agreed.[9]

Hughie stayed away from baseball and out of the news altogether until that day at the Polo Grounds—John McGraw Day, July 19, 1927—when he limped onto the field for one last ovation from his adoring fans. In August, he was so weak he went back to the sanitarium in Asheville, from where word came that he did indeed have tuberculosis. He recovered enough to go home and rallied for a time. He continued to make the bank board meetings and even felt well enough in early January of 1928 to help his brother with a court case. But a few days later, he was unable to get out of bed and was diagnosed with meningitis. Late in January he was to have attended a New York City newspaper banquet. He sent his regrets. "They're my best friends the newspaper boys. I wish I could have been with them. My associations with them have been one of the finest things in my in life." It was his last public statement.

During the evening on January 31 he drifted in and out of consciousness at his home in Scranton with his wife and daughter and four doctors at his side. Around midnight he became conscious and talked about baseball and his plans to write another series of articles about the game, but then slumped in the bed. One of the doctors bent over and eased him into a more comfortable position. Hughie opened his eyes, grinned a little, whispered hoarsely "atta-boy, doc," and died.[10]

26

The Saint in Uniform

Was Hughie Jennings mean or was he kind? Was he self-centered or was he selfish? Was he insulting and demeaning to other people or was he compassionate and helpful? Was he a vicious, anything-to-win competitor or was a he a fair-play, gracious loser? Was he serious or was he funny? Almost all of what we know about him comes from newspaper and magazine stories, many of them over 100 years old, and the Hughie that emerges, it would seem, was a complex personality who fit all of these descriptions. Because Hughie retired from baseball in 1924 when radio baseball broadcasts were in their infancy, there is no known recorded audio interview of him. No film of him was ever made. And because he died in 1928, people alive today would have to be near 90 years old to have known him when they were children.

Hughie's granddaughter, Grace Doherty of Scranton, is such a person. She remembers Hughie as a kindly, even saintly, figure in family lore who passed out five-dollar bills to the little children at family gatherings. Doherty also remembers a family story that illustrates that Hughie wasn't above using his celebrity to get what he wanted. Bob Keating, a young man from Scranton's neighboring town of Dunmore, married one summer when Hughie was in Detroit and planned to honeymoon in Detroit. When the couple wrote Hughie of their plans, he welcomed them and asked them to bring his teenaged daughter with them. As it was an overnight trip to Detroit from Scranton, it was a lot to ask of a newlywed couple, but they agreed.

"He expected them to do anything he wanted," Doherty said.

Aside from family stories such these, Hughie can only be known from what was written about him and by him. Hughie wrote numerous articles while he managed the Tigers, and a book ,"Our National Game." He also wrote a book-length series of syndicated newspaper articles called *Rounding Third*, which were published in 1925.

In the first two chapters of *Rounding Third* he wrote about his early life and his relationship with his father, but most of the book is pure baseball and Hughie reveals little of himself. The same is true of the *Our National Game*, wherein Hughie wrote about the development of baseball and about his favorite players. More helpful are the stories written about Hughie, especially those by Hugh Fullerton, Bozeman Bulger, and Malcolm Bingay.

Hugh Fullerton (1873–1945) was a baseball columnist and sports editor in Chicago, New York, Columbus, and Philadelphia for nearly half a century. He was the recipient of the 1964 J.G. Taylor Spink Award from the Baseball Hall of Fame. Fullerton once described Hughie this way: "Fiery-tempered, and uncultured, Hughey is the best type of fighting Irish. He can fight and forget. His best friends are those he fought with. He has a cheerful disposition and never lost the boyish spontaneous grin. Umpire Tim Horst called it 'the grin that echoed back from the stands.' As a player he was wiry, tough, agile and quick. It was said he could not hit yet he batted .300 or better for six seasons with high of .401. He wasn't fast but became a great base runner. He had no schooling yet became a college graduate and lawyer. Scoffed at as a manager, it was said he was too impulsive and too good a fellow to succeed, yet he reached the World Series in his first three seasons."

Bingay was born 1884. Though in the 1930s he became editor-in-chief of the *Detroit News* and the author of several books on Detroit history and the automobile industry, he was a young sports reporter and columnist when Hughie came to Detroit in 1907. Bingay became Hughie's most fervent admirer. He believed Hughie had a profound effect on the evolution of the Tigers and the city of Detroit. "It was he who built the great park at Michigan and Trumbull," Bingay wrote in one of his columns. "Not his strong arms, not his baseball skill, not his money, but his spirit. Hughie Jennings came to Detroit in the beginning of this city's transition from small town to roaring metropolitanism. He played no small part in that change. The city's metamorphosis during his 14 years astounded the world."

Bingay also saw Hughie as a man who could easily fit into any strata of society, and a man who was loyal, gentlemanly and spiritual. "His gentility was innate. Ask not the members of the cloisters clubs of Detroit who knew him well, but the newsboys of the streets, the inmates of the orphanages, the old baseball fans, and above all the hard-handed, bent men of the mines in the blackened hills and valleys of Pennsylvania.

"I have met many people, some world famous, some great scholars, some of great wealth, but none ever taught me more about the ways of life than did Hughey Jennings.

"A redheaded Irishman who would fight at the drop of a hat, but he had a spiritual understanding I think some of the superior saints possessed. Not that Hughey always made use of that understanding in his own way of life."

By that last sentence, Bingay was referring to Hughie's behavior on the field. From the time the umpire said "play ball" until the last out, Hughie was a different man and he believed that was the way it was supposed to be. "Whatever the game he played it to the letter and spirit of the rules," Bingay wrote. "In handball he always conceded a disputed point. So it was in tennis, cards and golf, it was always sportsmanship, but he used to say 'baseball is different. In professional baseball one must concede nothing.'"

Hughie certainly conceded nothing to the umpires. Though not in McGraw's league as an umpire baiter, Hughie confronted umpires regularly, but he rarely cursed. To Hughie "you lump of cheese" was an epithet. It wasn't just that he thought umpires made bad calls. He sometimes thought they were out to get him. "If the umpire is incompetent or biased, I'm justified in making a scene," he once said.

Yet once the game was over, Hughie instantly changed back to his real personality. Not even the umpires could hold a grudge against him. Billy Evans, a Cornell player under Jennings and later an umpire, took abuse from Hughie on disputed calls, but never said anything negative about him. "Jennings was first ballplayer described as colorful," Evans said. "Every game was a honorable battle to Hughey. His opponents admired him for his style of play as he was even-tempered and extremely personable."

Stoney McLinn, a sportswriter with the Philadelphia *Evening Public Ledger* once put it this way, "Hughey had that happy faculty of always being the same. In defeat, as well and victory, he was, on the surface, a smiling happy-go-lucky individual, seemingly without a care."

In that vein he was a joker. "There are thousands of laughs in baseball," he often said. Why even the ball itself wears a perpetual smile." To prove his point he'd pick up a baseball and put two dots of mud for eyes above an upturned seam which made a smile.[1]

Hughie could toss off a one-liner, as when he called it the Michigan State League "a tennis shoe league" and said, "the teams had one cap and each fellow who went to bat wore it."[2] In his favorite oft-told joke, he explained baseball was 2,500 years old. "It's not generally known," he'd say, "that Nebuchadnezzar was the first pitcher mentioned in history. The Bible mentions it in the last chapter of the Second Book of Kings, which says, 'And it came to pass in the ninth year of his reign in the tenth month and in the tenth day of the month, that Nebuchadnezzar the king of Baby-lon came and he and all his hosts against Jerusalem and pitched against them.'"

Bingay noted how he left his rivalries on the field. "Though known as the most fierce fighter on the diamond and one so game that it was said of him that they would have to cut off his head before he would quit, I do not think Hughey ever hated a living soul."

He couldn't hate and stay true to his religion. A devout Roman Catholic, he was sometimes called the "Saint in Uniform." He attended Mass daily when he wasn't on the road. At home in Scranton or Detroit after a day's work in his law office or Tigers' manager's office he knelt before a makeshift tabernacle and said the rosary. On the road it wasn't easy to get to church regularly, but Hughie usually managed to find a Mass. When he did he took the players with him. There were more Catholics in professional baseball than in the general population, 50 percent by one esti-mate. This was because of the large amount of Irish players, and because Catholic schools took more interest in athletics than public schools in the late 19th and early 20th century.[3]

Another Detroit writer who wrote fondly of Hughie was H.C. Walker. On August 18 in 1920 in his Sportology column in the Detroit Times, he recalled a day when Hughie made sure his Tiger ball players got to Mass.

> If I were the mother of a ballplayer I would rather see my son sign up to play with Hughey Jennings' club than with any other club. He was guide, counselor and friend to each of the boys. He is a good solid 18 carat gold man himself and he wants his boys to be so. No man ever took the advice of Hughey Jennings or followed his example and made a moral mistake.
>
> On Saturday nights when the team was traveling I heard him urge the boys to get up early and go to church. On long jumps through the south on spring training trips he studied the train schedule to see where the train would be during church hours the following morning. Once the train stopped at a little sliding in South Carolina for an hour between 4 and 5 o'clock Sunday morning. Hughey had telegraphed ahead to the town and learned there was a mass at 4 o'clock in the morning. Hughey went through the train the night before, canvassed the Catholic players and urged them to be ready to leave the train when it stopped at the siding. He personally led the small band of his own faith out through the railroad yards before the sun was up. It was Palm Sunday and each of the boys brought back a palm.
>
> That was characteristic of Hughey. He believed that a man who was true to his faith was a better man and a better ballplayer. He didn't care what a man's faith was for Hughey was the most tolerant of men, but he wanted each man to be true.
>
> Scores of times I have seen similar actions. It is not easy to go to

church when one is flying through the country often not stopping on Sundays save for an hour at some obscure station and most of the boys admitted they would have slept peacefully on if not for the personal interest of Hughey. It was Hughey their friend not their manager who acted on such occasions."[4]

On a trip to Rome in 1924 he visited 110 churches in 10 days. At home in Scranton, Hughie's Catholicism was legendary. He went to mass daily at St. Peter's Cathedral, where both his marriages and his funeral were public spectacles. One off-season he was asked to write a piece for the Scranton Diocese newspaper, the *Catholic Light*. Hughie chose the perils of being a big league ballplayer as his theme.

When I consider the snares and pitfalls in the path of a young man in baseball the percentage of lapses from the straight and narrow is small. He may have been born and brought up, and frequently is, in a country town. Suddenly he is transplanted in a large city, and paid a salary three or four times more than he could make at home. Companionship around hotels and the lures of the city are constantly inviting to him.

It is possible for a manager to go to bed with the chickens and tell the next morning which members of the team were out late. A player has to be in the pink of condition to give his best efforts to his team. If he retires at a reasonable hour and is refreshed with good sleep his face bears unmistakable evidence of that. He is not only able to play his best, but when the crucial test comes he can meet it because his nerves are not strung.

The team that has a few 'lushers' on its roster very rarely gets high in the race. Many a good player has cut his career short by overindulgence in worldly pleasures and acting the part of the good fellow.

The behavior of players is giving managers less trouble every year. This is true in other lines of enterprise. Railroads have no use for boozers.

If I find a player burning the candle art both ends, I advise him that even the best behaved player has a limited career. As a player he should make hay when the sun shines. I endeavor to convince him that carrying his month's salary around is a hazard from several standpoints. If he doesn't lose it outright, it will go away from him in other ways. I try to get him to bank it or send it to his mother, if he is fortunate to have one living.

Fierce loyalty was another of Hughie's personality traits. He never forgot the miners back home. One off-season he was visited in his Scranton law office by a Detroit writer. During their conversation, Hughie checked his watch, then suddenly jumped up and ran to the door. The writer followed. With Hughie driving his brand new E-M-F automobile they drove to a trolley stop where they packed as many miners into the car as they could and drove them to work at a breaker 10 miles away. Later, at the end of their shift, Hughie went back and picked them up.[4] Hughie knew that it was the miners and other ordinary men like them who made him, and he never forgot that. "It has long been a hobby of mine that the man who comes out to the game with 25 or 75 cents or maybe a dollar in his pocket should be given all the attention," he once said in a newspaper interview. "Treat him as kindly when he is trying to fight his way to a spot to stand in a crowd of 25,000 as if the stands were practically empty and he had his choice of 1,000 empty seats. The thing we must never let out of our sight is that if there were no baseball fans there would be no baseball games. Were I a magnate I would instruct every player, every subordinate, every employee to remember that it is from the men, women and children who love the sport that we get the authority to live and have our being."[5]

Though Hughie was not a racist or anti-Semite, he did accept the stereotypes of nonwhite and non-Christian people, which were almost universal among white males during his lifetime. He saw nothing wrong with the premise of the Vaudeville skit he performed with the blackface actor Ben Smith, which depicted a black man as an ignorant lackey, and he had this to say when asked about the lack of Jews in baseball: "From the ages of six to 12 is the most important period in the development of a ball player. He must master the fundamentals and train the muscles used in baseball. It is an absolute physical impossibility for a boy to shun baseball until he is 14 or 15 and then hope to become proficient. During the period when a youngster should be playing baseball if he wants to be a star, the Jewish boy is learning the fundamentals of business and the art of making money."[6]

Despite his lack of an early education, Hughie had an innate wisdom about dealing with people and a clever way of expressing them. Bingay collected a group of sayings which he called "maxims of Hughey." He wanted to turn into a book, though he never did. Here's a sampling of Bingay's Maxims of Hughie which ran in his columns.

Never waste your time scolding a man who has not got the goods. It is not his fault.

Never rebuke a man in anger, because when you are angry your reasoning is not sound; your emotions are speaking and not your heart. Let him know by scolding him you are paying him a compliment. Let him know if you didn't think he had the right stuff you wouldn't be wasting time and energy on him.

Above all things: you can not demand respect, you must earn it. Lip loyalty is a sin in the eyes of God, for the man who gives it and receives it."

* *Never scold a man for making mistakes. Merely explain to him. The man who never makes mistakes is the man who never does anything.*

* *No one in this world has ever batted .1000 in any walk of life.*

* *When the fight is over get it out of your system. If you don't the good fighting spirit sours and turns to hate, then you poison yourself and not the other fellow.*

* *Play the game the best you can then, win or lose, you will have no regrets down inside yourself. It isn't the winning that counts so much, but the way you have played that tells through the years.*

* *Time and energy are limited. You have just so much of both.*

* *Instill into every player that errors are as much a part of baseball as hits. If the executive in other walks of life could be made to realize this his lot in life would be a lot happier.*

* *As soon as the ninth inning has been played remember that tomorrow is another day. Keep that in mind whether you have won or lost. If you have won that thought will keep you from being overconfident. If you have lost it will give you courage.*

While Hughie was well-known and respected across America and to an extent in Europe during his lifetime, in the Scranton area he is still revered and has left a legacy. Among his 11 great grandchildren is Chris Doherty, Scranton's mayor.

27

Hughie in the Hall

When the results of the first Baseball Hall of Fame ballot were announced on January 29, 1936, Hughie Jennings appeared on just four of 226 ballots filled out by the baseball writers. While at first glance that sounds like a slight for a man who had been so beloved by the scribes, it wasn't. After all, the writers had been charged to select inductees from anybody in baseball since 1870 and of hundreds of eligible men only five — Ty Cobb, Babe Ruth, Walter Johnson, Honus Wagner, and Christy Mathewson — made the cut. Joining Hughie on the list of men who did not appear on 75 percent of the ballots needed for election were Cy Young, Rogers Hornsby, Grover Alexander, Jimmy Foxx, and Lou Gehrig.

Hughie appeared on a higher percentage of ballots in each of the next four elections: 8.7 percent in 1938; 12 percent in '39; 27 percent in '42; and 37 percent in '45. In the January 1945 elections Hughie was the 12th highest vote-getter after Frank Chance, Rube Waddell, Ed Walsh, Johnny Evers, Miller Huggins, Roger Bresnahan, Mickey Cochrane, Jimmy Collins, Ed Delahanty, Clark Griffith and Frankie Frisch, none of whom received the required 75 percent. Since that followed an election in '42 where only one man, Rogers Hornsby, was elected, a log jam of deserving players was piling up at the door to the Hall.

In August of 1944, three months before his death, Commissioner Kenesaw Landis, who ruled the hall as dictatorially as he did major leagues, gave the veterans' committee the power to elect members on its own. Previously the group, which included Connie Mack, and was officially called the Hall of Fame Committee, was only able to make recommendations and vote along with the writers. In April of 1945 the committee made its first selections, and Hughie Jennings joined the Cooperstown baseball immortals along with James O'Rourke, Dan Brouthers, King Kelley, Wilbert Robinson, Ed Delahanty, Jimmy Collins, Hugh Duffy, Fred Clarke, and Roger Bresnahan.[1]

Based on Hughie's overall career as a player, a statistical argument against his inclusion in the Hall of Fame could be made. His career average was .318 and he hit just 18 home runs in 4,903 at bats. On the plus side, in 1,285 games he had 1,527 hits and scored nearly 1,000 runs. And, of course, he is still the all-time leader in being hit by pitches with 287. He was hit 51 times in 1896 and 46 times each in 1897 and 1898, good for three of the top four spots on the single-season leader board.

Whatever the value of his lifetime numbers, Hughie earned his plaque during his five full seasons in Baltimore in the 1890s. From 1894–1898 he never batted below .328 and hit a high of .401 in 1896, a record for short-stops. In the seventh edition of *Total Baseball* Hughie had the highest Total Player Rating in the major leagues in 1895, '96, and '97. In 1895 he had 124 RBI with four home runs and in '96, 121 RBI with one home run. Hughie's ability to hit a ball a 400 feet with a fungo bat showed he likely had much more power as a than his statistics would indicate. In addition, he stole between 28 and 70 bases in each of those five peak seasons, and was the leader in fielding average four times and shortstop putouts three times. But his contribution as a fielder at shortstop went beyond the statistics. He revolutionized the position. From a 1907 newspaper story: "He was the best fielder the game has ever known. Absolutely without regard for his record which means he didn't care whether or not the official scorer chalked up an error against him. He went after drives that other shortstops wouldn't dream of and though he did not always do the impossible, he did do it enough times to stamp him as the wonder of the decade. He covered more ground than any other shortstop. No shortstop of his day or since had more chances than Jennings and the record shows he had an average of 6.43 per game for 12 seasons. It's rare for a shortstop to average over six for a single season. He was able to get what came his way without wasting a second and able to get the ball away from almost any position the body can assume."[2]

In the book *A Baseball Century, the First 100 Years of the National League,* published by Macmillan in 1976 for the 100th anniversary year of the National League, Hughie was selected as the shortstop on the league's first quarter century (1876–1900) all-star team. In The *Bill James Historical Baseball Abstract,* James selects Hughie as the shortstop on his 1890s major league all-star team.

Though Hughie is in the Hall as a player, Mack and the veteran's committee could not have ignored his managerial and assistant managerial career or his personality. His managerial record, including 76 games as manager of the Giants, was 1184–995 for a .543 winning percentage. His 1131 wins as manager of the Tigers was a franchise record which lasted over 70 years until Sparky Anderson got win number 1132 on September 27, 1992. As a player Hughie played on five pennant winners and as a manager and coach he was on seven pennant winners.

His managerial style was player-friendly. McGraw put it this way: "The player who feels humiliated by his comrades has a friend in Jennings. Hugh always patted him on the back and told him never mind it and play all the harder. In 1907 he took hold of a team when it was disorganized and torn by internal dissentions. By sheer force of character and energy he captured the American league pennant."[3]

Hughie was by all accounts was a great motivator, batting tactician, third-base coach, and baserunning and fielding instructor. As a manager he had a major flaw — in an era when all managers burned out pitchers, Hughie was one of the worst offenders.

In 1907 four Tiger pitchers pitched 1205 of 1370, or 89 percent of all available innings. Beginning in 1908 Hughie had 24-year-old Ed Willett pitch an average of 250 innings per season, through 1912. A year later Willett was out of the major leagues by age 29. When Ed Summers came to the Tigers as a 23-year-old in 1908, Hughie pitched him over 301 innings as a rookie and 280 his second year. In 1912 Summers was released after three games and 16 innings. He was 27.

Hughie's mishandling of pitchers wasn't just about the statistics, it was the way he thought about them. To Hughie if a pitcher was good, he was good and he was better than the alternative in the 17th inning of a game or the 340th inning of the season.

He wrote extensively about pitchers and pitching in several chapters of *Rounding Third* where he revealed that relief pitching was ruining the game, that the ability to pitch mega-innings was more in the pitcher's head than his arm, and that strikeouts by pitchers were not necessarily a good thing.

> One thing that often disgusts followers of base ball in these days is the frequent changing of pitchers. In my opinion the fellow that invented the bull pen did not do the game any good. The manager who first thought of using relief pitchers contributed nothing to the advancement of base ball.
>
> Not since the days of Walsh and Chesbro, 15 and 20 years ago, have pitchers thought they could do much work. When two or three hits are made off them, they immediately look to the bench in an appeal for help. Surely the race has not changed; men are as strong today as they were 20 years ago. It has simply become the custom to yank pitchers. Two, three and four are used in a game, sometimes five. If a manager gets one man each week to pitch nine full innings he is doing well. Pitchers have fallen into the habit of thinking that it is impossible for

them to pitch nine innings. They do not make men bigger today than they made them 30 years ago; rather they did not make them bigger 30 years ago than today. At that time a pitcher thought nothing about working every other day. Imagine the present pitcher working every third day. The fact that a pitcher strikes out many batters does not always signify greatness. It means that he has a lot of stuff but it does not mean that he is putting much thought behind his pitching. He is not pitching every ball with purpose.

Hughie wasn't much of a fan of batters either. He never reconciled himself with what he called the "modern game." He wrote the following passage at a time when only Ruth had ever hit more than 27 home runs in a single season.

Scientific batting has been gradually going out of the game. In batting practice a man hits the ball over the fence. Watch the result! The next batter tries to imitate him, and the next. You will find them all trying for distance; all wanting to hit home runs. There is something exhilarating about driving a ball over the fence; players like the thrill and the public also likes it.

Batters get to swinging on the ball in practice and they do the same thing in games. They no longer choke up on their bats. The lively ball has squeezed much of the sacrifice and hit and run work out of base ball. There are few good bunters in the game today and there are few men who are effective on the hit and run. The reason is simple. Hitting comes natural to a ball player while bunting and running do not. It takes long and hard practice to master the art of bunting and to get the knack of chopping a ball and pushing it through an opening on a hit and run. Players do not like to bother with the fine points involved in executing these moves, preferring to stand up at the plate and swing, for that is simpler and easier."

Simpler and easier was not Hughie Jennings' way.

Appendix A
1896 National League Hitting Leaders

Runs

1. Jesse Burkett	160		6. George Van Haltren	136
2. Willie Keeler	153		7. Mike Tiernan	132
3. Billy Hamilton	152		8. Ed Delahanty	131
4. Joe Kelley	148		9. Bill Everitt	130
5. Bill Dahlen	137		**10. Hughie Jennings**	**125**

Hits

1. Jesse Burkett	240		6. Ed McKean	193
2. Willie Keeler	210		7. Mike Tiernan	192
3. Hughie Jennings	**209**		8. Billy Hamilton	191
4. Ed Delahanty	198		9. Joe Kelley	189
5. George Van Haltren	197		10. Bill Everitt	184

Singles

1. Jesse Burkett	191		T6. Bill Everitt	153
2. Hughie Jennings	**173**		T6. George Van Haltren	153
3. Willie Keeler	171		8. Gene Demontreville	146
T4. Patsy Donovan	155		T9. Ed McKean	145
T4. Billy Hamilton	155		T9. Mike Tiernan	145

Doubles

1. Ed Delahanty	44		7. Sam Thompson	28
2. Dusty Miller	38		T8. Jesse Burkett	27
3. Joe Kelley	31		T8. Mike Griffin	27
4. Bill Dahlen	30		**T8. Hughie Jennings**	27
T5. Jack Doyle	29		T8. Tommy Tucker	27
T5. Ed McKean	29			

RBI

1. Ed Delahanty	126		7. Jack Doyle	101
2. Hughie Jennings	**121**		T8. Joe Kelley	100
3. Hugh Duffy	113		T8. Herman Long	100
4. Ed McKean	112		T8. Kip Selbach	100
T5. Cupid Childs	106		T8. Sam Thompson	100
T5. Heinie Reitz	106			

Stolen Bases

1. Joe Kelley	87		**6. Hughie Jennings**	**70**
2. Bill Lange	84		7. Willie Keeler	67
3. Billy Hamilton	83		8. Jake Stenzel	57
4. Dusty Miller	76		9. Eddie Burke	53
5. Jack Doyle	73		10. Bill Dahlen	51

Average

1. Jesse Burkett	.410		6. Billy Hamilton	.365
2. Hughie Jennings	**.401**		7. Joe Kelley	.364
3. Ed Delahanty	.397		8. Elmer Smith	.362
4. Willie Keeler	.386		9. Jake Stenzel	.361
5. Mike Tiernan	.369		10. Cupid Childs	.355

SLG

1. Ed Delahanty	.631		6. Bill Joyce	.518
2. Bill Dahlen	.553		7. Mike Tiernan	.516
3. Tom McCreery	.546		8. Elmer Smith	.500
4. Joe Kelley	.543		9. Willie Keeler	.496
5. Jesse Burkett	.541		**10. Hughie Jennings**	**.488**

OBA

1. Billy Hamilton	.477		6. Cupid Childs	.467
2. Hughie Jennings	**.472**		7. Jesse Burkett	.461
3. Ed Delahanty	.472		8. Elmer Smith	.454
4. Bill Joyce	.470		9. Mike Tiernan	.452
5. Joe Kelley	.469		10. Bill Dahlen	.438

Total Bases

1. Jesse Burkett	317		7. Ed McKean	267
2. Ed Delahanty	315		8. Bill Dahlen	262
3. Joe Kelley	282		**9. Hughie Jennings**	**254**
4. George Van Haltren	272		T10. Fred Clarke	246
5. Willie Keeler	270		T10. Bill Joyce	246
6. Mike Tiernan	269			

Total Average

1. Joe Kelley	1.430		6. Bill Dahlen	1.254
2. Ed Delahanty	1.405		7. Bill Lange	1.177
3. Billy Hamilton	1.316		8. Jesse Burkett	1.176
4. Bill Joyce	1.306		9. Mike Tiernan	1.164
5. Hughie Jennings	1.263		10. Elmer Smith	1.155

Hit by Pitches

1. Hughie Jennings	51		T6. Fred Clarke	14
2. Bill Joyce	22		T6. Tommy Tucker	14
3. Joe Sullivan	20		8. Dummy Hoy	13
4. Steve Brodie	18		9. Joe Kelley	12
5. Jake Beckley	15		10. Patsy Donovan	11

Appendix B

Playing Career Statistics

Year	Tm	Lg	G	AB	R	H	2B	3B	HR	RBI	SB	BB	SO	BA	OBP	SLG	OPS	OPS+
1891	LOU	AA	90	360	53	105	10	8	1	58	12	17	36	.292	.339	.372	.712	104
1892	LOU	NL	152	594	65	132	16	4	2	61	28	30	30	.222	.270	.273	.543	70
1893	LOU	NL	23	88	6	12	3	0	0	9	0	3	3	.136	.174	.170	.344	-5
	BLN	NL	16	55	6	14	0	0	1	6	0	4	3	.255	.339	.309	.648	71
	TOT	NL	39	143	12	26	3	0	1	15	0	7	6	.182	.240	.224	.464	26
1894	BLN	NL	128	501	134	168	28	16	4	109	37	37	17	.335	.411	.479	.890	110
1895	BLN	NL	131	529	159	204	41	7	4	125	53	24	17	.386	.444	.512	.957	143
1896	BLN	NL	130	521	125	209	27	9	0	121	70	19	11	.401	.472	.488	.960	152
1897	BLN	NL	117	439	133	156	26	9	2	79	60	42		.355	.463	.469	.932	146
1898	BLN	NL	143	534	135	175	25	11	1	87	28	78		.328	.454	.421	.876	149
1899	BRO	NL	16	41	7	7	0	2	0	6	4	9	0	.171	.346	.268	.614	68
	BLN	NL	2	8	2	3	0	2	0	2	0	0		.375	.375	.875	.250	232
	BRO	NL	51	175	35	57	3	8	0	34	14	13		.326	.424	.434	.859	134
	TOT	NL	69	224	44	67	3	12	0	42	18	22	0	.299	.408	.420	.827	125
1900	BRO	NL	115	441	61	120	18	6	1	69	31	31		.272	.348	.347	.694	87
1901	PHI	NL	82	302	38	79	21	2	1	39	13	25		.262	.342	.354	.696	100
1902	PHI	NL	78	290	32	79	13	4	1	32	8	14		.272	.330	.355	.685	111
1903	BRO	NL	6	17	2	4	0	0	0	1	1	1		.235	.316	.235	.551	60
1907	DET	AL	1	4	0	1	1	0	0	0	0	0		.250	.250	.500	.750	134
1909	DET	AL	2	4	1	2	0	0	0	2	0	0		.500	.500	.500	1.000	210

Appendix C

Managerial Career Statistics

Managerial Record

Standing	Year	Team		G	W	L	PCT		
1	1907	DET	A	153	92	58	.613	693	531
1	1908	DET	A	154	90	63	.588	647	547
1	1909	DET	A	158	98	54	.644	666	493
3	1910	DET	A	155	86	68	.558	679	584
2	1911	DET	A	154	89	65	.577	831	777
6	1912	DET	A	154	69	84	.450	720	777
6	1913	DET	A	153	66	87	.431	625	716
4	1914	DET	A	157	80	73	.522	615	618
2	1915	DET	A	156	100	54	.649	778	597
3	1916	DET	A	155	87	67	.564	670	595
4	1917	DET	A	154	78	75	.509	639	577
7	1918	DET	A	128	55	71	.436	476	557
4	1919	DET	A	140	80	60	.571	618	578
7	1920	DET	A	155	61	93	.396	652	832
1	1924	NY	N	44	32	12	.727	238	163
2	1925	NY	N	32	21	11	.656	189	145
Total				2202	1184	995	.543	9736	9087

World Series Managerial Record

Year	Team		G	W	L	PCT
1907	DET	A	5	0	4	.000
1908	DET	A	5	1	4	.200
1909	DET	A	7	3	4	.428
Total			17	4	12	.250

Chapter Notes

Preface

1. Description of the funeral was taken from the *Scranton Times*, February 3–6, 1928.
2. William Kashatus, *Diamonds in the Coalfields* (McFarland, 2002).
3. There are several sources for this Harris story. It appeared in the *Scranton Times* February 1, 1928.
4. Eulogies were reprinted in the *Scranton Times*, February 3–6, 1928.

Chapter 1

1. Rosamond D. Rhone, *Anthracite Coal Mines and Mining, The American Monthly Review of Reviews*, November 1902.
2. James Kugel, *North with Lee and Jackson: The Lost Story of Gettysburg* (Stackpole Books, 1996).
3. Rhone, *Anthracite Coal Mines and Mining*, November 1902.
4. Jennings' father's obituary, the *Baltimore Sun*, November 21, 1898.
5. Peter Roberts, *Anthracite Coal Communities*, pages 174–181 (Macmillian Company, 1904).
6. Susan Campbell Bartoletti, *Growing Up in Coal Country* (Houghton Mifflin, 1999).
7. *Ibid.*, and John Brown, *Hughie Jennings: Live Wire of Modern Baseball* (Baseball Magazine, December, 1911).
8. From an article found in the family scrapbook, without a date.
9. Hugh Jennings, *Rounding Third* (a series of syndicated newspaper articles published in 1925 in several newspapers including the *Bridgeport Telegram*).

10. Brown, *Hughie Jennings: Live Wire of Modern Baseball*.
11. There are several sources for this story. It appeared in *Baseball Magazine*, December 1911, page 35.

Chapter 2

1. There are several sources for this story. Oriole manager Ned Hanlon told it in the *Scranton Times*, December 3, 1911.
2. Bozeman Bulger (story in the *New York Evening World*), found in family scrapbook, date unknown.
3. Anthracite team stories are from several sources, including the *Scranton Times*, February 1, 1928.
4. Megan Barry, *Lehighton History* (from an essay by at lehighton.cpals.com).
5. Bozeman Bulger (story in the *New York Evening World*), found in family scrapbook, date unknown.
6. *Ibid.*
7. Jim Zbick, Lehighton baseball information taken from *Early Times Capsule, the Times News Online*.
8. Sol White, *History of Colored Baseball*, page 18 (University of Nebraska Press).

Chapter 3

1. Fr. Clyde F. Crews, *From Spirited City: Essays in Louisville History* (Cathedral Heritage Foundation 1996).
2. Philip Lowry, *Green Cathedrals* (Addison-Wesley, 1992).
3. *Baseball Magazine*, August 1908.
4. *Washington Post*, June 20, 1915.

5. Sam Crane, *Series of stories on 50 greatest players — no. 18*) from family scrapbook publication unknown.

6. Jennings, *Rounding Third*.

7. *Sporting Life*, March 26, 1916, page 10.

8. Carl Warton, in the *Boston Herald*, date unknown.

9. Burt Solomon, *Where They Ain't* (Doubleday 1999), pages 26–27; *Total Baseball, Seventh Edition* (Total Sports Publishing), page 4.

10. Tales of Old Time Players, the *Boston Garter*, June 1, 1912.

Chapter 4

1. *www.hickoksports.com*.

2. *www.baseball-almanac.com*.

3. Solomon, *Where They Ain't*, page 38.

4. Solomon, *Where They Ain't*, pages 44–45.

5. Information about Ned Hanlon from *Baseball Magazine*, July 1911, page 59; Charles Alexander, *John McGraw* (University of Nebraska Press), page 29; Solomon, *Where They Ain't*, pages 24–25; *Cooperstown: Hall of Fame Baseball Players* (Publications International, Ltd), page 46.

Chapter 5

1. Solomon, *Where They Ain't*, page 46.

2. Solomon, *Where They Ain't*, page 47.

3. Hanlon was quoted in the *Boston Garter* in 1912 in *Tales of Old Time Ball Players*.

4. Solomon, *Where They Ain't*, page 50.

5. *Ibid.*, page 52.

6. Chapman was quoted in an undated story in the Jennings family scrapbook by *Boston Herald* writer Carl Warton, date unknown.

7. Various sources list Hughie's birth year as 1869, 1870 and 1871. Toward he end of his life he told the *Scranton Times* he was born in 1871. St. Bonaventure records also list 1871.

8. Hanlon's theories on scientific baseball are from various sources including Solomon, *Where They Ain't*, pages 50–56; Fredrick Lieb, *The Baltimore Orioles: The History of a Colorful Team in Baltimore and St. Louis* (G.P. Putnam and Sons, 1955); and Alexander, *McGraw*, pages 38, 39.

Chapter 6

1. *Sporting News*, March 8, 1934, page 6.

2. *Sporting News*, April 4, 1891, page 1.

3. Blanche McGraw, *The Real John McGraw* (David McKay Co., 1953), page 55.

4. Alexander, *McGraw*, much of he McGraw biographical information chapter 2.

5. Solomon, *Where They Ain't*, page 49; an article by Vincent De Paul Fitzpatrick found in Kelley's Cooperstown file.

6. *The Baltimore Sun*, February 25, 1903, page 9.

7. Solomon, *Where They Ain't*, much of the Keeler biographical information came from chapter 1, pages 3–18.

Chapter 7

1. Alexander, *McGraw*.

2. Hughie was quoted in *Sporting Life*, July 5, 1902, page 6.

3. *The Washington Post*, September 23, 1894, page 15.

4. Alexander, *McGraw*, page 40.

5. Solomon, *Where They Ain't*, pages 70–71.

6. *Ibid.*, page 96.

7. McGraw's claim from a *Liberty Magazine* article cited in *Where They Ain't*.

8. *The Los Angeles Times*, January 13, 1924, page 13.

9. *Washington Post*, September 26, 1894, page 6.

10. *Baltimore Morning Herald*, October 3, 1894.

11. *Washington Post*, October 3, 1894, page 6.

12. From a story by The Associated Press, October 4, 1894. Appeared in *Los Angeles Times*, page 3.

13. *Washington Post*, October 4, 1894, page 6.

Chapter 8

1. *Washington Post*, October 4, 1894.

2. *Washington Post*, September 30, 1894.

3. Information about the fifty-fifty split was taken from *Where They Ain't*, pages 82–86.

4. *Rounding Third*.

5. Information about McGraw and Jennings at St. Bonaventure came from Alexander, *McGraw*, pages 36–44; Solomon, *Where They Ain't*, page 61; Eleanor B. English and Joseph C. English, Olean Youth Bureau, St. Bonaventure University, story at: *http://www.aafla.org/SportsLibrary*.

6. Alexander, *McGraw*, page 43.

7. *Ibid.*

8. Accounts of the 1894 and 1895 Temple Cup, Frank Ceresi, *www.baseballlibrary.com*, *Baltimore Morning Herald* and *Washington Post*; Solomon, *Where They Ain't*; Jerry Lansche, *Glory Fades Away: The Nineteenth Century World Series Rediscovered* (Taylor Publishing), pages 235–279; *Sporting Life*, October 1894 and 1895.
9. *Washington Post*, September 26, 1895.
10. Alexander, *McGraw*, page 48.

Chapter 9

1. *Sporting Life*, February 22, 1896.
2. *Sporting Life*, February 1, 1896.
3. *Sporting Life*, January 18, 1896.
4. *Sporting Life*, April 15, 1896.
5. Solomon, *Where They Ain't*, pages 104–105.
6. *The Pittsburgh Press*, May 6, 1896.
7. *Sporting Life*, July 28, 1896.
8. *The Pittsburgh Press*, June 3, 1896.
9. *Sporting Life*, July 28, 1896.
10. *Sporting Life*, August 15, 1896.
11. *Sporting Life*, August 29, 1896.
12. Bozeman Bulger in the *New York Evening World* from family scrapbook, date unknown.
13. Much of the Temple Cup description came from Lansche, *Glory Fades Away*, pages 279–285.
14. *Sporting News*, October 17, 1896.
15. *Washington Post*, September 26, 1896, page 8.

Chapter 10

1. *Sporting Life*, October 16, 1896.
2. *Baltimore Sun*, November 19, 1896; Alexander, *McGraw*, page 51.
3. Alexander, *John McGraw*, page 51.
4. *Washington Post*, February 4, 1897, page 8.
5. *Indiana Evening Gazette*, October 25, 1918.
6. *Washington Post*, March 15, 1904, page 8.
7. *Washington Post*, September 3, 1897.
8. *Chicago Daily Tribune*, September 25, 1897, page 4.
9. *Ibid.*
10. *Sporting News*, October 9, 1897, page 3.
11. Lansche, *Glory Fades Away*, page 291.
12. *Ibid.*, page 299.
13. *Washington Post*, October 15, 1897, page 8.
14. *Washington Post*, November 8, 1907.

Chapter 11

1. Solomon, *Where They Ain't*, page 126.
2. *Baltimore Morning Herald*, February 20, 1898, page 7.
3. *Evening Telegram*, June 8, 1909.
4. *Washington Post*, February 27, 1910.
5. Solomon, *Where They Ain't*, pages 132–133, 146–147.
6. *The Washington Post*, November 28, 1898, page 8.
7. *Baltimore American*, December 20, 1898, page 4.
8. *Brooklyn Daily Eagle*, March 12 1899, page 11.
9. *Chicago Tribune*, April 16, 1899, page 6.
10. *Washington Post*, June 18, 1899.
11. *Sandusky Star*, August 26, 1899.
12. *Washington Post*, July 17, 1899.
13. *Baltimore American*, August 4, 1899.
14. *Ibid.*
15. *Rounding Third.*

Chapter 12

1. *Rounding Third.*
2. *Sporting Life*, June 13, 1912.
3. *New York Times*, April 14, 1900.
4. *Sporting Life*, March 31, 1901, article by Joyless Jennings.
5. *Washington Post*, July 30, 1900, page 8.
6. *Chicago Daily Tribune*, December 8, 1901, page 7.
7. *Associated Press*, January 9, 1901.

Chapter 13

1. *New York Times*, June 22, 1901, page 10.
2. Solomon, *Where They Ain't*, page 209.
3. *Philadelphia Inquirer*, June 18, 1901.
4. *Philadelphia Inquirer*, June 20, 1901.
5. *Philadelphia Inquirer*, June 18, 1901.
6. *Philadelphia Inquirer*, June 21, 1901.
7. *Sporting Life*, June 21, 1901.
8. *Washington Post*, August 10, 1901, page 8.
9. *Washington Post*, August 12, 1901, page 8.
10. *Philadelphia Public Ledger*, July 14, 1901.
11. *Brooklyn Eagle*, July 1 1902.

Chapter 14

1. *Washington Post*, April 8, 1903, page 8.
2. *Washington Post*, June 28 1903, page 8.

3. *New York Times*, January 3, 1903, page 7.

4. *Rounding Third.*

5. *Los Angeles Times*, July 3 1903.

6. *Washington Post*, July 5, 1905.

7. *Washington Post*, July 16, 1905.

8. Lieb, *The Baltimore Orioles*, pages 122–126.

9. *Atlanta Constitution*, March 29, 1904.

10. Lieb, *The Baltimore Orioles*, page 125.

11 *The Laurel*, St. Bonaventure's, vol. 6, no. 9, June 1905, page 387.

12. Larry Gerlach, writing in *Baseball's First Stars* (Society of American Baseball Research, 1995); *www.baseballlibrary.com.*

13. *Trenton Evening Times*, August 28, 1906.

14. *Washington Post*, August 29, 1906.

15. Fredrick Lieb, *The Detroit Tigers* (Putnam, 1946), page 85.

16. *Middletown Daily Times-Press*, August 4, 1915.

17. Watson Spoelstra, *Detroit News: A series about Golden Jubilee of Tigers.*

Chapter 15

1. Bartoletti, *Growing Up in Coal Country*, page 36.

2. *Baseball Magazine*, August 1911, page 58.

3. *Baseball Magazine*, December 1911, page 35.

4. *Washington Post*, July 4, 1909.

5. *Washington Post*, January 22, 1911.

6. Cobb, from a series of articles by in the *Atlanta Constitution* in 1913.

7. *Detroit News*, December 12, 1907.

8. *Conshocton Daily Times*, August 27, 1909.

9. Billy Evans, one of a syndicated series of articles in November 1915.

10. Fredrick Lieb, *Detroit Tigers*, page 89.

11. Lawrence Ritter, *Glory of Their Times* (William Morrow, 1966), page 51.

12. *Detroit News*, December 5, 1907.

13. Hugh Fullerton, *Liberty Magazine*, article April 14, 1928, page 49.

Chapter 16

1. Much of the information about the Bungy affair and attempts to trade and Cobb came from Stump, *Cobb.*

2. *Washington Post*, March 21, 1907, page 9.

3. *Rounding Third.*

4. *Ibid.*

5. W. Bingay column in the *Detroit News*, January 16, 1908.

6. Joe Williams column in the *Detroit News*, July 1, 1941.

7. *Rounding Third.*

Chapter 17

1. *Washington Post*, November 18, 1906, page 8.

2. *Washington Post*, February 5, 1907.

3. *Washington Post*, March 8, 1907.

4. *Chicago Daily Tribune*, March 31, 1907 page D4.

5. Stoney McLinn, in a column in the *Philadelphia Evening Public Ledger*, from family scrapbook, date unknown.

6. Al Stump, *Cobb* (Algonquin Books, 1996), page 146.

7. *Washington Post*, June 15, 1907.

8. *Washington Post*, August 4, 1907.

9. *Washington Post*, September 1, 1907.

10. Arthur Daley in the *New York Times*, April 24, 1949, page S2.

11. *The Washington Post*, October 3, 1907.

12. *Ibid.*

13. *Detroit Free Press*, October 2, 1907.

14. Billy Evans Stories, in the *Indianapolis Star*, January 7, 1912.

15. *Detroit Free Press*, October 5, 1907.

16. *Chicago Tribune*, October 7, 1907, page 10.

17. *Detroit News*, October 8, 1907.

18. *Chicago Inter Ocean*, October 1907.

Chapter 18

1. *Detroit News and Tribune*, October 7, 1907.

2. Lieb, *The Detroit Tigers*, pages 87–99.

3. Lieb, *The Detroit Tigers*, page 99.

4. Accounts, stories and quotes from the 1907 World Series came from the *Detroit News and Tribune* and the *Chicago Tribune* October 7–14.

Chapter 19

1. Lieb, *The Detroit Tigers*, page 105.

2. *Washington Post*, December 15, 1907.

3. *Chicago Daily Tribune*, March 30, 1908 page 12.

4. *Ibid.*

5. *Chicago Daily Tribune*, March 31, 1908 page 8.

6. *Chicago Daily Tribune*, April 14, 1907 page 12.
7. Al Stump, *Cobb*, pages 160–161.
8. *Ibid.*, pages 162–163.
9. *Washington Post*, August 23, 1908, page S1.
10. *www.baseballlibrary.com*, from the Baseball Chronology.
11. *Detroit News*, October 9, 1908.
12. *Chicago Daily Tribune*, October 11, 1908.
13. *Detroit News*, October 15, 1908.

Chapter 20

1. *Nevada State Journal*, April 1, 1925.
2. *Washington Post*, August 11, 1909.
3. *Chicago Tribune*, October 10, 1909, page D-1.
4. *Washington Post*, October 4, 1909.
5. *Atlanta Constitution*, September 5, 1909.
6. Stump, *Cobb*, pages 170–175.
7. *Washington Post*, September 26, page S1; and September 27, page 1, 1909.
8. Glenn Stout, *Signs of the Miraculous* (Houghton Mifflin, 1993).
9. *Pittsburgh Press*, October 10, 1909.
10. *Ibid.*
11. *Detroit News*, October 12, 1909.
12. *Pittsburgh Press*, October 9, 1909.
13. *Ibid.*, October 12, 1909.
14. *Pittsburgh Press*, October 13, 1909.
15. *Washington Post*, October 23, 1909.

Chapter 21

1. *Washington Post*, June 4, 1911.
2. E-M-F home page, *www.dreamwater.org/emfauto.*
3. *Washington Post*, October 30, 1910.
4. *Scranton Times*, December 2, 3, 6 and 8, 1911, description of the accident and Hughie's quotations were taken from a series of stories.
5. *Scranton Times*, December 18, 1911.
6. *Washington Post*, December 18, 1911.
7. *Baseball Magazine*, December 1911, page 39.
8. *Ibid.*
9. *Scranton Times*, February 2, 1911, page 1.
10. *Scranton Times*, January 1, 1911, page 1.
11. *Atlanta Constitution*, March 10, 1912.
12. Stump, *Cobb*, pages 206, 207.
13. Tom Granahan, *Philadelphia Inquirer Magazine*, "The Unlikely Heroes of Shibe Park," September 16, 1984; Stump, *Cobb*, pages 207–210; and newspaper accounts.

Chapter 22

1. *Scranton Times*, January 3, 1910.
2. E.A. Batchelor, Personal and Confidential column in *Detroit Saturday Night*, October 4, 1919, and January 24, 1925.
3. *Scranton Times*, January 7, 1910.
4. John Brown, "The Live Wire of Modern Baseball," story in *Baseball Magazine*, December 1911.
5. *Washington Post*, September 21, 1924, page S8.
6. Arthur Daley, column *New York Times*, March 30, 1947, page S2.
7. *Mansfield News*, October 25, 1911.
8. *Scranton Tribune Republican*, November 13, 1912.
9. *Detroit News Tribune*, September 30, 1910.
10. Bert Walker, column in *Detroit Times*, February 1, 1928.
11. *New York Times*, October 1, 1910, page 11.
12. *Detroit News*, March 9, 1908.
13. *Washington Post*, April 28, 1915.
14. *Washington Post*, April 10, 1918.
15. Maurice Francis Egan and John B. Kennedy, *The Knights of Columbus in Peace and War and www.worldwar1.com/dbc/knightsc.htm.*

Chapter 23

1. Lieb, *The Detroit Tigers*, page 152.
2. *Sporting Life*, August 17, 1912.
3. *Washington Post*, June 26, 1912.
4. *Washington Post*, December 3, 1915.
5. Bill Dow, *Detroit Free Press*, April 17, 2002.
6. Stump, *Cobb*, pages 308, 309.
7. *Trenton Evening Times*, October 5, 1920.

Chapter 24

1. *New York Times*, July 20, 1927, page 17.
2. *United Press*, October 30, 1920.
3. *Newspaper Enterprise*, April 8, 1921.
4. *New York Times*, August 24, 1921, page 17.
5. *Rounding Third.*
6. *New York Times*, October 11, 1923, page 17.
7. *Detroit News Tribune* and *Washington Post* issues in March 1921.
8. Alexander, *McGraw*, page 253.
9. *New York Times*, May 22, 1924.

10. *Mine Boy to Manager*, chapter IV, a series of syndicated articles, 1925.

11. *New York Times*, November 8, 1924, page 13.

12. *Chicago Tribune*, November 3, 1924, page 29.

13. *Chicago Tribune*, Foreign News Service, November 6, 1924.

14. *New York Times*, December 3, 1924.

15. *NEA News Service*, October 2, 1922.

16. *New York Times*, July 16, 1923, page 7.

17. Alexander, *McGraw*, page 268.

18. Norman E. Brown, *Central Press Syndicate*, April 1926.

Chapter 25

1. *Gastonia Daily Gazette*, April 9, 1926, front page.

2. *New York Times*, April 11, 1926.

3. *Washington Post*, April 12, 1926.

4. *Gastonia Daily Gazette*, April 8, 1926.

5. *Lancaster Daily Gazette*, February 24, 1926.

6. *New York Times*, December 10, 1926.

7. Accounts of the feud are from the *New York Times* and the *Gastonia Daily Review*, December 11, 1926, and Alexander, *McGraw*, page 277.

8. Bozeman Bulger, *New York Evening World*, from family scrapbook, date unknown.

9. Alexander, *McGraw*, page 279.

10. Hugh Fullerton, *Liberty Magazine*, April 14, 1928.

Chapter 26

1. *Harper's Weekly*, August 27, 1910.

2. *Atlanta Constitution*, July 31, 1910.

3. H.C. Walker, Sportology in the *Detroit Times*, October 18, 1920.

4. Watson Spoelstra, *Detroit News*, series about golden jubilee of Tigers.

5. *Washington Post*, May 23, 1909.

6. *Rounding Third*.

Chapter 27

1. Information about Hughie's voting record and election came from the Baseball Hall of Fame website, *www.baseballhalloffame.com*; Ken Smith, *Baseball's Hall of Fame* (Grosset and Dunlap, 1974).

2. *Washington Post*, October 6, 1907.

3. *Washington Post*, October 13, 1907.

Bibliography

Alexander, Charles. *John McGraw*. New York: Viking, 1988.
_____. *Ty Cobb*. New York: Oxford University Press, 1984.
Bartoletti, Susan Campbell. *Growing Up in Coal Company*. Boston: Houghton Mifflin, 1996.
A Baseball Century: The First 100 Years of the National League. New York: Macmillan, 1976.
Cobb, Ty, with Al Stump. *My Life in Baseball*. New York: Doubleday, 1961.
James, Bill. *Historical Baseball Abstract*. New York: Villard, 1988.
Kashatus, William. *Diamonds in the Coal Fields*. Jefferson, N.C.: McFarland, 2002.
Lieb, Frederick. *The Detroit Tigers*. New York: G.P. Putnam's Sons, 1946.
Smith, Ken. *Baseball's Hall of Fame*. New York: Grosset & Dunlap, 1974.
Solomon, Burt. *Where They Ain't*. New York: Doubleday, 1999.
Stump, Al. *Cobb*. Chapel Hill, N.C.: Algonquin, 1994.
Thorn, John. *Total Baseball*. 7th edition. Kingston, N.Y.: Total Sports, 2001.
Wolff, Rick, Editorial Director. *The Baseball Encyclopedia*. 4th ed. New York: Macmillan, 1990.

Periodicals

Baltimore Morning Herald, 1894–1898
Baltimore Sun, 1894–1898
Baseball Magazine, 1908–1920
Brooklyn Eagle, 1900–1902
Chicago Tribune, 1907–1920
Detroit Free Press, 1907–1920
Detroit News, 1907–1920
New York Times, 1896–1928
Philadelphia Inquirer, 1901–1902
Pittsburgh Press, 1909
Scranton Times, 1896–1928
Sporting Life, 1894–1896
Sporting News, 1896–1928
Washington Post, 1896–1928

Index